A HISTORY of the ROMANIAN COMMUNIST PARTY

HISTORIES OF RULING COMMUNIST PARTIES
Richard F. Staar, editor

A HISTORY of the
ROMANIAN COMMUNIST PARTY

Robert R. King

HOOVER INSTITUTION PRESS
Stanford University, Stanford, California

Hoover Press Publication 233

© 1980 by the Board of Trustees of the
   Leland Stanford Junior University
All rights reserved
International Standard Book Number: 0–8179–7332–X
Library of Congress Catalog Card Number: 80–8327
Printed in the United States of America

Designed by Elizabeth Gehman

to
Nathan, James, Daniel,
and especially to Kay

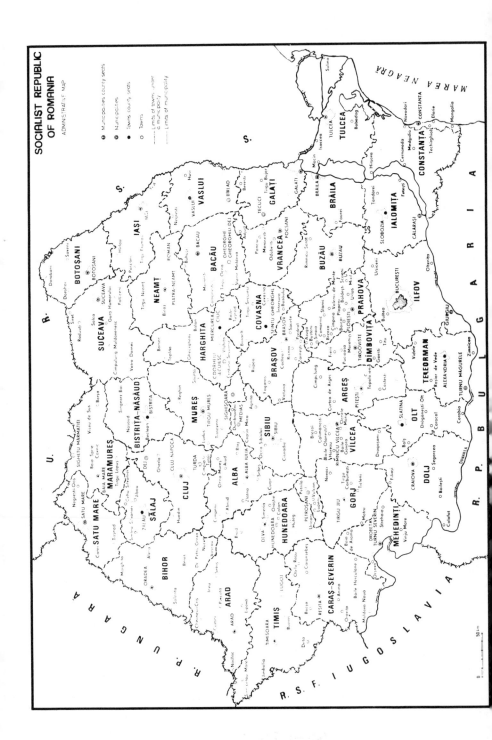

SOCIALIST REPUBLIC
OF ROMANIA
ADMINISTRATIVE MAP

Contents

Organization and Structure of
the Romanian Communist Party

(Personnel and Organization in December 1979)

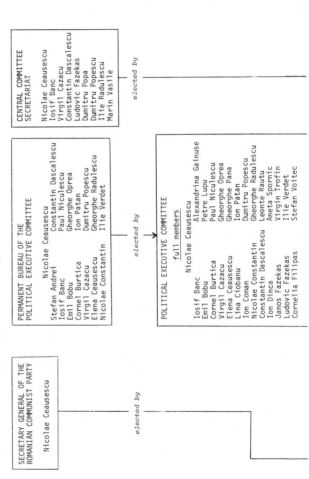

CENTRAL COMMITTEE SECRETARIAT

Nicolae Ceausescu
Iosif Banc
Virgil Cazacu
Constantin Dascalescu
Ludovic Fazekas
Dumitru Popa
Dumitru Popescu
Ilie Radulescu
Marin Vasile

elected by

PERMANENT BUREAU OF THE POLITICAL EXECUTIVE COMMITTEE

Nicolae Ceausescu
Stefan Andrei   Constantin Dascalescu
Iosif Banc   Paul Niculescu
Emil Bobu   Gheorghe Oprea
Cornel Burtica   Ion Patan
Virgil Cazacu   Dumitru Popescu
Elena Ceausescu   Gheorghe Radulescu
Nicolae Constantin   Ilie Verdet

elected by

POLITICAL EXECUTIVE COMMITTEE

full members

Nicolae Ceausescu
Iosif Banc   Alexandrina Gainuse
Emil Bobu   Petre Lupu
Cornel Burtica   Paul Niculescu
Virgil Cazacu   Gheorghe Oprea
Elena Ceausescu   Gheorghe Pana
Lina Ciobanu   Ion Patan
Ion Coman   Dumitru Popescu
Nicolae Constantin   Gheorghe Radulescu
Constantin Dascalescu   Leonte Rautu
Ion Dinca   Aneta Spornic
Janos Fazekas   Virgin Trofin
Ludovic Fazekas   Ilie Verdet
Cornelia Filipas   Stefan Voitec

elected by

SECRETARY GENERAL OF THE ROMANIAN COMMUNIST PARTY

Nicolae Ceausescu

elected by

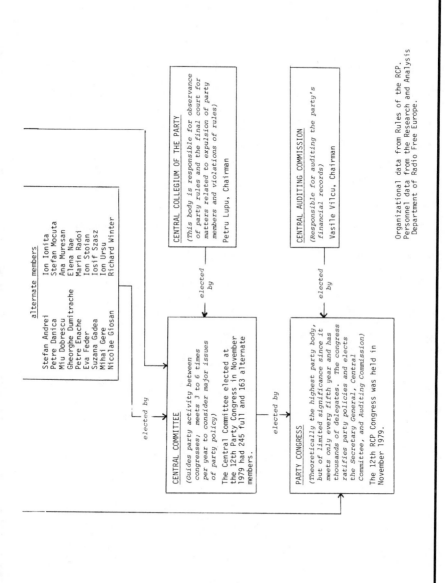

alternate members

Stefan Andrei   Ion Ionita
Petre Danica   Stefan Mocuta
Miu Dobrescu   Ana Muresan
Gheorghe Dumitrache   Elena Nae
Petre Enache   Marin Radoi
Eva Feder   Ion Stoian
Suzana Gadea   Iosif Szasz
Mihai Gere   Ion Ursu
Nicolae Giosan   Richard Winter

CENTRAL COLLEGIUM OF THE PARTY

(This body is responsible for observance of party rules and the final court for matters related to expulsion of party members and violations of rules)

Petru Lupu, Chairman

CENTRAL AUDITING COMMISSION

(Responsible for auditing the party's financial records)

Vasile Vilcu, Chairman

elected by

CENTRAL COMMITTEE

(Guides party activity between congresses; meets 3 to 6 times per year to consider major issues of party policy)

The Central Committee elected at the 12th Party Congress in November 1979 had 245 full and 163 alternate members.

elected by

PARTY CONGRESS

(Theoretically the highest party body, but of limited significance since it meets only every fifth year and has thousands of delegates. The congress ratifies party policies and elects the Secretary General, Central Committee, and Auditing Commission)

The 12th RCP Congress was held in November 1979.

elected by

Organizational data from Rules of the RCP.
Personnel data from the Research and Analysis Department of Radio Free Europe.

Name	Born	Date Elected
Permanent Bureau of the Political Executive Committee		
Stefan Andrei	1931	November 1974
Iosif Banc	1921	March 1978
Emil Bobu	1927	November 1979
Cornel Burtica	1931	January 1977
Virgil Cazacu	1927	November 1979
Elena Ceausescu	1919	January 1977
Nicolae Ceausescu	1918	November 1974
Nicolae Constantin	n.a.	November 1979
Constantin Dascalescu	*ca.* 1920	November 1979
Paul Niculescu	1923	March 1978
Gheorghe Oprea	1927	November 1974
Ion Patan	1926	November 1974
Dumitru Popescu	1928	November 1979
Gheorghe Radulescu	1910	January 1977
Ilie Verdet	1925	January 1977
(Central Committee Secretaries not members of the Permanent Bureau)		
Ludovic Fazekas	1920	November 1979
Dumitru Popa	1925	March 1979
Ilie Radulescu	1926	March 1979
Marin Vasile	1929	March 1978

SOURCE: Personnel files of the Research and Analysis Department of Radio Free Europe.

PARTY LEADERSHIP
1979)

Party Office	Government or Other Positions
	Minister of Foreign Affairs
CC Secretary	Chairman, Central Council of Workers' Control of Economic and Social Activities
	Minister of Labor and Chairman, Trade Union Confederation
	Minister of Foreign Trade and International Economic Cooperation
CC Secretary	
	Chairman, National Council of Science and Technology
Secretary General	President of Romania; Chairman, Front of Socialist Unity
	Chairman, State Planning Committee
CC Secretary	Chairman, Council on Problems of Social and Economic Organization
	Minister of Finance and Comecon Representative
	First Deputy Prime Minister
	Minister of Technical-Material Supply and Control of Fixed Assets
CC Secretary	Chairman, Council for Radio and Television
	Chairman, Higher Court for Financial Control
	Prime Minister
CC Secretary	Ministry of Forestry and Construction Materials; Chairman, Council for Workers of Hungarian Nationality
CC Secretary	Minister State Secretary of the Chemical Industry
CC Secretary	
CC Secretary	Chairman, National Union of Agricultural Production Cooperatives

Editor's Foreword

The present volume, Robert R. King's *A History of the Romanian Communist Party*, continues the series of monographs on the histories of the sixteen ruling communist parties from their organization to the present. This series was initiated to fill an important gap in modern English-language historiography. Since the movement in Romania has not as yet produced its own official history, the gap is perhaps more evident in this case than in others.

Dr. King deals with the founding and interwar experience of the Romanian Communist Party (RCP). Externally, it was dominated by the Soviet party and government, because Moscow considered Romania a staging ground of imperialism in the struggle against the USSR. Initially, the membership of the RCP included a disproportionately large number of ethnic minorities. This, coupled with the Soviet demand that the RCP advocate the return of Bessarabia to the USSR and a self-determination that included secession for certain other Romanian territories, led non-communists to conclude the party an alien institution. Moreover, the RCP was outlawed for most of the interwar period, which further limited its influence on Romanian politics.

The RCP's accession to power was largely a function of the Soviet military presence in Romania in the closing months of World War II. Once the party began to play a major role in the country's political life, it underwent a significant organizational transformation. A dramatic growth in membership was followed by an extensive purge and other efforts to create a responsive, disciplined movement. The leadership likewise changed significantly as the party developed and new conditions arose. The most serious problems included establishment of elite coherence, which could be accomplished only through purge and organizational change. Successful institutionalization of the RCP and its elite prepared the stage for further stable growth and the adoption of new policies. Among the most significant developments has been the party's effort to alter its interaction with

Romanian society from a relation based on coercion to one based on persuasion and manipulation. The most important indicator of this change since the early 1960s has been the RCP's treatment of the Romanian national heritage.

A distinctive hallmark of the RCP has been its autonomy in pursuing international policies. The Soviet link remains the most important foreign connection, but the effort to diversify international contacts is increasingly apparent. The obvious purpose is to secure support from various other independently minded communist movements for the RCP's claimed right to pursue its own national policies.

Hoover Institution   RICHARD F. STAAR
Stanford University   *Director of International Studies*

_____ Preface _____

A number of books on contemporary Romania have been published in English. Because Romania has achieved extensive recognition for its considerable degree of foreign policy autonomy from the Soviet Union since the early 1960s, much of what has been written has focused on the country's international relations. Other Western treatments have considered the social and economic transformation that has taken place in Romania since the communist party came to power after 1944. Thus far, however, there has been no extended work in English that has focused on the history of the Romanian Communist Party (RCP), and even the party has not yet produced a comprehensive treatment of its past. When the Hoover Institution invited me to write the volume on Romania for its series on the histories of ruling parties, the task appeared to be not only challenging and entertaining but also a significant link in our chain of understanding of contemporary Romania.

I have approached writing this party history as a political scientist rather than a historian. My principal concern has been with the political and organizational development of the RCP that has influenced its current nature. I have not attempted to look at the country and society in general, but rather to focus specifically on the party, although one cannot analyze the party, of course, without considering its interaction with its environment. Furthermore, I have tried to avoid the temptation to highlight the party's international policies, as interesting and significant as they are. External influences—in particular the impact of the Soviet party and state—must be treated, but this interesting subject will be viewed from the perspective of the impact it has had on the internal development of the party.

I am grateful to Richard F. Staar, associate director of the Hoover Institution, for inviting me to write this volume for the series on ruling party histories that he is editing. He has given me a free hand in my approach to the topic and has made no attempt to impose a rigid topical or methodological framework.

The Research and Analysis Department of Radio Free Europe in Munich, West Germany, provided a particularly congenial atmosphere in which I did most of the research for this study. My former colleagues at Radio Free Europe have contributed much to my understanding of Romania and Eastern Europe. Two deserve special mention: J. F. Brown, now the director of the Radio, has given encouragement and helpful criticism to my work on Romania for several years; the Romanian Research Unit and its chief, Ion Gheorghe, have supplied me with obscure bits of information and assistance and have offered helpful criticism on many topics. The Radio Free Europe archives on Romania made my task easier, and the institutional support and encouragement were essential factors in the completion of this history.

Several individuals were particularly helpful with the less glamorous aspects of producing the manuscript. Unity Evans carefully edited and criticized the style of much of the manuscript, and also painstakingly prepared the tables. Ina von Boroevic located scores of obscure books and periodicals for me in the Bayerische Staatsbibliothek. Edith Bertel typed most of the manuscript.

While I owe much to all of these individuals and to Radio Free Europe, I accept full responsibility for the ideas and interpretations that are here expressed.

Introduction
History as Science, Myth, and Ideology

The dissident Yugoslav Marxist philosopher Svetozar Stojanovic once observed sarcastically that communist party officials were people for whom "the only absolutely certain thing is the future since the past is constantly changing."[1] For them, the certainty of the communist millennium—though its actual achievement appears to be receding into the ever more distant future—is much easier to deal with than the past. This is particularly true since in communist ideology the interpretation of the past holds a special place that endows it with certain mystical qualities. History is not simply a record of man's past but a science, and once its laws are understood, it can illuminate the present as well as the future. Marxism holds the keys that "make it possible to foresee . . . the general direction of historical development." Thus Marxists must undertake "a thorough study . . . of historical data, of historical facts. Only in this way can one discover the internal connection between events and explain each one, so as not only to understand the past and the present but also to foresee the future scientifically."[2] Furthermore, a communist party guided by Marxian ideology becomes an instrument of the forces that shape man's destiny; thus, its role and right to rule are very much a function of the proper interpretation of the past.

The Uses of History

In a communist state, history serves important functions that are a result both of ideology and the practical requirements of governing.[3] While some of these are similar to the service history performs for any political system, some are unique, and others assume a different character under communist ideological conditions. First, history is the repository of tradition and legend, as in any society, and can be used to legitimize the regime in power. This involves relating precommunist with postrevolutionary history, to confirm for the party its right to rule; it is a task very much affected by the party's path to power. In societies in which the communist party achieved power essentially on its own (for example, the Soviet Union, Yugoslavia, China) this task is easier than in Eastern Europe, where communist rule was imposed by force of Soviet arms. In Romania this was a particularly serious problem since the Romanian communists were a negligible political factor before 1944, dominated by non-Romanians, and manipulated by a hostile foreign power for its own interests.

A second function of history is its didactic use to exhort and inspire the masses. This function is one that has been given particular emphasis in contemporary Romania. The resolution of an important ideological Conference on Political Education and Socialist Culture in 1976, for example, noted that history is "a powerful element in patriotic education and advanced thinking":

> By cultivating gratitude to and appreciation of our forefathers—who defended our people's national existence at the cost of great sacrifice and raised the banner of the struggle for freedom and independence and national and social justice—education must instill in the people's minds a feeling of responsibility for our forefathers' inheritance and a determination to continue to carry the beacon of progress and civilization in Romania under new historical conditions.[4]

In Romania, history may play an even more important role in this regard than elsewhere since Romanian nationalism is very much involved in the idealization of the country's distant past.

History also serves to rationalize official policies and programs. In the march toward the ideal communist society the party is the cloud by day and the pillar of fire by night; hence, history must show that despite errors and miscalculations of individuals the party continues to lead the chosen toward the promised land. This requirement for party infallibility has imposed serious limitations on postwar Romanian historians, particularly in light of the significant changes that have been made in policies and programs in the 35 years since the party came to power. This is also one of the major reasons for the Romanian Communist Party's (RCP) inability to produce a comprehensive official history.

Another function, unique to communist systems, is that history is a vehicle for policy debates and political infighting among party leaders. Since open debates are considered to be inconsistent with the ideal of party unity, they frequently take place in the guise of discussions of history, which provides an ideal medium because of its ideological importance and its relevance to the present and future. The Chinese communists have been particularly adept at using discussions of their distant past to debate contemporary issues, but this is also done within other parties as well. One of the more interesting examples is the extensive use of history in Eastern Europe to raise questions involving ethnicity, territorial claims, and national minorities.[5]

The RCP's Problems in Dealing with Its Past

Because history serves many varied functions in a communist system, it is not taken lightly. General history is sufficiently sensitive and complicated that scholars who must write and teach under the ideological eye of the party face serious obstacles in practicing their profession. The problem becomes still more difficult for those who deal with the history of the party itself.

Reviewing what has been published in Romania on the history of the Romanian party, one finds extensive data on events prior to the founding of the party but considerably fewer materials on more recent and more significant developments. Furthermore, the materials on later periods have been subject to manipulation for political ends, and widely conflicting interpretations and data have appeared on the same events.

RCP leaders have frequently announced the intention to produce a definitive account of the party's past, but thus far, despite periodic reiterations of this commitment, no comprehensive account has yet appeared. The first step was the creation in 1951 of *Institul de istorie a partidului de pe linga C.C. al P.M.R.* (The Institute of Party History of the Central Committee of the Romanian Workers' Party [RWP]). In 1955 at the Second Congress of the RWP, party leader Gheorghe Gheorghiu-Dej announced that a party history would be written.[6] De-Stalinization, initiated by Nikita Khrushchev a few months later, however, raised a whole host of complicating factors that delayed implementation of this pledge. Between 1956 and 1960, the Institute of Party History published a volume entitled *Lessons for the Assistance of those Studying the History of the Romanian Workers' Party*.[7] A note at the beginning of the book specified that it had evolved from a series of lectures and dialogues, and criticism from students of party history was solicited. This was apparently a first-draft attempt at the party history, but the effort did not get beyond that stage. The writing of the history was not even mentioned at the 1960 party congress.

At the December 1961 Central Committee (CC) plenum at which Romania's Stalinist past was criticized and the blame placed on former party officials who had been purged between 1953 and 1957, Gheorghiu-Dej again called for a party history. On that same occasion Nicolae Ceausescu, a CC secretary at the time and subsequently secretary general of the party, said that a "scientific" history of the party should be written, which would "put an end to the idealization and superficial analysis on which it is today based."[8]

When the Gheorghiu-Dej era came to an end in March 1965, the party was still without a comprehensive official history. At the party congress in July of that year it was again announced that one would be produced, and in October 1965 a commission was established for that purpose, headed by Ceausescu, the party's new secretary general, and including all members of the party's Permanent Presidium and all CC secretaries with responsibilities in the ideological area. It was announced that a sketch of the party history would appear in 1966 and the complete work would be published by the end of 1967,[9] but due to the new issue of how to deal with Gheorghiu-Dej and his role in the party, the deadlines passed and nothing appeared.

In the context of the ideological revitalization in 1971 and 1975–1976, the lack of a party history was particularly evident. In 1975, there were indications that a new concept of the history was emerging. In an address to the party academy Ceausescu raised a number of ideological and historical issues and suggested that the party history be integrated into the history of Romania.[10] This approach would have two advantages: first, it would contribute to the effort to link the party more closely with the nation, a policy that has been pursued by the RCP since the early 1960s, and second, it would minimize the space that could be devoted to strictly party problems and thus make it easier to gloss over some of the more controversial and awkward aspects of the party's past. With the launching of the 1976 ideological campaign, the necessity and importance of a definitive party history was again stressed by Ceausescu,[11] but it still has not appeared.

Although the party has not published a comprehensive history, its past has been used frequently as a source of inspiration for the education of party cadres, and for propaganda work with the population. A number of articles on specific past incidents have been published; these serve party purposes without being endowed with the sanctity of official history.[12] Furthermore, the topics selected have generally not been controversial. Because earlier periods are less problematical than more recent times, it is easier to write about the party history before 1944 than the period since the RCP came to power. The safest era is the period of workers' movements before the party was founded in 1921. The history of peripheral organizations (trade unions, the youth organization, various antifascist front groups) is less controversial than that of the party itself. The Stalinist era (1948–1953) and its policies have been more awkward to deal with than developments during the period of the coalition government (1944–1948) and those after 1956. Biographies or "reminiscences" of individual party members who were active in the interwar period have been a ready source of inspiration from the past, and they can easily be structured to omit difficult topics. Although these tendencies have been noted and criticized,[13] it has been easier for party historians to stick with safe but mundane topics than to venture into significant areas and risk the wrath of party ideologues for "erroneous" interpretation.

A second means of providing data from the party's past, without the hazard of giving an official interpretation to events, is the publication of historical party documents. Even this seemingly innocuous alternative, however, has run into difficulties. One of the first tasks of the Institute of Party History after it was founded in 1951 was to publish documents from the period before 1944. The first such publication was a single volume of selected documents covering the period 1917–1944, which appeared in 1951. A larger selection was to appear in a subsequent multivolume collection.[14] The closer to the present the editors came, however, the longer the period of time required for the selection and editing process, and the more complete series never got past 1937.

Furthermore, a decade after its publication this collection of documents came under sharp criticism as a result of changes in the party's policies. An authoritative review of postwar Romanian historiography in the journal of party history in 1969 criticized "the tendency to make a fetish of the literal contents of documents, sometimes using unscientific criteria in their selection in such a way as to serve certain preconceived theses."[15] A subsequent review in 1972 specifically criticized the published party documents as "not based on completely scientific criteria in the research, selection, and printing of basic documents." Because of "their one-sidedness and omissions" they have "long since been left behind and refuted by [Romania's] concrete historical realities and by the demands of a vigorous scientific methodology."[16]

As a result of these problems, the party had in 1969 issued a new volume of documents covering events leading up to the party's 1921 founding.[17] This marked the beginning of a new series of documents. The inability to deal with more recent events, however, has also been evident in the publication of these documents. After ten years of editorial work, several volumes of documents on the prehistory of the party from 1829 to 1921 have been published, but only one volume (covering the years 1921–1924) has been published on the documents from the period after the founding of the RCP.

The Framework for This Approach to RCP History

In the writing of any history one faces two problems. The first is the question of what material to include and what to omit, and this becomes more problematical when the history is to be a brief account. In this treatment of the RCP, I have not looked at the history of Romania as a whole, but have attempted to focus specifically on the party. This requires analyzing the party's relationship with society and considering the broader impact of some of its policies, although the principal concern is the institutional and organizational development of the RCP rather than its impact on Romania's social, economic, or cultural life. The international policies of the party—and, in particular, its relationship with the Soviet party and state—are essential aspects in the evolution of the party that are taken into consideration. While the scope of this history of the party is intentionally narrowly focused, I hope it will provide broader insight into the evolution of the party and thus enhance understanding of postwar Romanian developments.

The second problem one faces in writing history is how to organize the material for logical presentation. Both topical and chronological approaches have their limitations. The approach I have chosen to follow takes some liberties with the strict chronology of events, but this has been done in the hope that a more topical treatment of party history will contribute to a greater appreciation of the political, sociological, and organizational developments that have shaped the RCP.

The party began as a small political movement that was declared illegal shortly after it was founded. It had little indigenous support among the general population and was composed largely of non-Romanian ethnic elements whose goals were inimical to Romanian national interests. In addition, it quickly came to be dominated by the Communist Party of the Soviet Union (CPSU) through the Communist International (Comintern), and the

RCP was manipulated to serve the interests of the CPSU and the Soviet state, with little consideration of Romanian conditions or concerns. The party then came to power in the aftermath of World War II through the military might of the Red Army, which occupied Romania in 1944. It achieved its monopoly of political power with Soviet support and under Soviet direction. The policies that the RCP followed during its early years were largely uncritical emulation of similar policies being pursued in the USSR and elsewhere in Eastern Europe, and they were carried out initially with little regard for conditions in Romania.

Over time, however, the RCP changed from one of the most loyal, orthodox, and dependent of the Soviet client-states in Eastern Europe into the Warsaw Pact member with the greatest degree of autonomy in its foreign policy. It began to pursue independent domestic policies that diverged in significant respects from the Soviet pattern. During this time the party also began to alter its relationship with the Romanian population, seeking to identify itself with the country's past and presenting itself as the champion of Romania's national goals. The party has achieved a measure of popular acceptance and national identification that is unique in Eastern Europe. While the party's policies are not fully congruent with traditional Romanian national interests, and popular support is limited by the party's unwillingness to go further in meeting the population's demand for consumer goods, the transformation has been significant.

Though this study follows a topical outline, the sequence of subjects has an underlying chronological rationale. The first chapter analyzes why the RCP won little popular support during the period between its founding in 1921 and the eve of its rise to power in 1944. Chapter 2 considers why and by which means the RCP came to dominate Romanian political life between 1944 and 1947.

After achieving power, the party's principal task was its own institutionalization: increasing membership, building organizational loyalty, and socializing members to the party's goals and procedures. This institutional transformation is discussed in chapter 3. This chapter considers not only the immediate results after the RCP came to power (initial growth in party membership and organizational development before 1948, followed by a period of retrenchment and consolidation between 1948 and 1955), but also traces the growth in membership and the development of the party organization since 1955. Chapter 4 considers the parallel development of the party elite. Many significant elements in the formation of the elite have changed over time, and this chapter compares developments since 1944, such as the changing requirements for holding leading positions in the party and measures to increase elite coherence.

The task of party institutionalization had been largely completed by the time of the party congress of 1955. After this the party began to turn its attention to building its authority and developing its relationship with Romanian society. Chapter 5 analyzes these changes, which have become increasingly evident since the late 1950s. The Romanian party is best known for its espousal of the Romanian national heritage and the development of a foreign policy that is autonomous from that of the Soviet Union. While these developments are in part related to the changing nature of the relationship between the party and Romanian society, they have achieved unique proportions in Romania and have become the hallmark of the RCP. These issues are treated in chapters 6 and 7.

1

The Legacy of the Interwar Period

$\mathbf{T}$he RCP played little role in the country's politics prior to 1944. What happened in and to the party during this period, however, had a significant influence on its leadership, policies, organization, and membership after the party was thrust into the forefront of the country's political life as a result of the coup d'etat of August 23, 1944. To some extent the party's lack of influence before that date can be attributed to the Romanian government's decision to outlaw it in April 1924, less than three years after it was founded. Police repression and the need to carry out most activities underground certainly hampered its effectiveness. At the same time, political, social, and economic conditions in Romania were such that the party's task would have been difficult even if it had not been banned.

The Soviet Union's insistence that the members of the Comintern must serve first the interests of Soviet foreign policy complicated the task of the RCP still further. The requirements of Soviet policy, as seen from Moscow, frequently conflicted with the requirements of sound political activity in Romania. In the first decade of the RCP's existence there were frequent differences both within its leadership and with the Soviet line, and it was not until its fifth congress in 1931 (held in Moscow) that these problems were generally resolved—along lines favored by the Soviets. As a result, the party was not particularly successful in meeting the specific needs of the Romanian population during the 1930s, although the atmosphere in this period was more favorable to party activity than in the previous decade.

The Romanian Setting

The Romania in which the party came into existence was a very different country from that which had existed only a few years previously.[1] On the eve of the Balkan Wars (1912–1913) Romania was a kingdom composed of the principalities of Wallachia and Moldavia, which had been united in 1859 and had achieved full independence from Turkey in 1877 (this area was referred to as the "Old Kingdom"). In the Second Balkan War (1913) Romania joined Serbia and Greece in attacking Bulgaria, for which it was awarded Southern Dobruja.

Romania's participation in the First World War permitted it to acquire still more territory. Although bound by secret agreement with the Central Powers (Austria, Germany, and Italy), Romania remained neutral during the first two years of conflict, and when it finally entered the war in 1916 it did so on the side of the Allies. Through skillful diplomacy and careful exploitation of its military position, Romania acquired Transylvania, part of the Banat, Crisana, Maramures, and Bukovina from the disintegrating Austro-Hungarian Empire. (These territories with the exception of Bukovina are usually referred to collectively as Transylvania.) Ethnic Romanians were the largest single nationality in all of these areas, but there were substantial Hungarian, German, Jewish, Serbian, and other minorities as well. With the collapse of Russia after the Bolshevik Revolution, Romania also obtained Bessarabia, which had been a part of Moldavia before its annexation by Russia in 1812. Romanians were the largest ethnic group in Bessarabia, but there were also large Russian, Ukrainian, Jewish, Bulgarian, Turkish, and German minorities.

In five years Romania had more than doubled both its territory (from 137,000 square kilometers in 1915 to 294,000 in 1919) and its population (from 7,625,000 in 1913 to 15,500,000 in 1919). Creating a unified state from these disparate parts was a difficult task. Before 1913 the country was overwhelmingly Romanian, but after 1918 there were large minorities. The 1930 census showed 72 percent (13 million) Romanians, 8 percent (1.4 million) Hungarians, 4 percent (.7 million) Germans, 4 percent (.7 million) Jews, 3 percent (.6 million) Ukrainians, 2 percent (.4 million) Russians, 2 percent (.4 million) Bulgarians, and 5 percent others. Furthermore, the new territories were quite different from the Old Kingdom in many respects. Those which had been part of the Hapsburg Empire were generally more socially and economically advanced than the Old Kingdom, while Bessarabia was probably less so. Also, the peoples of these newly acquired territories had rather different expectations for unified Romania. The old Romanian political leaders saw the new areas as provinces to be treated the same as those of the Old Kingdom, while leaders in Transylvania and Bessarabia expected some degree of regional autonomy; they were not anxious to replace the hegemony of Vienna or Petersburg with that of Bucharest. National integration was further hampered by the international consequences of the territorial acquisitions. Hungarians considered Transylvania an important historical part of their homeland, and of all territories taken from Hungary after the First World War, Transylvania was the most significant, and emotionally felt, loss. Hungarian-Romanian relations were further strained with the Romanian occupation of eastern Hungary and the suppression of the Bela Kun communist government in 1919. The new Soviet government likewise refused to accept the union of Bessarabia with Romania, and this controversy continued to sour relations between the two countries throughout the interwar period. Bulgarian claims to Southern Dobruja, though not as serious as those to Transylvania and Bessarabia, created problems between Bucharest and Sofia.

Irredentism exacerbated the difficulty of coping with substantial minority populations and forced Romania to adopt a defensive international stance. The Hungarian and Soviet threats to the unity of the Romanian state in the period before 1938 did not pose as serious a problem as politicians at the time claimed, but they did create a convenient opportunity for political leaders in Bucharest to ignore social and economic injustices and rally the population with nationalist programs and slogans. They also provided a convenient excuse for Old Kingdom leaders to undermine the economic and political leadership of the newly acquired territories.

The Romanian governments during the interwar period were not terribly successful in dealing with the multiple challenges they faced. Certainly stability was not a feature of Romanian politics during this era. Widespread poverty in the countryside and social and economic inequalities were major sources of insurmountable political difficulties. Among the most serious problems contributing to the political instability was the fact that the peasant masses were largely excluded from political life and were manipulated by political figures. Elections, with two notable exceptions, were determined in advance, and political corruption was endemic.

During the interwar period there were four major political groups, which at one time or another dominated Romanian political life: the Liberal Party, the peasant parties, King Carol with his supporters, and the fascists. Although all four groups were active during most of the period and competed with each other for political influence, the leading role was played by each in succession. The Liberal Party, under Ion I. C. Bratianu, led the first government of United Romania from December 1918 until September 1919. The Liberals, who had earlier espoused land reform, established the framework for expropriation and distribution of land to the peasants. Despite rather generous provisions on paper, however, there were enough loopholes in the legislation to prevent ruinous losses to the rural establishment. In the 1919 elections Bratianu's party lost heavily in the first of the two free elections in interwar Romania. A coalition of propeasant organizations formed a government under the leadership of a Transylvanian, Alexandru Vaida Voevod. Peasant disturbances, hostility of land owners to the new government's proposed agrarian policies, and general instability led the king, Ferdinand I, to dismiss the government within a few months and appoint as premier a popular but conservative war hero, General Alexandru Averescu. The general immediately called new elections, and by resorting to traditional manipulation gained a majority for his People's Party.

The agrarian legislation adopted under Averescu's tenure was far less liberal than the peasantry expected; nevertheless, it proved to be enough of a safety valve that Romania emerged from the period of revolutionary upheaval that rocked Central and Eastern Europe between 1918 and 1921 with its established order still intact. Under Averescu the conservative nationalist trend in domestic policy and antirevisionism in foreign affairs were established. In 1921 Romania entered a defensive alliance with Poland and Hungary against the Soviet Union, and then joined Czechoslovakia and Yugoslavia in the Little Entente directed against Hungarian revisionism.

The Liberals were called back to power by King Ferdinand in 1922 and through control of the electoral process insured their hold on the government for the next six years. The Liberals governed for the benefit of the middle class and the Romanian establishment, while avoiding social and economic reforms that would have benefited either peasants or industrial workers. The period, however, was one of economic growth and relative prosperity.

The deaths of Ion Bratianu and King Ferdinand, political manipulation involving the royal succession, and weakened Liberal leadership brought the Liberal era to an end in 1928. The regency asked the National Peasant Party under Iuliu Maniu to form a government, which was confirmed in the second honest election of the interwar period. Although Maniu and his associates were more democratically inclined than the other political leaders of the time, conservative forces were sufficiently entrenched, so that significant reform was difficult. National Peasant governments continued until 1933 (without Maniu, who resigned in 1930), but their influence was further undermined by the depression after 1930, the party's own internal weaknesses, and the activities of King Carol II.

King Ferdinand's son Carol had renounced his right to the Romanian throne in 1925 in favor of his own son, Michael. When Ferdinand died in 1927 a regency council was appointed to act in behalf of the new five-year-old monarch. Carol's renunciation of the throne had been due to Liberal pressures and his desire to continue living with his mistress, Magda Lupescu. In 1930, however, Carol suddenly returned to Romania, parliament revoked the law excluding him from the succession, and he assumed the throne as Carol II.

Political life between 1930 and 1940 was increasingly dominated by Carol. Largely as a consequence of the world-wide economic crisis, the first three years of his reign were marked by rapid changes in government, general instability, and the breakdown of older political parties. The period 1934 to 1937, during the premiership of Gheorghe Tartarescu, was somewhat more stable. The last three years under Carol was a period of royal dictatorship, emphasized by the dissolution of all political parties in 1938.

During the 1930s Romanian politics came to be affected by international events to a much greater extent than they had been during the previous decade. The rise of a revisionist Germany and the emergence of a more active Soviet foreign policy after 1933 brought Romania again into the vortex of great power politics. These developments were not only played out in diplomatic terms, but also internally, through the Soviet-dominated Romanian communists and Nazi Germany's efforts to establish links with Romanian fascists.

Carol's dictatorship came to an abrupt end in September 1940 when he abdicated and left the country, following the Soviet annexation of Bessarabia and the German-Italian decision to award Northern Transylvania to Hungary. Carol fell from power in large part because he had lost the confidence of the Germans, who had become an increasingly important factor in Romanian politics. He had also managed to alienate domestic political groups through his disregard for political freedom and his failure to take any action at the moment of national crisis when Romanian territory was seized.

The successor to the throne was Carol's son Michael, but real power was shared by military leader Marshal Ion Antonescu and the Romanian fascist organization, the Iron Guard. The alliance was an uneasy one, however, and lasted only until January 1941 when Antonescu used the army to suppress the unruly Guard. The Germans, now engaged in the Second World War, were more concerned to utilize the Romanian economy for the benefit of their war machine than to support a local fascist group; hence they acquiesced in the decimation of the Iron Guard.

The Antonescu regime can be referred to as "fascist" only in the general sense that it was in military alliance with Nazi Germany. Especially after the suppression of the Iron Guard in early 1941, the regime assumed more the character of a Balkan military dictatorship, although it did take on some of the trappings of fascism. Political life ceased altogether, and control of the country was in the hands of the army and the Germans. In June 1941 Antonescu brought Romania into the war by joining the German attack on the Soviet Union. The marshal was too deeply involved with Germany to call a halt when Romania had reoccupied Bessarabia; thus the Romanian army marched on to Stalingrad with the *Wehrmacht,* and then slowly retreated as the power of the Red Army grew.

Well before his rule came to an end, Antonescu must have known that Germany would lose the war. Nevertheless, he made no effort to extricate Romania from the German grasp, although he permitted representatives of the old political parties to contact the Allies. There was no effective internal opposition to his regime, which permitted him to remain in power until 1944. Then, as the Soviet army began its late summer offensive that carried the war into Romania and as American air raids increased, King Michael seized the initiative by arresting Antonescu, declaring war on Germany and Hungary, and seeking an armistice with the Allies.

It was only at this critical juncture in Romanian history that the communist party began to play a significant role in the country. Although Romanian politics between 1918 and 1944 were turbulent and unstable, the RCP was notably unsuccessful in exploiting these conditions. To understand why this was so, one needs to consider the nature of the party during the interwar period.

The Founding of the RCP

By the end of the nineteenth century socialist and Marxist ideas had acquired a limited following throughout the Old Kingdom (such ideas had appeared earlier in the more industrially advanced territories of Transylvania and Bukovina), and in 1893 the Romanian Social Democratic Party was founded in Bucharest. Its program, inspired by West European social democratic movements, was essentially moderate and nonrevolutionary. Recognizing Romania as an underdeveloped country, the Social Democrats saw their role as being to encourage the evolution of conditions that would eventually lead to socialism.[2] A number of socialist publications appeared during this period, though many of them were short-lived.[3]

Within seven years, however, the Social Democratic Party disappeared. Some of its members, anxious for more active and meaningful political participation, sought to expand their base, and in 1899 changed their name to National Democratic Party. Others, frustrated by their limited influence on Romanian politics, instead joined the Liberal Party, where they associated themselves with those members who successfully pressed for universal suffrage and agrarian reform during the period of Liberal Party rule immediately after World War I.[4]

The reviving of the socialist movement after its collapse at the turn of the century was primarily accomplished by two men, who continued to dominate it until after World War I. The first was Constantin Dobrogeanu-Gherea, a Russian Jew who had been forced to leave tsarist territory and subsequently settled in Romania. He played a prominent role in popularizing socialist ideas, and his writings had a lasting impact on Romanian socialism. The second was Christian Rakovsky, an ethnic Bulgarian from the Dobruja who had studied in Western Europe and established close contacts with West European and Russian socialists. He became editor of the Social Democratic newspaper, *Romania muncitoare,* and subsequently played a prominent role in the Soviet Union as head of government in the Soviet Ukraine and as ambassador to England and, later, France, before being purged in the late 1920s for his connections with Leon Trotsky. The impact of these two men on the Romanian socialist movement gave rise to two trends that were to have a profound influence on the development of socialism and communism in Romania. First, they had strong ties with the Russian revolutionary movement, whereas earlier socialist leaders had been more influenced by French and German socialism, and second, they were the first in a long line of non-Romanians to play leading roles in Romanian socialism and communism.[5]

After the 1917 Russian revolutions, and prompted by the conditions of economic and social unrest in Romania that accompanied the end of World War I, the socialists moved toward the left, and changed the party name again to Socialist Party in November 1918. To what extent the Socialists were responsible for fomenting or encouraging strikes and labor unrest in Romania during this period is unclear. It seems most likely that while they benefited from the radicalization of the political atmosphere, their role in causing it was limited.[6] During this period social and political changes led to the birth of a number of factions in the party.

The overthrow of the monarchy in Russia gave new impetus to the Romanian socialist movement and particularly to the party's left wing. A "Romanian Social Democratic Action Committee," of which Rakovsky was a prominent member, was established in Odessa in May 1917 by socialists who had fled there fearing imprisonment in Romania. Although the group was close to the Russian revolutionaries, it did not uniformly follow the Bolshevik line; nevertheless the Socialist Party in Romania was apparently sufficiently concerned about its Russian links and its radicalism to disavow the group. In early 1918 a Romanian Revolutionary Committee was formed, again with headquarters in Odessa, and a revolutionary battalion and a naval unit were established. The success of the local communists in Hungary under Bela Kun also resulted in the founding of a Romanian communist group in Budapest in December 1918, which included leftist Social Democrats from Transylvania. Various prisoners of war (including former officials from Transylvania and the Old Kingdom) who were being held in Russia were organized under Bolshevik influence.[7]

The conflict between these more radical groups organized under Bolshevik auspices, plus the left-wing faction of the Socialist Party in Romania (all of whom were called "maximalists"), and the more moderate factions of the party (known as "centrists" and "minimalists"), came to a head when the Comintern was established in March 1919. Among various factions within the party, views on association with the Comintern ranged from open hostility to insistence upon immediate affiliation. The maximalist group demanded the latter, and the launching of an insurrection. The Socialist Party leadership hammered out a rather moderate compromise program and sent it to the Comintern. They did not, however, request affiliation; nor did they—as the Comintern insisted—promise to include the word "communist" in the party's name.[8]

Following an attempted general strike and a terrorist action against the government, the more moderate groups broke away from the Socialist Party; at the same time a delegation representing the party leadership went to Moscow to negotiate affiliation with the Comintern. This delegation was composed of six individuals: Alexander Dobrogeanu-Gherea, Constantin Popovici, Gheorghe Cristescu, David Fabian, Eugen Rozvany, and Ion Flueras. In meetings with the Comintern executive committee in November 1920, Nikolai Bukharin severely criticized the Romanians for supporting the Averescu government, failing to aid the Hungarian communist government, refusing to call themselves a communist party, and failing to act against the existing Romanian government. The Romanian delegation ultimately engaged in self-criticism and pledged to bring the entire Socialist Party into affiliation with the Third International.[9] In a long letter written in December 1920 Grigory Zinoviev, chairman of the executive committee, reiterated at some length the accusations against the Romanian Socialists, criticized them for failing to support the Russian cause, and insisted that immediate steps be taken to bring the party into the Comintern.[10]

When the delegation returned to Romania in January 1921 the communist groups proceeded to prepare for a congress at which the party would accept affiliation with the Comintern and change its name as the Moscow officials had demanded. The congress was duly held in Bucharest on May 8–13, 1921; the question of affiliation with the Communist International was the major issue. In ex post facto reconstructions of the gathering, considerable difference of opinion was expressed with regard to the results and the significance of the event. C. Titel Petrescu, in his history of Romanian socialism, claimed that during the first days of the congress sentiment was against affiliation, but police provocateurs joined forces with the communist faction that favored it, in order to justify police intervention later.[11] Romanian communist accounts of these events before the mid-1960s maintain that the decision to affiliate with the Comintern was unanimous, but now the party—in line with its interests in emphasizing opposition to Comintern interference in internal party affairs—claims that 428 delegates voted outright for affiliation and 111 did so "with reservations." Party leader Nicolae Ceausescu has explained that the reservations had to do with "the mandatory nature of the decisions of the Communist International for member parties," but concludes, nevertheless, that "the May 1921 congress unanimously decided to transform the Socialist Party into the Romanian Communist Party."[12]

On May 12 the police closed the conference and arrested most of the participants who had voted for affiliation. Those who escaped arrest met on May 13 and sent a message of solidarity to Moscow. The arrests prevented completion of the task of organizing the newly created party, however, and it was not until the second congress in October 1922 that the leading positions were all filled and the name officially changed to "Romanian Communist Party, a Section of the Communist International" as demanded by the Comintern.

Although the majority of the delegates to the congress apparently favored the decision to affiliate with the Comintern, figures on party membership after the decision suggest that the newly founded RCP attracted considerably less than the entire membership of the Socialist Party. Current Romanian estimates place this at 100,000 on the eve of the split, while a Soviet estimate put it at about 45,000.[13] In 1922, however, the RCP had only 2,000 members—a small minority of the Socialists whichever figure one uses for their strength before the split.[14] Those who did not favor ties with the Comintern subsequently reorganized the Social Democratic Party, which was based largely on the trade unions and played a small role in Romanian politics until all parties were outlawed in 1938.

Factionalism and Internal Weakness

Less than three years after its establishment the RCP was banned by the Romanian government. Even before that the party suffered from considerable police harassment and government restrictions on its activities. In spite of being illegal, however, it continued to function underground, utilizing various front organizations to participate in elections and carrying on additional organizational work among certain groups of the population. Its membership, however, remained very small. As noted above, there were some 2,000 at the time of the fourth congress of the Comintern in 1922, and two years later, at the fifth congress, it had risen to only 2,500.[15] At the time of the fifth RCP congress in 1931 a party official said membership totaled only 1,200 and added that recruitment of new members was not progressing properly.[16] By 1936 the figure was estimated to have reached 5,000, but on the eve of the party's rise to power knowledgeable observers put it at about 1,000.[17] Similar problems affected the party's youth organization, which in April 1924 had fewer than 1,600 members.[18]

A report issued at the time of the sixth congress of the Comintern in 1928 reflected the weakness of the Romanian party. Its banning had "caused a temporary disorganization in its ranks," and as a result it had "no means of approach to the masses" and not even an illegal press. In the two years between 1926 and 1928 it did not issue "a single illegal manifesto, nor did any of its organizations show any initiative in this respect." Attempts to convene an illegal conference were made for two years without success, the leadership was accused of "treachery and betrayal," and the membership was described as suffering from "passivity and demoralization."[19]

One serious problem that hampered the party's effectiveness during the first decade of its existence was the factionalization of its leadership, which was compounded by the Comintern's efforts to gain full control over the RCP. Owing to the party's organizational weakness, however, the Comintern moved rather slowly. Its executive committee first dealt with the RCP in February 1926, when Chairman Grigory Zinoviev criticized party leader Gheorghe Cristescu in very strong terms, charging him with "rightist errors."

One representative of the leftist minority within the party complained that it did not yet have a leadership capable of guiding it "along a correct Marxist-Leninist line, of bolshevizing" it. A spokesman for the party leadership, while admitting some errors and criticizing Cristescu, was hardly repentant. But despite the strong directive from the executive committee, there was little improvement in the party's leadership.[20]

In 1930 the Comintern, taking up the matter of the "unprincipled factional struggle" within the RCP, issued directives removing three of the leaders it held most responsible, and gave instructions designed to bring about unity in the party.[21] Despite this vigorous intervention on the part of the Comintern, however, it was still over a year before the fifth RCP congress was convened and the situation more or less resolved. That congress marked a turning point in the party's interwar history. It confirmed Soviet control over the leadership and, to a great extent, marked the end of the factional struggles. The RCP's increasing organizational ability became apparent as it succeeded in exploiting labor unrest in the next few years, but although it had been successfully "bolshevized" it was still organizationally limited in capacity, and its membership remained small. Organizational weakness and the fact that it had to operate underground were among the main reasons for the party's poor showing in the elections that took place during the interwar period, although it received considerably greater support than the size of its membership would suggest. It was the prime motivating force behind the Workers' and Peasants' Bloc, an organization that enabled it to participate in the election campaigns.[22] In the 1926, 1927, and 1928 parliamentary elections the bloc received between 31,930 and 39,300 votes, but it never even reached 2 percent of the total vote cast.[23] The communist-led bloc made its best showing in the elections in 1931, when the serious economic problems besetting the country generated increased support for it in the industrial districts of Transylvania. The Workers' and Peasants' Bloc ran candidates in 47 electoral districts and received 73,710 votes—twice the average number it had received in three elections in the late 1920s. Five of its candidates, including Lucretiu Patrascanu, were elected to the parliament, although their election was subsequently invalidated and none of them actually functioned as a deputy.[24] In the 1932 elections, however, the bloc ran candidates in only nine districts and received only 9,941 votes.[25] During the 1937 elections, in keeping with the Comintern's policy of putting up "a united front of democratic forces" against fascism, the communists attempted to cooperate with the National Peasant Party, but the latter concluded an agreement with the All-for-the-Fatherland Party (the political party of the Iron Guard) to refrain from reciprocal attacks; the RCP again made a poor showing.

The Problem of Appealing to the Working Class

One of the party's major problems in gaining electoral support, as well as in increasing its membership, was the size of the working class, which in most other countries formed the mainstay of communist support. Because of the low level of industrialization in Romania, there was no large working class to which the party could appeal. The Old Kingdom, Bessarabia, and the Dobruja were economically underdeveloped, and Transylvania was only somewhat more advanced. During the first third of the twentieth century there was a concentration of industry in larger undertakings and a decline in the number of small shops employing only a few workers. Nevertheless, in 1930 there were 140,948 industrial enterprises in Romania, of which 130,433 were still small shops employing no more than five persons. In total less than 10 percent of the active population was engaged in industry.[26]

Not only was there a very small working class from which the party could seek support, but many workers still retained links with the countryside, which industrialization had only recently induced them to leave. Thus there was no developed working-class consciousness, a fact that is reflected in the small number of workers affiliated with trade unions. Between 1919 and 1929 union membership rose from 25,000 to 42,000, and by 1938 it was still only some 80,000. The former Austro-Hungarian territories of Transylvania and the Banat, which had a longer tradition of industrialization, comprised the largest proportion. Of total union members in 1929, some 60 percent came from these two areas, which had only 23 percent of the country's population; 26 percent of union members were from the Old Kingdom, which had over 44 percent of the population.[27]

Further complicating the communists' task of successfully appealing to the working class was competition from the Social Democrats. The latter based their party largely on the trade unions, and in fact many of their leaders were officials in the trade union movement, although complete separation of political and union activity was the general practice. The communists, on the other hand, were banned after 1924, which made it impossible for them to engage in open propaganda or organizational work. The RCP's revolutionary program contrasted sharply with that of the Social Democrats, who felt that objective economic and social conditions in Romania were not ripe for radical social transformation, and thus believed their role was to encourage capitalist and democratic evolution in order to generate "objective" conditions that would someday bud into socialism. This passive approach on the part of the Social Democrats did not inspire an enthusiastic following among the working class, but the radical activist policy of the RCP also failed to kindle much support.

The party did seek to seize the initiative in the trade unions from the Social Democrats. A confrontation between the two parties at a union conference in Cluj in the fall of 1923, however, resulted in defeat for the communists, and shortly thereafter the Comintern directed the party to establish separate organizations, which were called "unitary" trade unions.[28] This effort achieved only limited success. The following year, at its third congress, the party leaders again directed the membership to undertake an intensive campaign among the working class, at the same time acknowledging the absence of "deep bonds with the broad working class."[29] In July 1925, when the leadership issued an important resolution calling for the "bolshevization" of the party, it declared that "the base of the communist party is the industrial proletariat" and urged renewed activity in the trade unions.[30] But when the Central Committee reviewed this activity that December, it reported no progress in establishing cells within factories and trade unions, and again the party leaders were criticized and directed to intensify their efforts.[31] A Comintern report on the Romanian party in 1928 stated that "no great systematic communist party work had been carried out in the trade unions," and charged the RCP with opportunist deviations regarding the unions, noting that "generally speaking the party has too little grasp of what practical work in the trade unions means."[32]

A major event in the party's struggle to establish its links with the working class was the general congress of the Unitary Trade Unions held in Timisoara in April 1929, under the direction of Vasile Luca. It ended in a violent confrontation with the authorities, who sent troops to terminate the proceedings. One worker was killed and the other participants, who barricaded themselves in the trade union building, were arrested after a siege.[33] Thereafter the Unitary Trade Unions were dissolved. But efforts continued to be made to infiltrate the other unions. In a 1930 resolution issued by the Comintern's political secretariat, criticizing the leadership and activity of the RCP, one of the major complaints was the fact that the party organizations still had little strength among the unions and in the factories.[34]

Owing to its lack of influence on the working class, the party played a limited role in most of the strikes and other manifestations of labor unrest that marked a good part of the interwar period, including the upsurge of such demonstrations that accompanied the economic crisis of 1929–1933. The party has attempted ex post facto to identify itself with all interwar workers' demonstrations, but except for the railway workers' strike of 1933 there seems only a limited basis for such claims.[35] Contemporary criticism by Comintern officials was particularly pointed with regard to the party's ineffective role in promoting worker unrest. Bela Kun, in a scathing attack on its "unprincipled factional struggle," stated that in most cases the party had "no link with spontaneously developed economic struggles. It was incapable of leading the disabled movement in Bucharest, present or previous unrest, or such revolutionary strike movements as those that took place in Lupeni and Arad." In fact, Kun continued, when a strike at the Lupeni mine was being bloodily suppressed, the party leadership failed to call on other mines to join in a sympathy strike because it believed the action to be the work of provocateurs. But not only was the party chastised for playing no role in initiating worker unrest; it was accused of failing to take advantage of spontaneous outbursts and of being "far removed from the working masses, from their struggle, and from the political life of the country."[36] Another criticism reiterated the charge that worker unrest in Romania was spontaneous and that the party and the leaders of the Unitary Trade Unions had absented themselves from the struggle: "The workers seek leaders, but our party organizations and the Unitary Trade Unions remain sunk in deepest passivity."[37]

The Comintern's rebuke and the reorganization carried out under Moscow's guidance at the fifth RCP congress in 1931 apparently had the effect of stimulating the party to greater activity among the workers. The high point of communist success in the interwar period was its leadership of the railway workers' strike in early 1933; the party figure who benefited most from this action was Gheorghe Gheorghiu-Dej, a young railway worker whose rise to prominence in the party is attributable largely to the recognition he achieved as a result of the strike. In March 1932 he was elected secretary of the railwaymen's Central Committee for Action. The workers' dissatisfaction with government economic policies resulted in the call for a general strike on February 2, 1933, and King Carol and the National Peasant government then in power decreed a state of emergency. On February 4 Gheorghiu-Dej and a number of other leaders of the strike were arrested. On February 15 the strikers occupied the railway workshops at Grivita, a suburb of Bucharest, but the following day troops were called in. A number of workers were killed, and according to some reports 2,000 people were arrested. Although he was taken into custody before the main events of the strike took place, Gheorghiu-Dej's reputation in the party was greatly enhanced by the attention focused on him during the strike and at his trial. The durability of this reputation is apparent when one considers that he spent the years from 1933 to 1944 in prison and still emerged as one of the main contenders for the leadership of the RCP.[38]

The Party and the Agrarian Question

The second major socioeconomic group from which the RCP sought to win support was the small peasantry. Since the peasants constituted by far the largest social class, the rewards of a successful appeal to this group would have been considerable. In 1913 almost 80 percent of the Romanian population was engaged in agriculture, and even in 1934 it was estimated that 72.4 percent were dependent on that sector. Despite a series of extensive agrarian reforms, in 1930 three-quarters of all land holdings in the country were under five hectares (about twelve acres) in size, and owing to the density of the rural population and the low per capita production, radical solutions might well have elicited a favorable response.[39]

In its attempts to exploit the peasant situation the RCP faced a number of difficulties that limited its success. Among the factors that played a role in minimizing the appeal of radical programs to the peasantry were the land reforms carried out at the end of World War I. Though it is perhaps going too far to claim that the reforms created a barrier to bolshevism in the West, they did help to lessen the appeal of communism. Another difficulty was that the party found itself in conflict with the Comintern over peasant policy; it sought to adjust its policies and tactics to local peculiarities and needs, while the Comintern based its directives primarily upon the needs of the Soviet Union and on Soviet perception of the requirements of the international communist movement.

The theoretical writings of Constantin Dobrogeanu-Gherea also limited the impact of party activity on the peasantry and brought it into conflict with the Comintern. According to some party leaders, his major work, *Neoiobagia* [Neoserfdom],[40] which analyzed the problem of the peasantry from a Marxist point of view, influenced the party's program and tactics until the fifth congress in 1931.[41] The basic thesis of neoserfdom was that "the impact of capitalism upon a backward agrarian society such as that in Romania produced a hybrid in which there was a monstrous mingling of old and new." Thus one found a liberal bourgeois government and legal system coexisting with a peasant class. Bound to small plots of land that they could not leave owing to modern equivalents of feudal restraints, the peasants were condemned to the poverty of neoserfdom. Dobrogeanu-Gherea's Marxian analysis, however, did not lead him to expound a socialist program that could appeal to the peasantry. He regarded peasant uprisings like that of 1907 as tragedies to be avoided and warned against the consequences of unleashing the brutal passions of the peasant class. His solution was to clear the way for capitalist development by eliminating the neofeudal restraints that tied peasants to the land and encouraging the development of small farms, which he regarded as a more efficient form of cultivation than large landed estates.[42]

From the beginning Dobrogeanu-Gherea's viewpoint clearly permeated the RCP's peasant policy. His son Alexander, who was one of the founding leaders of the party, was influential in drawing up its first agrarian program;[43] in the debates at the fourth Comintern congress in the summer of 1922 Marcel Pauker argued with Eugen Varga, the Hungarian Marxist economist who delivered the report on agrarian problems, from premises largely based on the theory of neoserfdom.[44]

While Dobrogeanu-Gherea's analysis was compatible with Lenin's approach to the agrarian question, the former's essentially passive program contrasted with the latter's preoccupation with advancing the revolution. Lenin recognized the backward elements in peasant revolts, for example, but nevertheless favored them because they furthered the cause of revolution. With the Communist International dominated by Leninist ideas and the Romanian Marxists strongly influenced by Dobrogeanu-Gherea, conflict was unavoidable.

At the fifth Comintern congress in 1924, the Romanian party was criticized for failing to understand the need to attract the peasants and for not having drawn up a program for work among this important group; in reply Romanian representatives indicated that the party intended to study the peasant question and intensify its work in rural areas.[45] At about the same time the Red Peasant International, established under auspices of the Communist International, made an unsuccessful attempt to secure the adherence of the Romanian Peasant Party as well as that of the peasant parties in other Balkan states.[46] This failure, added to the Romanian government's decision to outlaw the RCP in April 1924, made it still harder for the party to attract the support of the peasantry.

The Comintern apparently did not subject the weak Romanian party to close scrutiny until some two years after it was outlawed. By the spring of

1926, however, when factionalism forced the executive committee to summon representatives of left and right to present their positions, agrarian policy and the question of whether to seek a coalition with the National Peasant Party constituted the crux of the controversy. The rightist faction insisted that revolutionary activity was unproductive under existing circumstances, and hence the most useful course would be coalition. The leftists, on the other hand, regarded entering a coalition as joining forces with "kulaks and reactionaries" and said that such a policy underestimated the revolutionary potential in the countryside. Not wishing to resolve the dispute by splitting the already weak party, the Comintern criticized both factions and called on the party to intensify its efforts.[47] A year later the Comintern was still complaining that "except for individual comrades [the members of] the communist party [of Romania] have failed to undertake any activity among the peasants of old Romania," and the party was once more instructed to adopt a more active policy vis-à-vis the agricultural areas.[48]

Changes on the domestic political scene in 1928 brought the agrarian problem to the fore again but Comintern policy was now shifting to the left, in keeping with the interests of the Soviet Union; as a result the policies imposed on the RCP were out of tune with Romanian conditions. The National Peasant Party launched a series of protest meetings that culminated in a massive demonstration in Alba Julia in May 1928. This gathering served to emphasize the revolutionary potential of the peasant masses and focused the attention of the Comintern on Romania and its weak communist party. The question that split the party was whether the RCP should oppose the National Peasant Party or remain neutral and possibly even support that party's accession to power. Although the Comintern enjoined opposition, the RCP did little either to help or to hinder the establishment of the National Peasant government under Iuliu Maniu in November 1928.[49]

Events in Romania prompted an in depth Soviet analysis of the causes behind developments there, and a wide-ranging debate over the attitude the RCP should adopt toward the new government.[50] The Comintern ultimately decided in favor of opposition to the National Peasant government, not because this was the most satisfactory way to further the communist party's efforts to appeal to the peasantry, but because it was consistent with the course upon which the Soviet Union was embarking at that time. At the RCP's fifth congress, held at the end of 1931, the Comintern's policy toward the National Peasant Party and the agrarian question was adopted *in toto*.[51]

Competition with and Opposition to
the Iron Guard

Another factor that limited the success of the RCP in the interwar period was the competition from the Iron Guard for the allegiance of those segments of the population that favored radical solutions. During the interwar period, in both Romania and Hungary, where the revolutionary left was weak and disorganized, the fascist movement had no need to guard its left flank or to compromise with the forces of moderation. Hence fascists were free to become "the radical and revolutionary movement they never clearly became in the West." The Legion of the Archangel Michael, also known as the Iron Guard, appeared "as a distinctly radical social force."[52] The radical and apparently revolutionary nature of the Iron Guard movement can in part be attributed to the weakness of the RCP and its failure to attract those groups in Romania that were predisposed to radical solutions. But at the same time it seems likely that competition from the Iron Guard made the revolutionary task of the communist party more difficult, since a radical alternative was available. Also, this alternative was linked with Romanian nationalism, while the communist party was identified with non-Romanian interests.

The workers and peasantry, two of the major groups the RCP sought to attract to its cause, were also groups to whom the program of the Iron Guard appealed. The working classes in Germany and other West European countries have been traditionally linked with the political left. In Romania, on the other hand, large numbers of workers identified with the Iron Guard. Eugen Weber concluded that in Bucharest alone "a special Legionary Workers' Corps founded in 1936 soon boasted eight thousand members," and although it was disbanded in 1938, shortly after its reappearance in the fall of 1940 it numbered 13,000 militants.[53] The Iron Guard was more successful than the communists in winning support among nationalistic and religious members of the peasantry because it was identified with Romanian nationalism and with the church, whereas the communist party was seen as an antinational, extraneous element and its ideological opposition to religion alienated many. The supernationalism of the Iron Guard, on the other hand, tended to drive the non-Romanian nationalities toward the communist party, which had the effect of reinforcing its image as an organization inimical to Romania's national interests.[54]

With the increase in influence of the Iron Guard, the Romanian communists took the lead in the antifascist movement, and succeeded in attracting some workers, intellectuals, and professional people into cooperation. Ana Pauker and Dmitri Kroshnev were the party leaders who actively led this program after 1934. The Romanian communists have sought to claim a monopoly on the antifascist movement,[55] but other forces and groups also opposed both the Iron Guard and King Carol's dictatorship. The antifascist campaign, however, did bring the party some support from writers and journalists, who contributed articles to its propaganda organs, and from lawyers, who defended communist leaders in their increasingly frequent trials. Among the lawyers was Ion Gheorghe Maurer (prime minister in the Romanian government from 1961 to 1974), who defended Ana Pauker in 1935.[56]

The Party's Policy on the National Question

Greater Romania, as it emerged from World War I, was considerably larger and more ethnically diverse than the Romanian state that existed in 1913. The traditional principalities of Moldavia and Wallachia were augmented by the acquisition of Southern Dobruja from Bulgaria (in the Second Balkan War, 1913), and the former Austro-Hungarian territories of Transylvania, Crisana, Maramures, part of the Banat, and Bukovina (after World War I). In the chaos and civil war that followed the Russian revolutions of 1917 Romania also acquired Bessarabia. The Old Kingdom was ethnically homogeneous; some 92 percent of the population were of Romanian descent. The addition of the new territories after 1918 changed the picture considerably, however. In the 1930 census Romania as a whole had a population that was 71.9 percent Romanian. Except in Southern Dobruja, Romanians were also the most numerous nationality in the new territories, but there were substantial minorities. In 1930 Transylvania (including the Banat, Crisana, and Maramures) had a Hungarian minority of 1,353,276 (24.4 percent of its total population) and ethnic Germans numbered 543,852 (9.8 percent). In Bukovina Romanians made up only 44.5 percent of the population, with Ukrainians (236,130, or 27.7 percent), Jews (92,492, or 10.8 percent), and Germans (75,533, or 8.9 percent) forming substantial minorities. The balance was similar in Bessarabia, where Romanians made up 56.2 percent of the total population in 1930; but there were 351,912 Russians (12.3 percent), 314,912 Ukrainians (11 percent), 204,858 Jews (7.2 percent), and 163,726 Bulgarians (5.7 percent).[57]

Almost as soon as it was founded, the communist party became involved in the question of how best to exploit the minorities to its advantage. Here again, however, it found that the interests of the Soviets differed from its own. The new communist government in Moscow was concerned about the loss of Bessarabia; this territory had been taken from Turkey by the tsarist government in 1812, and had been under Soviet jurisdiction for several months before becoming a part of Romania in 1918. Initially there were conflicting views on Bessarabia within the Soviet party. In 1919 the Soviet government handed the Romanian government an ultimatum demanding evacuation of its troops from Bessarabia within 48 hours, but took no action when the time limit expired. In 1920 Ukrainian Commissar of War Mikhail Frunze apparently proposed that the Red Army reconquer Bessarabia, since it had almost completed its action against the last of the White opposition in Russia. He was supported in this by Marshal K. Y. Voroshilov. Christian Rakovsky, at this time head of the Ukrainian government, opposed military action against Romania on the grounds that it would unite the major powers against the young Soviet state, and a Romanian collapse as a result of Red Army action could prove to be more than Soviet resources were capable of handling. In the summer of 1921 Trotsky proposed acknowledging Bessarabia as part of Romania, but Rakovsky argued that refusing to settle the question would enable the Soviets to utilize the issue in their Balkan maneuvering.

The question again came to the fore in 1924, as the Romanian and Soviet governments undertook negotiations on establishing diplomatic relations. On this occasion Maxim Litvinov favored recognizing Romanian sovereignty over Bessarabia and closing the issue, but again Rakovsky, supported by Commissar for Foreign Affairs Georgy Chicherin, argued against abandoning the claim to Bessarabia. This line prevailed, and the negotiations between the two governments collapsed because the Soviets refused to agree to any document that might imply recognition of Romania's right to the territory.[58]

From this point on the Soviet government followed a consistent policy of claiming Bessarabia.[59] In the summer of 1924, following the failure of negotiations with the Romanian government, the Soviet Union, with clearly irredentist intentions, established the Moldavian Autonomous Soviet Socialist Republic on the small, ethnically Romanian territory on the Soviet bank of the Dniester River. At the fifth Comintern congress in the summer of 1924 Dmitry Manuilsky, in a report on the national question, distinguished irredentism between "a workers' and peasants' " and a bourgeois state from irredentism between two bourgeois states. In the case of the former ("revolutionary irredentism"), the correct course would be to decide in favor of the Soviet state. Manuilsky noted that the communist parties in Poland, Estonia, and the Carpatho-Ukraine had already supported annexation of certain of their territories to the USSR. Although he did not mention the Romanian communists in this connection, at its third congress earlier that year the RCP had in fact approved a resolution favoring the return of Bessarabia to the Soviet Union.[60]

The USSR and Romania established diplomatic relations in June 1934, but no solution to the Bessarabian question was reached. An agreement was initialed in 1936 by Litvinov and Romanian Foreign Minister Nicolae Titulescu, which included Soviet recognition of Romania's possession of Bessarabia, but Titulescu was dismissed from his post by King Carol before the agreement was ratified, and nothing further was done. This conciliatory agreement had been conditioned by the growing Soviet concern about German influence in Eastern Europe, and it seems unlikely that the move represented any fundamental change in the Soviet position, which by 1924 had hardened to the view that Bessarabia should be restored to the Soviet Union. In 1944 the Red Army occupied Bessarabia and the territory was again integrated into the Soviet state.

The Soviet claim to Bessarabia established the Comintern's position on that aspect of the Romanian nationality question. The remainder of Romania's minority problems were decided on the basis of other reasoning. In the USSR the Bolsheviks had found ethnic dissatisfaction to be a powerful and disruptive force that could be utilized in bringing about revolutionary upheavals. They had advocated the slogan of self-determination for nationalities, including the right to secede from the existing state. Both Lenin and Stalin, however, made it clear that secession from the Soviet state ran counter to the interests of the nationalities, and where they were in a position to prevent separation they did so. In other words, the Soviets utilized the slogan of self-determination to topple the old system, but once the proletariat had succeeded in coming to power, self-determination, if it resulted in separation, became counterrevolutionary. In other countries, though, they transplanted their Russian experience directly, without considering the effect it might have, under different conditions, on the local communist parties.

In Romania the Soviet-inspired policy on the national question was a major reason for the RCP's lack of appeal. From the Soviet point of view, however, the primary concern was not the strength of the Romanian party but the role of Romania in terms of Soviet foreign policy considerations. The CPSU leaders regarded the Romanian and Polish governments as hostile to the new Soviet state—the Poles because of their defeat of the Red Army and annexation of Soviet territory, and the Romanians because of their annexation of Bessarabia and the role of the Romanian Army in bringing about the collapse of the Hungarian Soviet government. The Soviets saw Romania as an "outpost" or the "advance guard" of the imperialist countries. From this point of view, a primary consideration in Soviet foreign policy was to weaken Romania internally, in order to lessen its power to act against the USSR. A policy of inciting national unrest was thus directed toward short-run interests, while the long-term interests of the Romanian party suffered.

After the RCP was established problems arose with regard to establishing its own nationality policy. A draft program on the question was prepared, apparently for presentation at the founding congress of the party in 1921, and while the general analysis of the national question in Romania was couched in Marxist terms, the party's tasks in this connection were hardly revolutionary. Workers in the party and the trade unions should be able to use their mother tongue at meetings and in contacts with other groups, but the party should not be divided into segments by nationality; the workers should oppose action by those of Romanian nationality against the cultures of other nationalities; and the party should engage in work among organizations that encouraged national cultures.[61]

This mild document, however, was already out of tune with the Comintern's position. The theses on the national and colonial question drafted by Lenin and adopted by the Comintern at its second congress in 1920 called for vigorous exploitation of national discontent, involving the right of self-determination including secession, and the Comintern's executive committee pointed out to the Balkan communist parties that encouraging national unrest could play a particularly important role in that region.[62]

Romania was obviously one country where this principle could be applied. The RCP leadership, however, was divided over the issue. There were three main factions. Gheorghe Cristescu, secretary general of the party and an ethnic Romanian from the Old Kingdom, argued against the policy of self-determination including secession on the grounds that it could be interpreted by the authorities as treason and might result in the banning of the party. Elek Koblos, the central organizational secretary, and Sandor Korosi-Krizsan, both Hungarians from Transylvania, insisted on following the Leninist directives and adopting the self-determination slogan. A number of leading party members from Transylvania were in agreement with this view because they regarded their region as the most highly developed industrially and hence the area in which the party was most likely to achieve success, and the slogan of self-determination was likely to help the party cause there. A middle group led by Alexander Dobrogeanu-Gherea and including a number of intellectuals proposed that the question be referred to the Comintern executive committee. In September 1923 a delegation composed of Cristescu, Korosi-Krizsan, and Dobrogeanu-Gherea went to Moscow, where the issue was presented to Comintern officials. CPSU theorist Bukharin insisted that the Romanian party must support the principle of self-determination for tactical reasons, describing the Bolsheviks' success in disrupting the Kerensky government in 1917, although he did point out that after the revolution the unity of the state had been restored. The same Leninist principle of "breaking up and uniting again" on a new basis would also have to be applied in Romania. Cristescu was still reluctant to accept this, because it would make work among the Romanians more difficult, but in the end he capitulated and Korosi-Krizsan drafted a resolution expressing agreement.[63]

A resolution was drawn up in Moscow and approved by Bukharin and the Romanian delegation. It became official party policy the following year at the RCP's third congress, and laid the principles of the party's national policy for the remainder of the interwar period. With regard to Bessarabia, the Soviet claim was unequivocally admitted:

> The workers and peasants of Bessarabia, who came to life in the first vital period of the Russian revolution and now suffer under the boot of the Romanian military dictator, daily express the hope that their national revolution will make them one with the Union of Soviet Socialist Republics, which will guarantee the development and protection of their vital interests.[64]

At the same time the party undertook the task of propagandizing against the antinational ruling Romanian bourgeoisie and in favor of the rights of the minorities. The party leaders were aware that the slogan of self-determination for all nationalities was likely to create serious difficulties for them in their work among the ethnic Romanians, and therefore party members were directed

> to explain over and over again to the Romanian working masses that the national struggle against the power of the Romanian bourgeoisie advances the struggle for liberation of the Romanian proletariat and that it is in the vital interests of revolutionary victory . . . to support as a basic principle the right of self-determination of nations, including complete separation from the existing state.[65]

The resolution on the national question adopted at the third RCP congress brought the party into line with Comintern policy, which from 1924 on began to emphasize the national question as a major aspect of communist activity in the Balkans. Manuilsky's report to the fifth Comintern congress in the summer of 1924 and the resolution adopted at that gathering emphasized the obligation of all parties, and particularly those in the Balkans, to exploit national discontent by propagating the slogan of self-determination of nationalities, including the right of separation. Manuilsky criticized the RCP for advocating the establishment of an independent Transylvanian republic, which was contrary to the irredentism of the Hungarians in the region, who favored incorporation into Hungary. The party apparently took this position because it did not want to support a foreign bourgeois government's territorial claims. The RCP spokesman in the debate on the national question (Korosi-Krizsan, using the name Georgescu) denied Manuilsky's charges with regard to the party's national policy, but fully accepted the Comintern line.[66] Further emphasizing the importance of the Comintern views on the national question were the directives to the Balkan parties adopted by the Comintern-led Communist Balkan Federation at its sixth congress, also in 1924.[67]

The party continued to follow this policy throughout the interwar period, and it was periodically reaffirmed in resolutions adopted at party congresses and in other party documents. There were some deviations from the line set in 1923–1924, but these were criticized and apparently abandoned. At the fourth party congress in 1928, in addition to affirming the RCP's obligation "to support by all possible means the struggle of the working masses of Bessarabia for unification with the RASSM [Soviet Moldavia]," the party went further, agreeing to support "the tendency toward unification of the working masses of Bukovina with the Soviet Ukraine." On the same occasion the party leadership was criticized for "obscuring the revolutionary point of view on the national question" by substituting the slogan "a federative republic of the workers and peasants of Romania" for "self-determination including separation" and by occasional passivity in "carrying out [party] policy with regard to the 10-year occupation of Bessarabia."[68] It would appear that in the interest of appealing to ethnic Romanian elements some party leaders sought to play down the stridently anti-Romanian national policy. The fifth party congress in 1931 did not initiate any major departures, but the Soviet Union's way of handling nationality problems was particularly emphasized as a model for dealing with Romania's own national questions.[69]

The RCP's Success in Appealing to the Minorities

Of the three target groups the RCP sought to attract during most of the interwar period—workers, peasants, and "the oppressed nationalities"— the greatest success was achieved with the minorities. Although there is insufficient information to establish the point conclusively, there are strong indications that, to a significant degree, such success as the party achieved in the elections was supplied by dissatisfied minorities. In the parliamentary elections of 1926, 1927, and 1928, the party's strength clearly lay in areas with large non-Romanian ethnic populations. Although table 1 shows an apparently strong correlation between the proportion of non-Romanians and the communist vote, other factors must also be considered. Transylvania and the Banat, which provided the great majority of communist votes, were more industrialized than Bessarabia, Bukovina, and many parts of the Old Kingdom; and as noted earlier, these areas also had a higher degree of working-class consciousness. Despite all this, however, a large portion of

TABLE 1

Communist Vote by Region, 1926–1931
(in percent)

Region	Total Population (1930)	Non-Romanian Population in Region	Total Vote for Communists			
			1926	1927	1928	1931
Old Kingdom (including Dobruja)	48.7	11.5	9.9	17.3	12.3	9.7
Crisana-Maramures	7.7	39.9	*	*	2.6	*
Transylvania	17.8	42.4	38.6	46.6	44.6	70.5
Bessarabia	15.9	43.8	*	*	9.1	*
Banat	5.2	45.6	42.1	31.9	21.0	*
Bukovina	4.7	55.5	*	*	10.4	*

SOURCES: Al. Badlescu, "Gegen eine Welt von Feinden," *Die Kommunistiche Internationale* 10:2 (January 9, 1929), p. 61; and "Der Sieg des Arbeiter- und Bauernblocks bei den Wahlen in Rumanien," ibid., 12:20 (May 23, 1931), p. 888.

*Data not given.

the communist vote must be attributed to the party's appeal to the minorities.

A contemporary polemic over the 1931 elections between the Social Democrats and the communists also lends support to this view. In analyzing the success of the communist Workers' and Peasants' Bloc, which had almost doubled its votes over the figures for the 1928 election (reaching nearly 74,000 in 1931) the head of the Social Democratic Party claimed that the communists had "utilized the irredentist aspirations of the peasants in the border regions. Communists received most votes in areas on the Hungarian, Russian, and Bulgarian borders from the peasants of the national minorities."[70] In the Comintern analysis of the vote the Social Democrats were accused of lying and the votes for Social Democratic and Workers' and Peasants' Bloc candidates were compared, with the intention of showing communist strength in industrial areas. The evidence presented, however, shows that in industrial areas in minority regions the communists did better, but in ethnic Romanian areas the socialists were more successful. In the industrialized areas of Timis, Arad, Bihor, Mures, and Cernauti (Czernowitz; Chernovtsy)—all areas with substantial non-Romanian populations—communists outpolled the Social Democrats, but in Bucharest and in the Jiu Valley coal mining district—both areas of predominantly Romanian ethnic composition—the Social Democrats did better.[71]

The RCP not only found electoral support among the national minorities but also enrolled large numbers of them as party members. Two primary groups were attracted to communism in Romania for ethnic reasons. One was what R. V. Burks called "the rejected peoples": those without a territorial base or a clear-cut ethnic identity (in Romania the Jews were the primary ethnic group in this category). The second group was made up of the irredentists of neighboring states, who were dissatisfied with being included in Romania and with their treatment there.

To the Jews, communism's universal ideology promised a new identity transcending the ethnic or the national. The Jews who were attracted to communism were not those who sought to crystallize religious and cultural values, but those who believed assimilation was the answer to Jewish identity. As Burks points out, the Jewish communists of Eastern Europe were "assimilationists" who "tended to believe that genuine assimilation would become possible only if and when the existing society underwent some fundamental change."[72] The anti-Semitism of many Romanians, coupled with the sizable Jewish community (some 728,115 in 1930), gave the communists a large group to whom they could appeal. While the older generation tended to acquiesce in the status quo, many of the younger generation of Jews became members of the RCP, and a number of them found their way into the party leadership during the interwar period; Ana (Rabinovici) Pauker is perhaps the best known, but others included her husband, Marcel Pauker, and Alexander Dobrogeanu-Gherea.[73]

The irredentists saw the party as a vehicle not of assimilation but of ethnic protest. The communists were the political group most strongly opposed to continuation of the state in its existing form, and hence a number of dissatisfied Hungarians from Transylvania and Bulgarians from the Dobruja were drawn into the party. Its policy of calling for the right of self-determination of nationalities including secession was particularly important in attracting these groups.[74] In the leadership of the party during the interwar years there were a large number of ethnic Hungarians and Bulgarians. The former included Elek Koblos (who was secretary general between the third and fourth congresses and who represented the party at Comintern congresses under the name of Badulescu), Vasile Luca, Korosi-Krizsan, and many others. Among the Bulgarians who played leading party roles during this period were Boris Stefanov (who was a member of the RCP Central Committee during most of the interwar years), Gheorghe Crosneff (who in the 1930s was editor of the illegal party paper, *Scinteia*), Dimitur Kolev (Dumitru Coliu), and Dimitur Donchev.

The RCP enrollment of a large number of ethnic non-Romanian members and its espousal of the Comintern principle of self-determination for nationalities resulted in a division into regional organizations that focused on their own interests and many of which worked actively for separation of various territories from the Romanian state. One observer described the party as "more a confederacy of radical national minorities than a Romanian revolutionary movement."[75] The Bessarabian wing of the party, for example, was closely associated with the CPSU and in some cases was more under Soviet than RCP direction.[76] Unions of Bessarabian, Bulgarian, and Ukrainian peasants were organized under communist auspices and in fact carried out irredentist programs even before the RCP itself was fully organized. CC members led these groups but were only indirectly responsible to the party.

In the Dobruja, revolutionary irredentist groups associated with the Bulgarian Communist Party (BCP) and the Comintern followed policies quite independent of those of the RCP, although a number of the Bulgarians involved in these groups were leading officials in the Romanian party. Under instructions from the Comintern to foment revolution at all costs, they advocated the creation of a free and independent Dobruja, as called for in the fifth Comintern congress's statement on the national question in Central

Europe and the Balkans. In 1933 the Comintern changed its policy; the Dobruja was no longer to become free and independent but part of Bulgaria. At this time the BCP sent one of its CC members, Dimitar Ganev, who did not come from the Dobruja, to take charge of the communist front, the Dobruja Revolutionary Organization, and persuade it to begin encouraging reversion of the territory to Bulgaria. Ganev was co-opted as a member of the Romanian party's CC.[77]

Although during most of the interwar period the RCP encouraged the dismemberment of the Romanian state, by the end of the 1930s indications of some modification in its national policy appeared. The growing strength of Nazi Germany and fascist Italy was of sufficient concern to the CPSU to prompt it to direct communist parties to create united fronts in order to strengthen the antifascist forces in the various East European states, and apparently the Romanian party moved toward a minority policy that was more consistent with Romania's national interests. In 1938, for example, the BCP sent a representative to discuss with Romanian party officials the question of annexing the Dobruja to Bulgaria, but the Romanians refused to meet with him.

The shift in viewpoint was most apparent at the time of the territorial changes forced upon Romania in 1940. Although the party praised "the liberation of the peoples of Bessarabia, northern Bukovina, and the Baltic States," all of which had been annexed by the Soviet Union after ultimatums backed by the Red Army, it criticized the fact that northern Transylvania, which had over one million "Romanian workers and peasants," had been given to Hungary under terms of the Second Vienna Award. In a statement on this action, the RCP held Marshal Antonescu and the Iron Guard responsible for the loss of this territory and proclaimed that only through cooperation with the Soviet Union was there any hope of defeating imperialist power. It is interesting that the cession of the southern part of the Dobruja to Bulgaria was not mentioned in this context—at least not in the documents published after the war.[78] The Soviet position was also similar to that taken by the RCP. On the morning the Vienna Award was signed, the Soviet news agency TASS issued a communiqué expressing Soviet dissatisfaction at not having been consulted in the matter.[79]

After the German attack on the Soviet Union, in which Romania, under Antonescu, participated, the RCP intensified its efforts to form a united front with other domestic democratic parties in order to put an end to the country's participation in the struggle against the USSR. In numerous proclamations and action programs the party supported the Soviet view that

Romanian troops should evacuate Bessarabia and northern Bukovina, but advocated the return of northern Transylvania to Romania.[80] Negotiations between the RCP and other parties anxious to replace the Antonescu regime ran into serious difficulties over the issue of Bessarabia. The RCP refused to pledge itself to preserve Romania's prewar territorial integrity, and the other parties were reluctant to join a bloc of which it was a member unless it did so. Nevertheless, in June 1944 the National Democratic Bloc was constituted with communist participation, though no agreement on territorial integrity was reached. By this date Soviet troops had already reoccupied Bessarabia and had crossed the Prut River in some places, and a drive against the German and Romanian armies was imminent. With the prospect of a major role for the Soviet Union in postwar Romania, the participation of Romanian communists was considered useful by other Romanian political figures. The Soviets, supported by the British and American governments, also insisted on communist participation.

The change in the RCP's nationality policy during World War II had little impact upon its popular support. Although it opposed Hungary's annexation of northern Transylvania, it acquiesced in the Soviet seizure of Bessarabia and northern Bukovina, and this fact, plus the party's national policy in the fifteen years before the war and its close ties with the Soviet Union, did little to mitigate its image as a party opposed to Romanian national interests.

From its founding in 1921 until the arrival of Soviet troops in Romania in 1944, the RCP played a peripheral role in Romania's political life. Although during the first decade of this period Moscow's needs were not necessarily the determining factor in setting RCP policies, the organization was still unable to take advantage of the social, economic, and political instability in Romania to advance its influence largely because the organization was split into competing factions which were unable to combine their efforts. The "bolshevization" of the party at its 1931 congress reduced factionalism and resulted in the imposition of a greater degree of organizational discipline, but tighter control from Moscow meant that Soviet needs dictated RCP policy and did not permit the flexibility necessary to exploit indigenous conditions in Romania. Further hampering its success through most of the interwar period was the outlawing of the party in 1924, which forced it to work underground and utilize front organizations.

The most serious obstacle to RCP influence during the entire interwar period, however, was the fact that it was considered by Romanians to be the instrument of a hostile foreign power. This was significant from the time the party was founded and remained true until well after the communists had come to power in Romania. RCP policy on the nationality question, imposed by the Comintern in 1923, was interpreted by ethnic Romanians as an attack on Romania's national integrity, even though it was not consistently advocated or implemented by the party until after 1931. The attractiveness of the party to Jews and irredentist minorities, and the importance of such groups in the party leadership, further weakened the appeal it might have had to Romanians; in view of the popular emphasis on Romanian nationalism during the interwar period, the inability of the RCP to gain a significant following is not surprising. On the eve of its rise to power it had at most a few thousand members. In short, it would be difficult to find a political party less likely to gain power in postwar Romania than the RCP.

2
The Path to Power

The means by which a communist party achieves power exert a critical influence on that party's subsequent behavior. As Chalmers Johnson has observed, the "mode of coming to power" is significant because it leaves open certain options and forecloses others in the party's relationship with the population.[1] He notes that parties that come to power as leaders of popular movements are "trapped by their popularity" and must either sacrifice the popular appeal they have achieved or moderate their ideological goals so far as social transformation goes. A "derivative communist regime" faces no such conflict, and such a party imposed by external force is free to pursue its ideological goals with little concern for the effect upon its popularity.

The Romanian communists' road to power has been universally categorized as "derivative" or "imposed."[2] While there is no gainsaying the fact that the Romanian "revolution" was imposed by the Soviet Union through its dominant position in Romania following the arrival of the Red Army in 1944, the fact that the existing government structures remained intact (though considerably weakened) influenced the way in which the party came to power. In Poland and East Germany organizational disintegration was so complete that the communist parties there were quickly able to establish themselves in power, since they faced no competing institutions. In Romania however, such total disintegration was forestalled by the coup d'etat of August 23, 1944, which involved the arrest of Marshal Antonescu and leading figures in his regime, followed by the creation of a new government and the switching of Romania's allegiance from the Axis to the Allied powers. Thus, both monarchy and government structure retained a degree of vitality and legitimacy.

The Communist Role in
the August 23, 1944, Coup

The role played by the communist party and various of its leaders in the
August 23, 1944, coup is difficult to determine with precision. Yet this question is a critical one in assessing the party's route to power and the impact
that route had upon the subsequent evolution of the party's relationship
with Romanian society and institutions. The chaos and pace of events at
that time precluded detailed revelation, and the partisanship displayed by
procommunist and anticommunist apologists since that time has resulted
in exaggerated claims and denials regarding the role of the RCP and its
leaders.

Because Gheorghe Gheorghiu-Dej became the leader of those elements
in the party that were identified with the coup, he and his supporters claimed
they had played a major role in carrying it out. They maintained that in
August 1943 under the direction of Gheorghiu-Dej, the party leaders had
elaborated a plan "aimed at overthrowing the military-fascist dictatorship,
removing Romania from the Hitlerite war, and bringing the country into
the war against Nazi Germany."[3] Others even claim that the party's role was
set in CC decisions dating from 1941 and that the coup was thus the culmination of policies adopted some three years previously and then painstakingly implemented. According to these versions Gheorghiu-Dej's escape
from prison on August 9 set the stage for the coup fourteen days later:
"Heading the coalition of people's democratic forces, the Romanian Communist Party executed the armed insurrection which destroyed the military-
fascist dictatorship," and Antonescu was arrested "in accordance with a
plan drawn up by the party."[4]

Gheorghiu-Dej himself declared on a number of occasions that the party
had planned and carried out the coup. In a speech for the 40th anniversary
of the party in 1961, he repeated the claim that the party leadership had
done so as early as August 1943. He said other political parties had agreed
to join the communists when it became apparent that the Soviet Army was
at the gates and they feared opposition would cause isolation from the
masses. Furthermore, the king and his advisers saw acceptance of the communist plan and participation in the removal of Antonescu as "the only
hope of escaping their heavy responsibility . . . for dragging Romania into
the anti-Soviet war."[5] On numerous occasions before his death the Romanian party leader reiterated the claim that the communist leadership had
planned and implemented the entire coup.[6]

After the death of Gheorghiu-Dej in early 1965, however, certain changes in the historical accounts of the events surrounding August 23, 1944, were made. These changes were prompted not by interest in introducing greater veracity into the party's official accounts of the coup but by the political exigencies facing his successor. Nicolae Ceausescu, who followed Gheorghiu-Dej as party leader, was anxious to play down the cult of his predecessor. This would remove any obstacle to the building of his own image, and at the same time preclude his senior rivals benefiting from their long association with the past leader.

A second consideration that has gradually led to a different emphasis in post–Gheorghiu-Dej accounts of the coup is Ceausescu's attempt to win the support of all patriotic and national forces for his policy of encouraging social and economic development in Romania. This has resulted in a more favorable assessment of the role of various noncommunist groups and individuals (including the king) in various historical events, including the coup of August 23, 1944.

One of the more interesting examples of this was the treatment accorded the roles of the RCP and the king in the arrest of Antonescu. Various official party accounts during the Gheorghiu-Dej era reported that Antonescu had been apprehended by "patriotic struggle" units (*formatiunile de lupta patriotice*), which were set up by and functioned under the direction of the party. One of the most explicit accounts appeared in one of a series of articles in the journal of the Institute of Party History.

> On August 23, 1944, the chairman and vice-chairman of the Council of Ministers (Ion and Mihai Antonescu) were arrested at the Royal Palace by a patriotic struggle unit. They had come to inform the king about a decision of the Council of Ministers calling for full mobilization to support the Hitlerite army.
>
> The king and the leaders of the bourgeois parties were afraid lest they share the fate of the fascist regime. They agreed to the arrest of the fascist leaders, hoping in this way to curb the revolutionary *élan* of the masses, maintain the bourgeois-landlord regime, and bring Romania back under the rule of imperialist circles.
>
> So that the other ministers of the Antonescu government could be arrested, it was arranged that the Council of Ministers be summoned to the palace. The ministers were arrested by the patriotic struggle unit which was in the palace, one after another, as they arrived. These units, led by Emil Bodnaras, confined the fascist leaders to a clandestine house of the party in the Vatra Luminoasa district, where party-approved cadres kept watch. Thus the whole fascist government was arrested.[7]

Significantly, revision of this official view began within a few months of the death of Gheorghiu-Dej. The same party history journal published an article by Emilian Ionescu, the royal adjutant who had been involved in the events before and after the apprehension of Antonescu.[8] Ionescu discussed the attempts of the king and his advisers to find a satisfactory solution to the crisis and to separate the king from Antonescu, and concluded that in the end they were "compelled" to accept the communist plan. Although the party was described as "the initiator, organizer, and leader of the action to overthrow the military-fascist dictatorship," its role was somewhat reduced compared to the descriptions in earlier accounts. According to Ionescu, the communists had arranged for a patriotic struggle unit to try to penetrate the palace in order to seize Antonescu and others of his regime after he had been lured there by the king to discuss the military situation. Recognizing that the unit might not be able to enter the palace, a group of military men from the palace guard were also prepared for the task of arresting Antonescu. When the fateful moment arrived, on the afternoon of August 23, and the two Antonescus were summoned by the king, it was the palace guard that seized the dictator and his associate; only later that evening did the patriotic struggle unit, under the leadership of Emil Bodnaras, take custody of the prisoners and remove them to a secure location to prevent their recapture by German forces. The differences between this account and previous claims are quite striking.

Although more recent versions of the communist role in the coup seem to be much closer to the actual events than earlier ones,[9] they still differ markedly from noncommunist accounts. Various descriptions published in Western Europe and the United States, written for the most part in the late 1940s and early 1950s and thus suffering from the anticommunist fervor of those times, tend to play up the role of the king and the "historical" political parties while denigrating that of the communists.[10] Although the various accounts differ in detail, certain basic facts are clear. The coup was supported and to some extent planned by representatives of the Patriotic Front, a bloc composed of the four leading antifascist political parties: the National Peasants (led by Iuliu Maniu), the Liberals (led by Dinu Bratianu), the Social Democrats (led by C. Titel Petrescu), and the communists (who in these negotiations were represented by Lucretiu Patrascanu). How active or critical the communist party's role was in precipitating the actual coup is difficult to determine. The inclusion of a communist representative in the Patriotic Front and in the government, however, was only good politics in view of the imminence of the Soviet Army's entry into Romania and the leading role of the Soviet Union in armistice negotiations.

It seems most likely that the communists played a minor role in planning and carrying out the actual arrest, but that they took custody of the two Antonescus shortly after their seizure by the palace guard is firmly established in both Western and Romanian communist accounts. Support for the view of a limited communist role in the planning and carrying out of the coup is supplied by the accusation that in September 1944 Patrascanu told "bourgeois press correspondents" in Moscow (where he was negotiating with Soviet officials as a member of the Romanian armistice delegation) that the overthrow of Antonescu was the work of King Michael. He "did not even mention the heroic struggle of the Romanian Communist Party during the war, the party's drawing up of the plan for the armed insurrection, or the realization of this plan."[11]

The Significance of the Coup
for Subsequent RCP Development

In retrospect it appears that the inflated ex post facto assessment of the communist role in the events of August 23, 1944, and probably also that date's selection as the Romanian national holiday, has less to do with the importance of the coup in establishing communist power than with its significance as a focal point in the early postwar internal power struggle in the party. There were two principal factions within the RCP. The first, headed by Gheorghiu-Dej, was composed mainly of prominent members who had been imprisoned in Romania and included a large number of ethnic Romanians; the second, led by Ana Pauker and Vasile Luca, who headed the Romanian communist organizations in the Soviet Union, included a number of ethnic non-Romanians.

Thanks to the support of Emil Bodnaras, Constantin Pirvulescu, Iosif Ranghet, Chivu Stoica, and a number of others, Gheorghiu-Dej became the head of the party organization in Romania about 1943 or 1944, although he remained in prison. The first step was the elimination of Stefan Foris, at the time secretary general of the party. At a meeting in the Tirgu Jiu prison hospital on April 4, 1944, it was decided to reorganize the leadership; Foris was to be dropped and Gheorghiu-Dej designated head of the party. The purging of Foris was subsequently justified on grounds that he was "an agent of the bourgeoisie and the imperialists" and collaborated with the Romanian *siguranta* (secret police).[12]

While Gheorghiu-Dej and Bodnaras were seeking to organize partisan activity in Romania prior to the arrival of the Red Army,[13] Pauker and Luca were in the Soviet Union actively planning the communist route to power, on the assumption that existing governmental institutions would collapse in the wake of Romania's defeat by the Soviet armed forces. According to charges made after they were purged by Gheorghiu-Dej in 1952, Pauker and Luca organized a Romanian "Bureau" in the Soviet Union with themselves as party leaders. They were also responsible for setting up the Tudor Vladimirescu Brigade, composed of Romanian prisoners of war, which subsequently provided armed support for the party in its efforts to achieve power. The details of the Pauker-Luca plans, however, are somewhat obscure.[14]

It seems probable that the Soviet Union encouraged both the group around Gheorghiu-Dej and that around Pauker and Luca in order to increase its policy alternatives in dealing with Romania. Soviet interests, of course, constituted the primary consideration, and the Romanian communists were considered merely tools to be used as Soviet needs required; this applied to both factions of the Romanian party. At the time the Soviet Union's principal concern was to end the war against Nazi Germany as quickly as possible and on the most favorable terms, and it was therefore willing to consider entering into secret negotiations with representatives of the fascist Antonescu government, even though their talks with representatives of the antifascist political opposition (in which American and British representatives were also involved) were still going on.[15] Instructing Bodnaras to organize armed resistance and encouraging the party leaders in Romania to participate with other political forces in action against Antonescu were also consistent with broader concerns of the Soviet Union. That the latter would maintain a preponderant influence over Romanian affairs was established fairly early, and there is little evidence that the Soviets distrusted Gheorghiu-Dej and his associates. They thus could be flexible on the question of tactics.

For the two factions in the RCP leadership, however, the question of how Soviet influence would come to be exerted in Romania was a critical one. If a coup against Antonescu and reversal of Romania's alliances were to require a period of coalition with other political forces, it would be essential to keep Gheorghiu-Dej, along with Patrascanu and other ethnic Romanians of the nativist faction, in the RCP leadership; if the Antonescu government were to collapse in the wake of Romania's liberation by the Red Army, however, the Pauker-Luca group (which was probably better known to and more trusted by the Soviets) could be installed without concern for their popular appeal or their acceptability to other political parties. Thus the coup of August 23, 1944, gave Gheorghiu-Dej an opportunity to demonstrate his ability to the Soviet leadership, since his native faction was required in the coalition governments that ensued.[16] For Gheorghiu-Dej the coup was the event that made his rise to power possible, and it thus became hallowed in party history, much as Lenin's various interparty struggles in the Marxist movement in Russia subsequently became symbols quite unrelated to their real historical significance.

In fact, the criticism of Pauker and Luca expressed after they were purged, and particularly the massive attacks made on them at the November 30– December 5, 1961, Central Committee plenum, focused, among other things, on their disdain for the August coup. Gheorghiu-Dej was the most specific in this regard. He said of Pauker and Luca: "Instead of sharing the enthusiasm, joy, and satisfaction of the party, of the working class and the entire population, at this great victory—as would have been natural with true revolutionaries—on the contrary, they looked upon it with dissatisfaction and disapproval."[17] Gheorghiu-Dej also said that Pauker and Luca had "claimed it would have been better to leave the overthrowing of the military fascist dictatorship to the Soviet armed forces, because this would have enabled the working class to seize power immediately, avoiding the phase of collaboration with the bourgeois parties." On the same occasion Petre Borila accused Luca of denigrating "the events of 1933 [the railwaymen's strike that launched Gheorghiu-Dej into prominence] as well as those of August 1944." Also, "Pauker and Luca tried to discredit the August 1944 insurrection, going so far as to maintain that this revolutionary action had been a mistake which had been exploited by the bourgeoisie." Iosif Chisinevschi, a leading party official who was purged in 1957 and linked after the fact with the Pauker-Luca group, was also accused by Borila of having asserted in lectures at party schools that "the 6th of March [1945, when the communist-dominated government led by Petru Groza was installed] is far more important than the 23rd of August."[18]

The differences over the significance of August 23 have little to do with the historical importance of the event, but they are relevant because of their symbolism in the power struggle between Gheorghiu-Dej and his opponents. For the Romanian nation the date has a certain national and patriotic significance; for the Soviet Union and its Western allies it was significant since it resulted in the rapid disintegration of German-Romanian resistance on the southern part of the German-Soviet front and thus hastened the defeat of Nazi Germany. But from the point of view of the communist party's rise to power in Romania it was not a particularly significant event, and other dates (in particular March 6) were far more important.

The coup did, however, have a determining impact on the leadership of the party. As noted above, it gave Gheorghiu-Dej an opportunity to demonstrate his ability to the Soviet leaders, an opportunity he most probably would not have had if the Red Army had defeated and then occupied Romania, and the monarchy and government had collapsed. It gave him an opportunity to strengthen his position in the party, and without this initial advantage he would have found it much more difficult to outmaneuver his opponents. Historical speculation is risky and at best serves limited purposes, but it can be reasonably argued that without the August 23 coup Gheorghiu-Dej might well have been purged himself, and the Romanian party would have followed a very different course.

The Soviet Role in the
Communist Ascension to Power

Although the RCP demonstrated a certain initiative in its rise to power, there can be little doubt that the presence of the Soviet military and the key role the USSR played in Romania after August 1944 were the most important of the factors that contributed to its success. It had been clearly established by the three Allied powers even before the coup d'etat that the Soviet Union would play the dominant role in Romanian affairs. The American and British governments accepted this position. The U.S. ambassador in Moscow, W. Averell Harriman, observed with regard to the negotiations for the Romanian armistice, which were concluded in Moscow in September 1944: "The Russians entered upon these negotiations with the determination that the field should largely be theirs and that we should give them pretty much of a free hand in arranging the armistice terms and the subsequent treatment of the Romanians," and "the United States' attitude throughout the negotiations tended to bear them out."[19] America's policy toward Romania before 1947 continued to follow that line. Although the British were somewhat more active in presenting proposals with regard to Romanian affairs, they too accepted Soviet primacy. The Allied Control Commission, which was established by the armistice agreement and functioned on a formal basis until the peace treaty with Romania was signed in 1947, was dominated by the Soviets; American and British representatives had little influence over directives issued in the Council's name and carried out by Soviet troops. The two Western governments had no military forces in a position to influence developments in Romania, and realized that the question of Romania was of much higher priority to the Soviet Union than to themselves. Thus they limited their efforts to influence Romanian events to generally unsuccessful diplomatic measures.[20]

A key Soviet consideration was gaining control over the instruments of coercion: the army, the police, and the *siguranta*. Although the Red Army would have been adequate had a showdown taken place, the Soviets prevented such an eventuality by gaining control over or minimizing the effectiveness of these institutions. As soon as possible after the August 1944 coup, Romanian military units were reformed and redirected against German and Hungarian forces. All Romanians, including the leaders, not only accepted but desired this, in order to regain northern Transylvania and win cobelligerent status by making sacrifices for the Allied cause, thus reducing the penalties that might be imposed in the peace treaties. As Romanian military units joined in the fight against Germany, the Soviet Union began the process of bringing them under Soviet control and subjecting both officers and men to political education. Most military units, and particularly those in the vicinity of Bucharest, were sent to the front, and those that remained behind were in most cases disarmed. Under Soviet direction various other police and *gendarmerie* units were reduced in numbers, and all nongovernment groups were disarmed.

At the same time the many communist-formed and communist-led patriotic struggle units that had been organized and armed were not disarmed, disbanded, or sent to the front. Thus in the critical early period after the August coup, communist party influence was considerably magnified by Soviet actions that left armed communist groups virtually unopposed in Bucharest and other important centers. Meanwhile the Soviets insisted on placing communists in positions of control over the police and security forces; Teohari Georgescu, for example, became an undersecretary in the Interior Ministry in December 1944, and was named head of the ministry in March 1945. With the indigenous agencies of coercion under Soviet or Romanian communist control and with Soviet troops readily available "to maintain public order," the task of bringing the communist party to power was made considerably easier.

Steps toward Communist Control
of the Government

Hugh Seton-Watson has suggested the pattern by which the communist parties came to dominate the governments of postwar Eastern Europe.[21] In Slovakia, Hungary, Bulgaria, and Romania the local communist parties played little role in wartime resistance and the societies were not drastically altered by the events of the war or the subsequent Soviet occupation. In all these cases government institutions were still to some extent intact and retained a degree of legitimacy. In these cases the government came under communist domination in three stages.[22]

The first stage was the creation of a genuine coalition government, which of course included the communists as one of the coalition parties. In Romania the coalition came into being even before the end of the fascist regime when representatives of the four leading political parties worked together on the plot to overthrow Antonescu. Immediately after the coup of August 1944 King Michael designated a government headed by General Constantin Sanatescu, which included coup leaders Maniu (National Peasant), Bratianu (Liberal), Petrescu (Social Democrat), and Patrascanu (Communist). The first three were ministers without portfolio, while Patrascanu was Minister of Justice; this government lasted about two months.

A second Sanatescu government was formed in November with similar representation from the four coalition parties but with changes in other ministries. That government remained in power less than a month, until communist-led demonstrators demanded the dismissal of the Interior Minister, National Peasant N. Penescu. The king designated General Nicolae Radescu, a former chief of staff, to form a new government. Since control of the Interior Ministry, which had responsibility for police and internal security, was a controversial issue that had led to the collapse of the previous government, Radescu himself took charge of that ministry in addition to being prime minister.

During this period (the genuine coalition stage), the communists gained additional positions with each change of government and thus increased the areas under their influence. At the same time, the programs of these governments also contributed to the party's growing strength. Former Iron Guard leaders were arrested, fascist collaborators were prosecuted, and legal political activity was restored for the coalition parties. Since the Ministry of Justice under Patrascanu played the leading role in implementing these measures, many leaders who had not supported the fascist regime but who were hostile to the communists were harassed and prosecuted along with real collaborators. During this first stage of genuine coalition, freedom of expression was generally permitted, although no criticism of the Soviet Union was allowed. The parties were able to engage in political activity and criticize each other, but the Soviet occupation forces clearly assisted the communists and hampered the other groups.

Seton-Watson refers to the second phase of communist ascension as the "bogus coalition" stage. The government still included representatives of noncommunist political parties, but individuals from other parties were chosen by the Soviets or the RCP rather than by their own party, and they were selected because they had shown themselves willing to cooperate. During this period the principal vehicle of the RCP was the National Democratic Front (NDF), which was established in October 1944. In addition to the RCP, it included the Social Democratic Party, the Union of Patriots, and the Plowman's Front. The Union of Patriots was an amorphous group used to attract professionals, intellectuals, and nonproletarian elements, and it was never particularly important. The Ploughman's Front was founded in 1933 and had achieved something of a following in Transylvania in the 1930s. It cooperated with communist front organizations on occasion during that time, but by 1944 it had come under communist domination and functioned as the rural arm of the RCP. The leader of the Ploughman's Front, Petru Groza, had some political standing since he had participated in governments in the 1920s. Thus he was useful to the RCP as a candidate for leadership of the government when the NDF moved to consolidate its position.

The genuine coalition stage in Romania lasted less than seven months. The bogus coalition phase began with the installation of the NDF government under Groza on March 6, 1945. After a political crisis provoked by the Soviets and the Romanian communists at the end of February, Deputy Soviet Foreign Minister Andrei Vishinsky arrived in Bucharest and delivered an ultimatum to King Michael: dismiss Prime Minister Radescu and appoint Petru Groza to the post or Vishinsky could not guarantee the continuance of Romania as an independent state. In order to sweeten the imposition of Groza upon the country, however, the Soviets returned the administration of liberated northern Transylvania to the Romanian government as soon as he took office—something they had refused to do during the tenure of Groza's predecessors.[23]

The Soviets steadfastly supported the Groza government despite American and British protests that it did not represent all democratic forces in the country. After the Potsdam conference in the summer of 1945, King Michael asked for Groza's resignation. When it was refused, he ceased to recognize the legitimacy of the Groza government and appealed to the three Allied powers for help in establishing a truly representative government, which all three countries could recognize in accordance with the Potsdam declarations. The Soviets' unyielding support for Groza and his NDF government, however, resulted in its remaining in power.

With the installation of the Groza government, the National Peasants and Liberals went into opposition. Although this was tolerated by the communist-dominated government, it became increasingly difficult for the opposition parties. Some of the largest and most influential newspapers were suppressed by Soviet authorities. They also imposed strict control over the allocation of newsprint, with the result that most party newspapers, except communist and procommunist ones, either ceased publication or appeared in extremely limited editions. In 1945, for example, the National Peasant Party—at the time probably the party with the largest following— was allocated two rolls of newsprint per day for its national newspaper, while the communist daily, *Scinteia,* was given twenty. In addition, in many cases the Soviets prohibited political meetings of noncommunist parties "in order to maintain public order," and when rallies were permitted communist agitators disrupted the proceedings while Soviet troops or Romanian police forces under NDF control refused to intervene.

The Groza government program included a number of measures designed to build domestic support, undercut its political rivals, and bring Romania into a Soviet orbit. Agrarian reform legislation expropriated the farmland of war criminals and large land owners, and divided small parcels among the peasantry. This undermined the economic power of the most prosperous farmers and won the support of the masses of poor peasantry. Marshal Antonescu and his prime minister were brought to trial in May 1945, and the revelations of their misgovernance and crimes served to enhance the popularity of the Groza government. Also in May 1945 a long-term trade agreement with the Soviet Union was signed, which included provisions for the establishment of the infamous Soviet-Romanian joint companies that were used to exploit Romania economically until they were disbanded in the mid-1950s.

Elections had not been held since 1937, but the Groza government moved slowly in preparing for new ones in order to insure NDF control of the process. The voting finally took place in November 1946. The National Peasants and Liberals were permitted to field candidates, but they faced insuperable obstacles. The opposition parties were subject to legal and illegal harassment, the election laws gave every advantage to the NDF, and communist supporters had no difficulty being added to the electoral lists while many supporters of the opposition parties were disenfranchised for having fought against the Allies. On the eve of the elections the American and British governments protested these electoral practices, but since the

USSR did not join in the protest, the Groza government ignored them. The results were hardly surprising: the national assembly had 346 NDF, 33 National Peasant, and 3 Liberal deputies.

The signing of the allied peace treaty with Romania in February 1947 ended any moderating influence that the United States and Great Britain may have been able to exercise over the communist government. About mid-1947, the RCP moved from the "bogus coalition" to the "monolithic regime" stage with the suppression of all organized opposition. In the summer leaders of the National Peasant Party were arrested, and those who were not fled the country. The National Peasant and Liberal parties were dissolved by decree in August 1947, and in October Iuliu Maniu and other National Peasant leaders were brought to trial on charges of plotting against the security of the state. All were sentenced to harsh prison terms ranging from five years at hard labor to life imprisonment.

The Social Democratic Party was undermined and finally absorbed by the communists. After the installation of the Groza government in March 1945, Social Democrats willing to cooperate fully with the RCP were invited to participate in the government, while Petrescu and other leaders of the party vacillated about cooperation. The party finally split over the question of a single combined RCP-Social Democratic candidate list for the election, and on this issue Petrescu and others unwilling to work with the RCP left the party to join the parties in opposition to the NDF. The Social Democrats who joined the opposition suffered the same fate as the National Peasants and Liberals when they were banned, while those who cooperated with the communists were finally absorbed. In February 1948 the RCP and the remainder of the Social Democratic Party "merged" to form the Romanian Workers' Party (RWP). In actual fact this step merely formalized the Social Democrats' elimination by the communists.

The final step in creating the monolithic regime was the forced abdication of King Michael on December 31, 1947, and the proclamation of the Romanian People's Republic.

Imposing the Stalinist Model

During the 1944–1947 period the Soviet Union permitted considerable variation and diversity in the communist parties of Eastern Europe. In part this was a tactical expedient necessary to permit the Soviet forces and the communist parties to establish themselves in the individual countries, but it was also due to Soviet caution and uncertainty with regard to American and British reactions. By mid-1947, however, the peace treaties with the former enemy states in Eastern Europe (Bulgaria, Hungary, and Romania) had been signed, the patterns of the cold war were beginning to harden in U.S.-Soviet relations, and the communist parties were in relatively strong positions in all countries. Thus it was no longer necessary for the Soviet Union to postpone the full and unequivocal integration of these countries into its sphere, which involved insuring conformity not only in foreign policy, but in domestic matters as well. The Soviet political, economic, and social system was imposed uniformly across Soviet Eastern Europe.[24]

Several early steps had been taken that brought Romania closer to the Stalinist system, but only after organized political opposition was eliminated at the end of 1947 was the country fully brought into line with Soviet practice. During 1948 most aspects of the system were introduced. The foreign policy aspect included a treaty of friendship, cooperation, and mutual assistance between Bucharest and Moscow signed in February 1948. Although this treaty (as well as similar ones signed by the USSR with the other countries of Eastern Europe) was ostensibly directed against the possibility of a resurgent Germany, in fact it was aimed at the Western powers, and bound Romania and the Soviet Union to act jointly against any aggressor.

Another occurrence used to bring Eastern Europe into line was the expulsion of Yugoslavia from the Cominform in June 1948. The Cominform (Communist Information Bureau) was established in September 1947 under Soviet auspices, with the aim of furthering Soviet coordination of the ruling parties of Eastern Europe and the large communist parties of France and Italy. The expulsion of Yugoslavia from the organization followed an exchange between Stalin and Tito in which the Yugoslavs refused to accept Soviet domination. By purging the unwilling member, the Soviets were able to maintain firmer control over the parties that remained. A reflection of Romania's loyalty and subservience was the fact that the RCP played a major role in the Soviet-orchestrated campaign against Yugoslavia after 1948; significantly, the headquarters of the Cominform were moved from Belgrade to Bucharest.

Romania's government system was brought into line with Soviet practice with the adoption of the constitution of 1948. The document followed the pattern set by the 1936 Soviet constitution, although there was some effort to maintain at least superficial continuity with Romanian political traditions. (The parliament, whose structure and powers were very similar to the Soviet model, was called the Grand National Assembly, the term used for the Romanian parliament since the creation of an expanded national assembly upon the union of Transylvania with Romania in 1918.) The government structure established in 1948 has been altered somewhat in subsequent constitutions (1952 and 1965) and by amendments, but the pattern remains much the same. Formal government power was concentrated in the single house of parliament, but in actual practice power lay with the prime minister and other ministers chosen by parliament. A State Council, modeled after the presidium of the Supreme Soviet of the USSR, acted in behalf of the assembly when it was not in session (which was most of the time, since full plenary sessions lasted only a few days and were held only three or four times a year). Local government units, called People's Councils (analogous to the local soviets in the USSR) were provided for in the constitution and set up under legislation passed in early 1949, but were local extensions of central authority rather than autonomous representative bodies for dealing with local problems.

The economy likewise underwent significant changes after Sovietization began. In June 1948 industry, banking, insurance, mining, and transportation were nationalized. Although previously most public services and several major industries had been fully or partially state-owned, the wholesale nationalization marked the beginning of state control of the entire economy. This was furthered by the creation of the State Planning Commission in July 1948, which was to coordinate the economy and establish a national plan to guide all economic activity. A reflection of the importance given to establishing party control over the economy was the fact that the first chairman of the commission was Gheorghiu-Dej, who was at the time also first secretary of the RCP and minister of the national economy.

The first task of the Planning Commission, following the wartime disruption, was to get the Romanian economy back on its feet. In the last year of the war the Romanian economy had suffered considerable destruction as a result of ground fighting and Allied and German bombing. Postwar recovery was hampered by political and economic instability, disruption, and inflation; reparations to the Soviet Union called for in the peace treaty, costs of the Soviet occupation (which Romania was required to pay), and unofficial Soviet seizures of equipment and other goods caused further serious dislocation to the Romanian economy. The newly created Planning Commission drew up a one-year recovery plan for 1949 to bring the economy back to prewar levels of production.

The next task of the Commission was to initiate a long-term plan for the industrial development of the country. The first five-year plan was announced at the end of 1950, with extremely ambitious growth targets. The focus of investment was on heavy industry, with agriculture, consumer goods, and public services receiving considerably less attention. Though many of the ambitious goals of that plan were not achieved, it did begin the economic transformation of Romania, along Soviet lines.

Another major aspect of the Soviet economic model, the collectivization of agriculture, was begun in March 1949. Large land holdings not previously expropriated were seized, but rather than distributing land to the peasants, collective or state farms were created. The establishment of collective farms was initially envisaged as a gradual process, and the peasantry were to be won over to the concept rather than forced into the new collective units. Romania lagged behind the rest of Eastern Europe in the effort to follow the Soviet agricultural model, however, and in 1950 the pace of collectivization was considerably hastened by forcing peasants to join collectives. At the time the RCP praised the success of the collectivization drive, but when conditions changed and the forceable collectivization was criticized, the responsibility for these activities was added to the list of sins of Pauker, Luca, and their supporters, after they had been purged from the party.

In the social realm, the Stalinist pattern called for establishing control over education, the intelligentsia, religious organizations, and other institutions in order to direct their efforts to the political and economic goals of the party and to insure the party's monopoly of power. The communization of education was spelled out in a law passed in August 1948. In order to meet the RCP's economic goals greater emphasis was placed on technical schools, while the traditional liberal arts program of secondary education was decidedly downgraded. The content of courses at all levels was also altered to conform with accepted Marxist-Leninist ideology. The greatest impact was on such subjects as history, philosophy, and the social sciences. Russian language was introduced as a compulsory subject in the fourth grade, and text books were rewritten to present the Soviet Union and Russia in a highly favorable light. Universities and higher technical schools began to take class origin into consideration in admissions policies, with those of proletarian background being more readily admitted than those of bourgeois origins.

The new regime also sought to dominate the creative intelligentsia (journalists, writers, artists, musicians, academicians) in order to utilize their important talents in support of party goals. By controlling the rewards (no books could be published, works of art displayed, or music performed without party approval, and party-dominated creative associations fixed all compensation), the RCP was able to win support of some of these individuals. Those who cooperated had access to scarce commodities and received public acclaim. The watchword was "socialist realism," the term of approbation for creative works that supported party goals, such as novels that dealt positively with collectivization, journalism that inspired greater effort among industrial workers, paintings that elevated the worker and the new social order, and cantatas that praised the Soviet Union's "peaceful foreign policy." Many of those who cooperated with the regime were among the less talented, however, while some of the more gifted intelligentsia refused; others were too identified with precommunist works and were thus denied the opportunity to utilize their talents.[25]

Religious organizations presented a particular problem since the clergy were among the most hostile to the atheistic communists. The Romanian Orthodox Church had traditionally been dominated by the Romanian state (salaries of the clergy were paid by the government, for example), and the new communist government used the means at its command to bring the hierarchy under its control. All functions previously performed by religious groups (charity, general education, care of the sick, and so on), except the performance of religious rites, were prohibited by the state, and entry into the priesthood or religious orders was restricted. In 1949 a new patriarch of the Romanian Orthodox Church was elected with official support. The new church leader was closely connected with the RCP, although he was relatively unknown and rather young for the position. The most difficult religious group to bring under party authority was the Uniate or Greek Catholic Church in Transylvania. This group followed the Eastern Orthodox liturgy but had accepted the authority of the Roman Catholic pope in the seventeenth century when Transylvania was a part of the Hapsburg Empire. Because of this connection with Rome, the group was less subject to state control traditionally, and hence was seen as a more serious threat by the party. The Romanian Orthodox Church, at the direction of government and party authorities, held a congress at which the Uniates were "permitted" to return to the bosom of the orthodox mother church and ties with Rome were severed. Clergy who refused to accept this decision were incarcerated, and the government dissolved the four Uniate bishoprics and seized all property that was not passed to the orthodox church. This action not only took care of the troublesome link with Rome, but it also won the support of the Romanian Orthodox hierarchy, which had sought for some time to bring the Uniate group back into its fold. The various protestant denominations did not pose a particular threat and were rather quickly brought under control. Their principal strength was among the German and Hungarian minorities, their numbers were not great, and the protestant tradition did not include a strong centralized hierarchy around which opposition might crystalize.

Other organizations were either banned, brought under party control, or replaced with new party-directed groups. Youth organizations were replaced by party youth movements for various age groups. Women's organizations were combined into a single party-led group, which was accorded membership in the national front. The party also took over professional associations (for lawyers, physicians, and so on) by insuring the selection of party-approved officers. Even sports groups had to become part of the party-organized national sports league.

The Significance of the RCP's Road to Power

One of the critical aspects of a party's mode of coming to power is the degree to which it is linked with the population. The fact of the August 23 coup and the need for the party to compete for a time with other political parties seem to have had little lasting impact on the RCP. The most important factors in its rise were the overwhelming influence in Romania of the USSR—an influence bolstered by the presence of Soviet troops—and the fact that the United States and Great Britain played a minimal role. The imposed or derivative nature of the Romanian communist revolution is in no way altered by the events of August 23, 1944; in fact, the coup itself was precipitated largely by the successes of the Red Army. Despite a period of cooperation with other political forces, the RCP was never forced to seek popular support in the way the Yugoslav, Chinese, or Vietnamese parties were. Thus it was not hampered in its efforts to pursue the ideological goals of industrialization and social transformation.[26]

The subsequent actions of the party in gaining control of the government and imposing the Stalinist pattern upon Romania were not significantly different from what occurred throughout Eastern Europe. The step-by-step progression of the RCP from one of several participants in a genuine coalition government, through a communist-dominated bogus coalition, to the elimination of organized political opposition, was essentially the same pattern followed by the parties in Hungary, Bulgaria, and Slovakia. The Stalinist system imposed in Romania was also similar, and there are no indications that the reaction in Romania or the methods used were in any way unique.

No consideration of the RCP's road to power would be complete without mention of its impact upon the subsequent policy of autonomy from the Soviet Union, which began to become apparent in the early 1960s. Stephen Fischer-Galati argues that "the seizure of political power by the communists in Romania had unique characteristics that foreshadowed the 'Romanian independent course' adopted in later years" and "the prevention of the outright Soviet conquest of Romania by the *coup d'état* of August 1944, and the subsequent need for procrastination in the process of seizing power granted the Romanian communists the necessary respite which, in later years, allowed them in turn to assert their independence from the Soviet occupiers."[27] This view is consistent with his thesis that "at least as early as 1955 Gheorghe Gheorghiu-Dej and his associates were cautiously pursuing national policies first formulated in 1945 and envisaging a possible eventual assertion of independence from the Kremlin."[28] Kenneth Jowitt, however, has more convincingly shown that Romania's independent course can far more justifiably be regarded as beginning after 1962.[29] If one accepts this later date, the significance of the August 23, 1944, coup is even further diminished.

Although it is not possible to make any direct connection between the events of 1944 and the autonomous policy adopted some twenty years later, one can argue that there were certain indirect effects. Since Gheorghiu-Dej played a key role in initiating the deviation from Soviet policy, the coup was significant in that it bolstered his chances in the struggle for party leadership. One can also argue that since they increased his ability to deal with Pauker and Luca, the events of August 23 contributed to the Romanianization of the party leadership. This was certainly important in furthering the policy of autonomy under Gheorghiu-Dej and his efforts to link the party to Romanian nationalism. Thus the coup may have helped to create preconditions that favored an independent course, but there is little evidence to support the view that it had any significance beyond that.

The death of Gheorghiu-Dej and Ceausescu's attempts to play down the personality cult that had surrounded his predecessor engendered certain changes in the party's attitude toward the commemoration of August 23, 1944. The shift in the party's relationship with the population since the mid-1960s, and the related attempt to play up the party as an element of Romania's national tradition, however, have meant giving continued prominence to the coup; it is useful in emphasizing Romania's efforts to achieve its own liberation, for instance. The need to stress the party's role in the coup, however, has declined somewhat. Whereas Gheorghiu-Dej, motivated by the vanguard concept of the party and his personal identification with the event, felt it necessary to stress the party's role in planning and executing the coup itself, Ceausescu has sought to broaden the significance of the party's role. The commemorations over the last decade, while reaffirming the party's direct role, have stressed the broad support of the masses and the historical forces that were essential to its success.

3

Institutional Transformation

It has generally been established that for any political system to be viable it must be institutionalized; that is, "organizations must be created and sustained that are specialized to political activity."[1] While political scientists are in general agreement on the need for political institutionalization, they have shown less unanimity with regard to the essential aspects of this process.

The first basic problem in the process of institutionalization is how to differentiate the organization, in this case the party, from its environment; in other words, how to establish boundaries between the party and its surroundings. Boundary development and maintenance are essential to organizational development in order to prevent the organization's being overwhelmed by its environment. Indicators that reflect this aspect of institutionalization include the degree to which members are easily identifiable, the relative difficulty of becoming a member, and the extent to which leaders are recruited within the organization. As an organization becomes more institutionalized, membership becomes more stable, admission becomes relatively more difficult, and turnover is less frequent.[2]

For the RCP, whose membership grew from 1,000 to 800,000 in the four years after emerging from illegality in 1944, institutionalization was a serious internal difficulty. The problem was compounded by the other political, social, and economic tasks that had to be carried out simultaneously. The presence of the Soviet Army and the predominant influence of the Soviet Union in Romania after 1944, however, made it possible for the RCP to deal with the urgent requirements of the seizure and consolidation of power without first having to come to grips with institutionalization. By early 1948, with Soviet assistance, it had succeeded in eliminating all organized opposition, and thereafter concentrated on developing a higher degree of institutionalization. At no time, however, could the RCP follow this program single-mindedly, since it was seeking simultaneously to reorder the structure of the countryside, reorganize and industrialize the economy, and carry out a social transformation in keeping with Soviet practice.

The very rapid expansion of the RCP's membership between 1944 and 1948 was achieved at the expense of boundary establishment. Members were admitted, frequently in groups, with relatively little formality, and membership requirements were minimal. Gradually the party began to exhibit concern about its admissions policy, however, and by February 1948 rigid admissions standards had been established and were conscientiously enforced thereafter. The requirements remained relatively unchanged between 1948 and 1962, but since the latter year they have been relaxed to some extent. This has not resulted in the party's becoming less well bounded, however. Qualifications for membership are still stringent, and the fact that the party has in the meantime succeeded in differentiating itself from its environment means that the relaxation of admission requirements has had little impact on its level of institutionalization.

Another important aspect of the process of establishing organizational boundaries is the ideological training of party members. Philip Selznick has pointed out that ideology is a key instrument in the process of securing full commitment of members to the party cause.[3] Ideological indoctrination creates a separate moral and intellectual world for the party member, which helps to insulate him from external influences and at the same time facilitates his integration into the party.[4] From the beginning the Romanian party showed itself concerned about the instruction of party members. Before 1947 the need to consolidate the seizure of power was more pressing, and hence party education was given a lower priority. After 1948, however, the training of party members increased in importance. By 1955 most party members had completed at least evening courses in ideology and other topics considered essential by the party. This concern with education continued, though with less urgency, until 1971, when a new emphasis was placed on ideology, which continues to be an important concern of the leadership. Ideological education remains essential in maintaining boundaries, and proper ideological preparation is now prerequisite for admission to party membership.

A significant occurrence in the process of establishing boundaries in the early period was the purge of almost 200,000 party members carried out after 1948. This began with the "verification" of party members in late 1948, and it apparently continued even after that campaign had formally ended. The purge served to emphasize the newly imposed and more stringent membership requirements, and also confirmed the higher standards required of those already in the party. It helped as well to increase institutionalization. As Gheorghiu-Dej put it, "the verification was in fact an experience in growth for party members and activists" that led to an improvement in party work and to increased criticism and self-criticism, and "stimulated the party aktif and membership to study Marxism-Leninism."[5] While such a massive purge of the membership has not been repeated, individual members are still expelled, and this continues to help in defining the boundaries between the party and its environment.

The second main feature of institutionalization is complexity. Generally speaking, the more complicated an organization the more highly institutionalized it is.[6] Since 1944 the Romanian party has grown increasingly complex as both vertical and horizontal subunits have become differentiated. The mere growth in the number of local party organizations is an indicator of the increased complexity of the party. In July 1945 there were only about 2,500 local party organizations, but this number rose to nearly 70,000 by 1974. The growing complexity of the party organizations is also apparent from the internal specialization of subunits. Initial steps in this direction were taken in early 1947, with the creation of Central Committee sections for trade unions, women, peasants, and youth; these were paralleled by similar subunits on the district level. Since then the party bureaucracy on all levels, from central to local, has grown in size and complexity.

The third aspect in the institutionalization of the Romanian party is the effort to increase the party's coherence and reduce disunity within the organization.[7] Samuel P. Huntington has observed that "rapid or substantial expansions in the membership of an organization or in the participants in a system tend to weaken coherence."[8] This was certainly the case with the Romanian party between 1944 and 1948. Gheorghiu-Dej's frequent complaints about the lack of party discipline and unity reflect the incoherence that plagued the party during this period. The membership purge after 1948, and the emphasis on instruction, were major steps in the process of increasing consensus and unity within the party's ranks. One of the important sources of membership incoherence, however, was the high degree of disunity among the elite, which was not reduced until the purge of Ana Pauker, Vasile Luca, and Teohari Georgescu in 1952. A second source of incoherence within the party, and particularly within the leadership, was the lack of autonomy from the Soviet Union, and as Huntington has pointed out, coherence and autonomy "are often closely linked together."[9] As the party established its boundaries more clearly and as party organizational work progressed, internal incoherence was considerably reduced.

In the context of these political and sociological processes by which the RCP became increasingly institutionalized after coming to power, the remainder of this chapter will consider in greater detail and in chronological sequence the organizational changes in the party.

Initial Growth in Party Membership and Influence, 1944–1948

Once it was legalized after the coup of August 23, 1944, the RCP faced formidable obstacles to becoming a viable political force; it had been outlawed since 1924, its membership was small, and it had had very limited success in attracting popular support throughout the interwar period. After the establishment of the Antonescu regime in 1940, the party was subject to continuous and in some regards increased harassment from the security forces. Since a large number of its leaders were incarcerated and many others were in exile in the Soviet Union, the party lacked effective leadership; these factors severely handicapped organizational efforts prior to August 1944. Even after the party was recognized as a legitimate participant in the political system, there were serious obstacles to its growth. The social groups (workers and poor peasants) that might be most attracted to its programs had only limited previous experience with the party, and its record of pro-Soviet sympathies and policies that ran counter to Romania's national interests were obstacles to popular support. The most serious problems, however, were the party's organizational weakness and its lack of trained cadres; although some members of the party aktif had functioned in the underground and others had been trained in the Soviet Union during World War II, their numbers were small.

Within a few months of its return to legal status, however, the party started to function. Its newspaper, *Scînteia*, began to appear daily beginning in mid-September 1944.[10] It was published in an edition of 180,000 copies in October 1945, and by December 1947 this figure had risen to over 2,000,000. Party organizations were reorganized between April and October 1944, and by the fall of that year there were twelve regional party committees; a much larger number functioned at lower levels. But the party apparently insisted on being organizationally prepared before it began to recruit or even admit new members. A U.S. intelligence report on the political situation in Romania in late 1944 noted that "communist party rolls seem to be virtually closed to new recruits."[11] In October, however, the party did begin to admit new members.[12]

Initially its ranks grew relatively slowly. By February 1945 there were only some 16,000 members, but the March installation of the communist-dominated National Democratic Front government, headed by Dr. Petru Groza, began a period of much more rapid growth; in the six months that followed the advent of the Groza government nearly 240,000 new members came into the party, and by the time of the National Party Conference in October 1945 membership totalled 256,863. This rapid growth continued through June 1946, by which time membership had reached nearly 720,000. In the following year and a half—until the merger of the communist and Social Democratic parties in February 1948—membership increased only slightly, reaching some 800,000 on the eve of the unification congress (see table 2).

Those who joined the party came from varied social groups, and their reasons for affiliation differed considerably. The party made a deliberate effort to recruit industrial workers, and apparently had considerable success. Its efforts with this group were motivated by a number of considerations. Although Leninist doctrine with regard to the party and its social composition, and the ultimate goal of industrialization to which the party was committed from the beginning, provided strong ideological and practical reasons for recruiting workers, other considerations were probably equally important at first. One of these was the fact that workers were concentrated for the most part in urban areas, and in the struggle for political power a reliable membership core that could be mobilized for demonstrations and other political activities was a critical factor. Reflecting this concern was the fact that almost one-third of the party members in October 1945 (some 80,000 out of 250,000) were in Bucharest alone, and some 75 percent of these members in the capital were workers. Other major centers of party strength were also industrial areas: Cluj, Brasov, Timisoara, and the Jiu and Prahova valleys.

The proportion of workers who came into the party has probably been inflated—both in statistics dating from that time and in current analyses of the period—but there is no doubt that the party had considerable success among this group. The proportion of workers in the party ranks in June 1945 is given as over 55 percent, although as the rapid expansion of membership continued this figure declined; it was reported to be 42 percent on the eve of the unification congress in February 1948.

The peasantry were the second group the party sought to recruit; al-

TABLE 2

Membership and Social Composition of the Romanian Communist Party, 1944–1975

Date of Figures	Number of Party Members[*]	Social Composition (in percent)		
		Workers	Peasants	Others
Before August 1944	About 1,000	(a)	(a)	(a)
February 1945	16,000	(a)	(a)	(a)
March 1945	35,000	(a)	(a)	(a)
April 1945	42,633	(a)	(a)	(a)
June–July 1945	101,810	55	33	12
October 1945	256,863	53	31	16
June 1946	717,490	44	33	17
January 1947	704,857[b]	46[b]	37[b]	17[b]
September 1947	720,000	44	39	17
December 1947	803,831	42	38	20
February 1948[c]	1,060,000	39	(a)	(a)
May 1950	720,000	42	(a)	(a)
December 1955	595,398	42	(a)	(a)
June 1958	720,000	53[d]	(a)	(a)
June 1960	834,600	51	22	27
December 1961	900,000	52	22	26
December 1964	1,377,847	44	33	23
December 1965	1,518,000	40	32	28
December 1967	1,630,000	42	30	28
March 1968	1,761,000	42	29	29
March 1970	1,999,720	43	27	30
December 1970	2,089,085	44	26	30
December 1971	2,194,627	45	24	31
December 1972	2,281,372	46	23	31
December 1973	2,386,819	48	22	30
December 1974	2,500,000	50	20	30
December 1975	2,577,434	50	20	30

NOTES:

(a) Not available.

(b) These figures seem slightly inconsistent with others in the series which are from later sources and may be more accurate; the percentage of workers would appear to be a bit too high. In a speech at the December 1961 Central Committee plenum, however, Nicolae Ceausescu said party membership in November 1946 was 675,000, and the percentage of workers 46 (*Scinteia*, December 13, 1961). His figures also differ from those contained in the party archives, on which the table is based.

(c) After the merger of the Romanian Communist Party and the Social Democratic Party and the formation of the Romanian Workers' Party.

(d) This figure is inconsistent with others and may be based on social origin rather than current position, which would make it higher (many officials who would ordinarily be classed as functionaries come from working-class backgrounds).

SOURCES OF DATA:

Before August 1944: *International Press Correspondence* 16:50 (November 1936), p. 1371; and Henry L. Roberts, *Rumania: Political Problems of an Agrarian State* (New Haven: Yale University Press, 1951), p. 243.

February 1945 through June–July 1945: *Analele* 16:6, p. 6, citing party archives.

October 1945:   Gheorghi Tutui, "Conferinta nationala a P.C.R. din octombrie 1945. Consolidarea puterii populare," in Gheorghe Zaharia et al., eds., *1944–1947—Romania in anii revolutiei democrat-populare* (Bucharest: Editura politica, 1971), p. 178.

June 1946:   *Analele* 16:6, p. 6, citing party archives.

January 1947:   *Analele* 9:5, p. 30, citing party archives.

September 1947:   Gheorghe Gheorghiu-Dej, "Kommunisticheskaya Partiya rumynii v borbe za demokratizatsiyu strany," *Informatsionnoe soveshchanie predstaviteley nekotorykh kompartiy v polshe v kontse sentyabrya 1947 goda* (Moscow: Gosudarstvennoe izdatelstvo politicheskoy literatury, 1948), p. 253.

December 1947:   *Analele* 16:6, p. 6, citing party archives. In his speech before the December 1961 Central Committee plenum Ceausescu gave a figure of 800,000 members on the eve of the unification congress in February 1948, and he put the percentage of workers at that time at 42, the same figure as for December 1947.

February 1948:   Ceausescu speech to December 1961 Central Committee plenum (*Scinteia,* December 13, 1961).

May 1950:   Gheorghe Gheorghiu-Dej, *Artikel und Reden* (Berlin: Dietz Verlag, 1955), p. 261; and *Rezolutii si Hotariri ale CC al PMR, 1948–1950,* vol. 1 (Bucharest: Editura pentru literatura politica, 1952), p. 245.

December 1955:   *Congresul al II-lea al PMR* (Bucharest, 1956), p. 132; and *Congresul al III-lea al PMR* (Bucharest, 1960), p. 76.

June 1958:   *Scinteia,* June 27, 1958.

June 1960:   *Congresul al III-lea al PMR,* pp. 76–77; and Nicolae Ceausescu, *Romania re drumul desavirsirii constructiei* (Bucharest, 1968), vol. 1, p. 65.

December 1961:   Ceausescu speech, *Scinteia,* December 13, 1961.

December 1964 and
December 1965:   *Scinteia,* April 17, 1965 and April 14, 1966.

December 1967:   Virgil Trofin speech, *Scinteia,* December 8, 1967.

March 1968 through
December 1972:   *Scinteia* on the following dates: April 25, 1968; March 20, 1970; February 17, 1971; April 25, 1972; June 22, 1973.

December 1973:   *Era socialista* no. 6 (March), 1974, p. 4.

December 1974 and
December 1975:   *Scinteia,* July 25, 1975 and April 28, 1976.

*Figures for 1948 through 1965 include candidate members.

though the initial focus of party efforts was in the cities, work in the countryside was not long neglected. Legislation on agrarian reform was introduced within a few weeks of the installation of the Groza government in March 1945, and one of its aims was to secure the support of the peasantry for the new government.[13] The proportion of peasants in the party ranks increased from 31–33 percent in the fall of 1945 to 38–39 percent at the end of 1947. In those areas (Moldavia, Oltenia, the Dobruja, etc.) with a predominantly rural population, the peasantry became the largest single social group in the party.

Although no doubt large numbers joined the party out of ideological conviction and others did so because they felt that the communists would better their social and economic situation, a great many "opportunists" and "careerists" (the party's own terms) also joined its ranks. These included former supporters of the Iron Guard and the Antonescu regime, who saw active participation in the communist movement as a way to atone for their previous activities. Others in the bureaucracy were anxious to further their careers and share in the perquisites of power, and flocked to the party as its position gradually strengthened. These careerists and opportunists had been unwilling to commit themselves in the early months after the August 1944 coup, particularly since the traditional Romanian political parties still played a prominent role in the government. The establishment of the Groza government in March 1945, however, marked the clear ascendancy of the communist-led National Democratic Front and emphasized Soviet influence over any future Romanian government, and this prompted large numbers to join the RCP. As the communists' position strengthened and the traditional political parties were increasingly forced to fight a rear guard action to stave off further erosion of their positions, still more climbed onto the communist band wagon. Between October 1945 and the summer of 1946 almost half a million new members were admitted.

The party was by no means unwilling to accept these opportunists and careerists into its ranks. In fact, there is substantial evidence that it actively sought the adherence of certain former Iron Guard elements and supporters of the Antonescu regime. Since the RCP lacked a hard core of disciplined and dedicated cadres around whom it could organize other party members, it needed devoted people who would follow instructions and take the lead in the actions required for the seizure of power. But the Iron Guardists not only possessed certain skills and attributes the communists needed, they were also extremely anxious to prove their loyalty to the new rulers, and were thus more willing to carry out party instructions faithfully. In this initial period, when the communists had insufficient time to train needed cadres, these self-seekers provided a more reliable base than the members recruited from among the working class and the peasantry on the basis of ideological commitment and socioeconomic considerations. When the party had consolidated its position and eliminated organized opposition, these careerist elements were either retrained or purged as they became a liability, but initially they were important to the party's success.

That the party not only accepted but actively sought these people as members has been admitted by a number of its leaders, most specifically and in greatest detail at the CC plenum of November 30–December 5, 1961. On that occasion Ana Pauker and others associated with her, including Teohari Georgescu, Miron Constantinescu, and Iosif Chisinevschi—all of whom had been purged from the party leadership before 1961—were criticized for having encouraged undesirable types to join the party. The charges included reports of deals between Pauker and Iron Guard leaders to admit whole groups to communist membership, and organized competitions to enroll members without proper regard for Leninist precepts regarding selective party membership.[14]

Although Pauker and Constantinescu apparently were responsible for the recruiting campaign in this early period, it is doubtful whether their activity with regard to membership was opposed by other party leaders at that time. As noted above, the admission of opportunists and careerists was useful to the party while it still lacked trained cadres of its own. The revelations at the December 1961 CC plenum, coming as they did in the wake of the 22nd Soviet party congress with its vigorous renewal of the anti-Stalin campaign, were intended to justify Gheorghiu-Dej's claim that Romania had previously purged its antiparty and Stalinist elements; the charges of improper admissions under Pauker and her associates thus constituted a convenient indictment.

The faults laid at Pauker's door when her purge was initiated in 1952 had not included irregularities in regard to the admission of new party members before 1948. In 1950 Gheorghiu-Dej had discussed the party's admissions policy at some length in an article that reviewed the results of the verification campaign (in which some 20 percent of the party members were expelled), but he gave no indication that Pauker or anyone else bore personal responsibility for these policies.[15] Only some six months after she was purged did the first statement connecting her with them appear,[16] and the indictment was only made in full nine years later, at the December 1961 plenum. She became a convenient peg on which to hang the blame for the admissions policy before 1948, and once she was dropped from the leadership there was little she could do to defend herself. That these failings were ex post facto justification for decisions taken on other grounds is further indicated by the fact that Miron Constantinescu, who was criticized in the strongest terms by Ceausescu and Gheorghiu-Dej for his role in admitting "hostile, careerist, and opportunist elements" into the party, was not purged until 1957—and the real reasons for his removal then appear to be totally unrelated to his connection with member recruitment before 1948. Constantinescu was in fact subsequently reclaimed from oblivion and ultimately promoted to the post of CC secretary, after Gheorghiu-Dej's death and Ceausescu's assumption of the party leadership.

Although between 1944 and the end of 1947 the RCP expanded its membership considerably, this alone did not account for its political strength. In addition to the support it received from Soviet military forces, which remained in Romania until 1958, the party also relied on a number of front organizations that it established, or came to dominate, in order to increase its power. Realizing that the concentration of workers in urban areas was a circumstance of strategic political importance, the communists quickly sought to establish control over the trade union movement; the rapid expansion of union membership, which the RCP encouraged, helped it achieve this goal. In the 1946 union enterprise committee elections of some 25,000 trade union officials, almost 58 percent were communist party members; 14 percent were Social Democrats, and 17 percent had no political affiliation.[17]

In rural areas, Petru Groza's Plowman's Front became the party's principal instrument for mobilizing mass support. By the summer of 1945 its membership numbered over one million, making it possibly the fastest-growing organization in Romania at the time. Among the Hungarians of Transylvania the party worked through the Hungarian People's Union, which by August 1945 had a membership of 250,000, organized into over 500 branches.[18] Other front organizations were oriented toward intellectuals and academicians, engineers and technical specialists, women, youth, and so on. These organizations enabled the party to extend its political influence well beyond the growing circle of party members.

The increase in numbers and influence of the party and its front organizations was furthered by a number of factors. Soviet support and encouragement was certainly an element that should not be minimized, but social and political conditions in Romania at that time were also conducive to the growth of communist influence. Six years of dictatorship and war had resulted in the collapse of most traditional political organizations. According to Henry L. Roberts, "To a considerable degree the political leaders in Bucharest were generals without armies," and large segments of the population were politically inert or skeptical of the traditional parties.[19] In such a political vacuum communist organizational skills and discipline, and the support of workers in urban areas, were the main factors behind the party's success.

Organizational Development of the Party before 1948

In the first four years of its legal existence one of the party's major tasks was to maintain organizational growth and coherence at a pace commensurate with the turbulent growth in party membership. In July 1945 there were reported to be some 2,500 basic party organizations, of which 1,284 were in towns and 1,210 in rural areas.[20] By the time of the National Party Conference only three months later, the number had grown to 8,251, besides 58 *judet* (county) and 12 regional party organizations.[21] On the eve of the RCP's merger with the Social Democrats in February 1948 the number of basic organizations had mushroomed to 21,854, and the number of judet party organizations stood at 61.[22] Such rapid growth coupled with the lack of trained and tested party cadres created serious organizational problems. Many of these problems were discussed at the National Party Conference in October 1945. This was the first general party gathering after the party's return to legal status, and it provided a major opportunity to reorganize and establish the RCP leadership and lay down its political line.[23] The CC's political report to the gathering, read by Secretary General Gheorghiu-Dej, noted a number of shortcomings in organizational work.[24] The report confirmed that the party's "political influence considerably exceeds its organizational growth," that "the ideological and political growth of cadres has not kept pace with the development of the party," and that "organizational work leaves much to be desired." Among the problems Gheorghiu-Dej enumerated were that some officials were failing to maintain "live and permanent contact with the masses"; that some cadres were guilty of leftist deviation, going beyond party directives regarding industrial and agrarian reforms; and that a tendency toward "anarchosyndicalism" was apparent in some cases. He also charged both Hungarian and Romanian party officials with national-chauvinist deviations in Transylvania, citing the evil effects of Hungarian autonomist tendencies and Romanian reaction.[25] He ended by listing tasks in the organizational sphere designed to eliminate "the gap between the political influence and the organizational situation of the party." Among these were to ensure that leading party organs would exercise stricter control over the manner in which assignments were carried out, help party members to develop a greater sense of personal responsibility, encourage them to pay attention to organizational detail, strengthen party discipline, and encourage criticism and self-criticism so that weaknesses could be assessed and overcome.

One task that was given particular emphasis was "raising the political level of both the cadres and the entire party," and to this end Gheorghiu-Dej provided a separate list of duties with regard to political instruction. The reorganization of party education was decided upon: a six-month course was instituted at the higher party school and regional party school curricula were overhauled (one of the main topics dealt with in these party schools was to be the national question, treated on the basis of Marxism-Leninism). The party's press and other publications were also to be improved, and its propagandizing was to be intensified. In line with these directives the Stefan Gheorghiu higher party school was opened with an enrollment of 100 students in February 1946, and other schools were established in various regions. The need for agitators prior to the November 1946 elections, however, resulted in temporary cutbacks in the party's training programs.[26]

After the elections of November 1946 the position of the RCP was considerably strengthened, since it had managed by its dominant position to manipulate an overwhelming electoral victory for the National Democratic Front. The rate at which new members were admitted was sharply cut back, and the party again turned to its organizational problems. A CC plenum on January 8–9, 1947, was devoted to them, and a number of important measures for the institutionalization of the party were adopted.[27] In an attempt to strengthen control over the lower party organizations, those on the regional level were dissolved and those at the district and county level reorganized and placed directly under the CC. At the same time sections for trade unions, peasants, women, and youth were established in the CC bureaucracy, and parallel sections were planned for the district level; these measures were designed to consolidate and coordinate the party's leadership of and relations with these groups. Consistent with the plenum's decisions, the communists took steps in the spring of 1947 to consolidate work among the trade unions, the peasantry, and organizations for women, youth, and the minorities. In early 1947 the Union of Working Youth was established and the Plowman's Front was reorganized. At the same time the party also began to expel "hostile and dubious elements" from its ranks, although apparently on a much more limited scale than was later the case.

This initial spurt of growth culminated in the decision to merge the RCP and the Social Democratic Party and form the Romanian Workers' Party (*Partidul Muncitoresc Romîn* [RWP]). Despite some genuine grass-roots support for the creation of a single, unified working-class party, the RCP rejected the idea at first; the communists, though, who had begun to cooperate closely with the Social Democrats even before the August 23, 1944, coup, maintained their links with the latter. It was not until the founding of the Communist Information Bureau (Cominform) in September 1947 that they began actively working for unification of the two parties; the decision was clearly made by the Soviet leaders and it was implemented by all the East European states in 1948.[28] The Social Democratic Party was divided on the question of unification. C. Titel Petrescu, one of the Social Democratic leaders, and a group of followers favored maintaining independence. Other factions, however, favored the merger, and at a party congress in October

1947 the proposed merger with the RCP was approved. The leaderships of the two parties worked out the details, and the Romanian Workers' Party came into existence at a founding congress in February 1948.[29]

The RWP was not really a merger but rather the absorption by the communists of a segment of the Social Democrats, and the dissolution of that party. The resolution adopted at the founding congress, and Gheorghiu-Dej's address,[30] for example, specified that the new party would base its activity on the teachings of Marx, Engels, Lenin, and Stalin. It also specified that the party's basic principle would be class consciousness. Such ideas were not consistent with earlier Social Democratic positions, but were among the fundamentals of the communist party platform. The RWP leadership also remained firmly in communist hands. Of the 44 full and alternate members of the Central Committee of the Social Democratic Party elected in October 1947, 10 became full and 4 became alternate members of the CC of the RWP. By contrast, 20 of the 27 RCP CC members chosen in 1945 were full or alternate members of the RWP CC chosen in February 1948. The strength of communist influence was even more apparent in the higher party bodies; only 1 of the 5 party secretaries was a former Social Democrat, the 13-member Politburo had 10 former RCP members and only 3 former Social Democrats, and Gheorghiu-Dej remained the secretary general of the united party.

Not all Social Democrats became members of the new party. At the last congress of the Social Democratic Party, just a few months before the merger, its membership was reported to be 560,201;[31] communist party membership on the eve of the merger was put at about 800,000. In fact Gheorghe Vasilichi, an RCP representative at the last Social Democratic congress, enthusiastically said that the combined strength of the two parties would approach 1,500,000 members. After the merger, however, Ceausescu stated that the combined organization had a membership of only 1,060,000.[32] Since it is unlikely that the merger resulted in any voluntary withdrawal by communist party members, some 260,000 Social Democrats would seem to have become members of the RWP while as many as 300,000 did not. It is not clear how many of these Social Democrats chose not to become members and how many were excluded from membership; in his speech at the founding congress Gheorghiu-Dej was particularly concerned about eliminating rightist elements in the former Social Democratic party,[33] and some may have been excluded at the time of the merger.

The blanket addition of some 260,000 Social Democrats had a negative effect on the social composition of the party from the standpoint of the proportion of workers. As reported at the Social Democratic Party's congress in October 1947, the party at that time was made up of 28 percent workers, 45 percent peasants, and 27 percent other categories. During 1947 the communist party saw a decline in the proportion of workers in its membership, from 46 to 42 percent, and when the two parties were merged the proportion of workers dropped still further, to 39 percent, a fact that gave rise to some concern.

Steps to Create a "Party of the New Type": The Verification Campaign and Party Education, 1948–1955

The absorption of some 260,000 members of the Social Democratic Party was an expedient required by both the Soviet Union and the need to consolidate the RCP's power. Even before the unification congress, however, the party leadership was concerned with the problem of consolidating the party organizationally and strengthening the membership. By early 1948 it had generally eliminated any organized opposition on the part of other political parties, the king had been forced to abdicate, and the communist-led National Democratic Front (renamed the Popular Democratic Front after the creation of the RWP) was fully in control of the government. The kind of party required in such circumstances was quite different from that needed to seize power in the face of political competition from other viable and independent political institutions.

Well before the unification congress, the rate at which party membership was increasing had declined sharply; membership rose from approximately 700,000 to only 800,000 during the entire year of 1947. At the second RWP congress in 1955 Gheorghiu-Dej reported that in 1947 admissions had been stopped completely,[34] and apparently there were no new admissions to the party at all between 1948 and 1952.[35] At the unification congress much stricter membership requirements were set in the party statute. No members of the "former exploiting classes" were to be admitted, a mandatory six-month period of candidate membership would henceforth be required, and those applying for admission were to be carefully screened on an individual basis.[36]

A much more serious effort to cleanse the party and consolidate it was the so-called "verification" campaign, which was initiated by a CC decision in November 1948. The project, as the 1950 CC resolution on the completion of the campaign put it, was carried out by some 200,000 workers "representing an aktif outside the party."[37] As Ghita Ionescu has suggested, this probably indicates that it included members of the security forces, the Ministry of Justice, and the armed forces.[38] This group acted under the direction of a triumvirate: Constantin Pirvulescu, head of the party Control Commission; Alexandru Moghioros, head of the party's Organizational Bureau; and Iosif Ranghet, who was responsible for cadres.

Although the CC resolution stated that 192,000 members were expelled between November 1948 and May 1950, party membership was reported to be 720,000 at the end of the verification campaign. If the figure for February 1948 given by Ceausescu in December 1961 is correct (1,060,000), membership dropped by some 340,000 between February 1948 and May 1950. In fact, Ceausescu said in 1961 that "after the verification and in the ensuing years we expelled 300,000 alien, careerist elements."[39] Thus the verification campaign was considerably more extensive than even the CC's report indicated.

Not only did the party lose almost one-third of its membership between 1948 and 1950, but the purge apparently continued until well after the latter year. That it would do so was implied in the May 1950 CC resolution assessing the verification campaign. Although the evaluation was generally favorable, it was noted that some nonproletarian, petit-bourgeois, and foreign elements remained in the party, and party organizations were called upon "to rid themselves in a systematic manner of those who do not deserve the lofty title of party member."[40] Membership declined from 720,000 in May 1950 to 595,398 in December 1955, a further drop of over 17 percent. Although the CC resolution on the results of the verification campaign said conditions were again such that new members could be accepted, admissions did not begin until some time in 1952.[41] How many individuals were admitted between 1952 and 1955 is not known. One report, which said the percentage of workers increased by 5.9 percent during this period, implied a sizable number of new members,[42] and admissions between 1952 and 1955 must at least have compensated for party members who died during this period. On the basis of this minimum assumption, between 1950 and 1955 an additional 125,000 party members were dropped from the membership rolls. Thus, between 1948 and 1955 up to 465,000 members, or 44 percent of the total, were expelled.[43]

The 1950 report on the campaign noted that the purge had resulted in an increase in the proportion of workers from 38 to 42 percent (though the report still considered this unsatisfactory, and set a goal of raising this figure to 60 percent in the following two or three years). In the leading party and state organizations the working-class elements were further strengthened.

The proportion of workers in leading party bodies increased from 53 to 64 percent, and in leading state bodies it rose from 24 to 40 percent.

The campaign also prepared the way for the admission of new members, but new conditions were imposed. The CC specified that 80 percent of new party members should be from the working class, with the remaining 20 percent to cover all other social categories. In order to encourage workers (particularly in heavy industry) to join the party, different requirements were established for various social categories regarding length of candidate membership, number of recommendations, and the length of time those making such recommendations had been party members. These three social categories, in order of preference, were workers in heavy industry, other industrial and agricultural workers, and all others.

In addition to the thorough and extensive purge of the ranks of the party, a number of measures were taken at the same time to strengthen it organizationally. The youth organization was one of the first institutions to be reorganized after the merger with the Social Democrats. While the party was still struggling for power a variety of youth organizations had been set up to appeal to various groups of young people, but in December 1948 all these were united in the Union of Working Youth (*Uniunii Tineretului Muncitoresc* [UTM]), and party control over this organization was consolidated and strengthened.[44] Also during 1948 party work among women was consolidated; the women's front was reorganized into the Union of Democratic Women of Romania.

The most significant steps to strengthen party organization were taken at a plenary session devoted to organizational matters, some six months before the CC reviewed the success of the verification campaign.[45] A number of serious shortcomings were noted: failure to observe party discipline or to carry out CC instructions, antiparty methods of work, the stifling of criticism and self-criticism, dictatorial attitudes, nepotism, and so on. These were ascribed to a failure to apply Leninist standards with regard to the proper social structure of the party, and the verification campaign was praised as helping to resolve these problems. It was nevertheless deemed useful to introduce certain organizational changes in the party's structure. An Organizational Bureau (Orgburo) was established to supervise party organizational work, and at the same time the Control Commission was directed to take a stronger stand in punishing members who violated party discipline. Certain changes were also made in the structure of the CC apparat. Directorates were established for administration, cadres, and propaganda and agitation. In addition to the CC sections dealing with industry, transportation, domestic trade, and other matters, sections were created to deal with workers, peasants, youth, and women. Lower party organizations were to be structured along parallel lines.

The CC plenum of August 1953 also devoted considerable attention to organizational matters, and again the party's structural weaknesses were apparent in the CC resolution.[46] The links between party and population were criticized as inadequate; the CC apparat failed to check on how CC decisions were implemented; regional organizations (particularly that of Bucharest) were guilty of stifling criticism from party cadres; organizational failings were noted in the trade unions, the youth union, and rural party organizations. The party also undertook certain organizational changes. The Orgburo, which had been established only three years before, was abolished and its functions were taken over by the Politburo and the CC secretariat. Regional party organizations were to hold conferences every two years to elect new committees, and lower level organizations were to hold them annually. The CC also decided that a party congress would be held in March 1954 at which a new party statute would be adopted. (This congress was subsequently postponed, and was ultimately held in December 1955.) Perhaps the most important step—and the most revealing indication of the party's low level of institutionalization—was the decision that "within the shortest possible time . . . a party aktif of 80,000 to 100,000 comrades" should be recruited from among the best qualified party members. The fact that a party with 600,000 members did not have an aktif of 80,000, plus the anxiety conveyed in this CC resolution, were indications that the party was still organizationally weak as late as 1953.

In the process of creating a party of "the new type" the education of party members was a crucial factor. Along with the purge and the strengthening of its organizations, a number of steps were taken to intensify and improve party education. At the founding congress of the RWP in 1948 Gheorghiu-Dej had cited party instruction as an area in need of considerable attention, and the CC resolution on organizational problems issued in January 1950 noted that there were still problems in this area. In October 1948 the party established the A. A. Zhdanov School for the training of ideological cadres, and in July 1949 this was transformed into a higher school of social sciences with a two-year curriculum, to prepare higher-level cadres who were to become directors and instructors in party schools and professors and lecturers in the social sciences. The need for such specialists was great, but there were to be only 100 students per year (200 at any one time).[47]

In July 1950, shortly after the results of the verification campaign had been assessed, a CC plenum launched a major effort to intensify the education of party members. The relevant CC resolution reported that some 100,406 party members had received instruction during the 1948–1949 school year, and 249,125 during 1949–1950. It was noted, however, that the quality of instruction was low and that the ideological and theoretical preparation of instructors was unsatisfactory and it would become a major task of the party to provide them with adequate training. In the 1950–1951 school year the number of party members attending courses was to increase by 30 percent, to 325,862; the A. A. Zhdanov School was to increase its student body to 250; the Stefan Gheorghiu Party Academy (for training leading cadres for the party organizations) was to have 200 students; and higher party schools were to be set up in important regional cities to train 1,893 students. Special seminars lasting from three to six months were to be held in Bucharest to train the instructors who would participate in these programs. The CC resolution conveys the urgency of the task as well as the extent of the undertaking.[48] Three years later, on the eve of the 1953–1954 school year, concern was still being expressed about the education of party members: party organizations were again enjoined to consider instruction a central preoccupation; the quality of teaching was again criticized; a new series of seminars for teachers was set up; and various additional measures were to be undertaken.[49]

The second congress of the RWP, held in December 1955, seems to mark the turning point in the struggle to create a "party of the new type." Serious shortcomings were still reported, but apparently enough difficulties had been overcome and a large enough loyal cadre created to permit the party to expand its membership. The admission of new members had begun in 1952, though the number taken in before 1955 was apparently not large. As noted above, the CC resolution on the verification campaign set a goal of 80 percent of new members from the working class.[50] At the congress, however, the party leader reported that only 48 percent of the candidates admitted to the party since 1952 were workers. This, together with the reduction in membership that occurred during that period, was sufficient to raise the proportion of workers from 37 percent in 1951 to 43 percent in 1955.[51]

The results of the massive efforts to provide instruction were also more modest than might have been expected. Gheorghiu-Dej reported that "over 500,000 members and candidate members of the party and activists outside the party had participated in courses on Marxism-Leninism and basic problems of party policy" after working hours. But he also said that in the seven years since 1948 over 48,000 party members had completed three-month basic party courses, fewer than 12,000 had completed middle-level party schools, and only 2,400 had completed higher party schools, while an additional 31,000 had finished "evening school and university courses on Marxism-Leninism."[52] Despite this limited success in altering the social composition of the party and raising the educational level of its membership, the party leader reported that the task set by the CC in August 1953, to create a party aktif of 80,000 to 100,000 individuals, had been accomplished.

A major difficulty in creating the aktif after 1948 had been the divided loyalty of party members. As Jowitt has pointed out, before 1952 the party elite was fragmented, with each leader maintaining fiefs within his own sphere, staffed by loyal retainers.[53] But by 1953 Gheorghiu-Dej was in a position to create the loyal party aktif he desired. He had succeeded in removing the most serious challengers in the party leadership by purging Pauker, Luca, and Georgescu; the verification campaign had eliminated many less-disciplined elements from the party, and no doubt made those who remained more responsive to the leadership. This, coupled with the campaign to provide instruction for party members, permitted the creation of the aktif Gheorghiu-Dej sought.

The Growth and Development of the Party after 1955

The creation of an aktif of 100,000, which was announced at the second RWP congress, was a crucial turning point in the further expansion of the party. The process of creating the "party of the new type" demanded by Gheorghiu-Dej was sufficiently advanced so that after this congress, party membership was again permitted to increase. As can be seen from table 3 (and also from table 2), membership has risen significantly since 1955. This is not to say that the leadership has abandoned its earlier concern about the membership, but by 1955 the institutional pattern was established and expansion could proceed without facing the serious problems that plagued the period from 1944 to 1955. Certain matters continued to be of concern to the leadership—the quality of newly admitted members, their social composition, party education, and the need to strengthen party organizations—but they were less urgent and less difficult to deal with than those that marked the initial period of party institutionalization.

The admission of new members, once it was resumed in 1952, was apparently carried out at a rather slow pace, and until 1955 those dropped

TABLE 3

Growth in Party Membership
(in five-year intervals 1950–1975)

Year	No. of Members	Percent Under or Over Previous Figure
1950	720,000	
1955	595,398	− 17.3
1960	834,600	+ 40.1
1965	1,518,000	+ 82.0
1970	1,999,720	+ 31.7
1975	2,577,434	+ 28.9

SOURCE: Table 2.

outnumbered those admitted. After the second congress the pace quickened, although at the congress both Gheorghiu-Dej and Ceausescu emphasized the need for careful screening and the desirability of increasing the worker element. Changes in the party statute adopted at the congress also made conditions of admission more stringent. As in 1948 and 1950, requirements varied somewhat according to occupation, reflecting the party's priorities. Sponsorship requirements were not changed for applicants in Category 1 (workers in heavy industry who had been active in production for at least five years), but for those in Category 2 (other industrial workers, workers in machine tractor stations and state agricultural enterprises, engineers, and technicians) and Category 3 (other workers, working peasants, and officials) those recommending them for admission were required to have been full party members for longer periods. The duration of candidate membership was also extended: from six months to a full year for those in Category 1, and from one year to one and one-half and two years for those in Categories 2 and 3, respectively.[54]

The drive to increase the proportion of workers was successful after 1955. A CC resolution issued in June 1958 reported that of the 145,000 candidate members in the party 72.5 percent were workers, and in industrial areas (Bucharest, Brasov, Ploesti) the proportion was even higher. At the same time greater emphasis was placed on drawing engineers and technicians into the party, a logical requirement in view of the growing sophistication of the economy. The need for more such members was also pointed up by Gheorghiu-Dej at the third RWP congress in 1960, although workers were still the first priority.[55]

Gheorghiu-Dej's comments on party admissions at the third congress reflected a rather strict stand, and in fact between June 1960 and April 1962 the rate of admissions was below that maintained between 1955 and 1960.[56] In April 1962, however, the RWP deemed desirable a relaxation in this regard. There appear to be several reasons for the change. First, the collectivization of agriculture had been completed (at least on paper) in early 1962. This reorganization of the rural sector of the economy, while it failed to resolve many of the problems besetting Romanian agriculture, in many respects marked the completion of the first steps in the communization of Romania. (The nationalization of industry had been carried out much earlier.) Second, the initial differences with the Soviet Union and the Soviet-led Council for Mutual Economic Assistance (Comecon) were beginning to emerge. The Romanian leaders must have calculated that if they were to enjoy a certain degree of autonomy from the Soviet Union, a broadening of the party's base of support among the population would be essential, and expanding party membership was part of this strategy. Finally, fifteen years of dominance had given the party greater confidence in its relationship with the population.

A CC plenum in April 1962 adopted a number of changes making admission easier. The three-tiered classification of individuals was replaced by a simpler, two-category system; the period of required candidate membership was reduced; provisions were made for direct admission to the party, without candidate membership, in exceptional cases. The ban on individuals who had been members of "bourgeois" and "other" political parties in the past, including those who held responsible positions in such parties, was relaxed. At the same time the CC resolution recommended greater restraint with regard to the expulsion of members. Perhaps most significant, a reduction in the proportion of workers in the party's social composition was anticipated, as peasants in newly collectivized areas were recruited, and engineers and technicians (usually placed in the category of intellectuals and officials) were brought in.[57] Significantly, between April 1962 and the end of 1965 party membership rose by some 600,000, an increase of over 68 percent.

Since the initial upsurge in new members between 1962 and 1965, party growth has been gradual and regular.

Admission requirements were further relaxed in the changes to the party statute approved at the ninth congress in July 1965. Categories were abolished; all those seeking admission were to be treated equally, and all would henceforth be required to produce the minimum number of recommendations previously called for. Also, the candidate probation stage was eliminated.[58] Since that time the requirements for admission to the party have been changed in only minor respects.[59] Party organizations are still periodically enjoined to adhere strictly to admission requirements and to consider each case individually, but the procedures that have been established have resulted in considerable stability in regard to admissions since the mid-1960s. According to party statistics for the end of 1975, over 17 percent of Romania's adult population and almost 24 percent of the active labor force are party members. The growth of the party is reflected in the fact that only ten years earlier 10 percent of the adult population were members.[60]

The social composition of the party has undergone considerable alteration since the early 1950s, reflecting both a change in attitude on this issue and demographic changes in the country. As a result of the deliberate effort to recruit workers and the discriminatory admission procedures that favored them, they represented more than 50 percent of the membership between 1958 and 1962 (see table 2). With the decision to follow a more liberal admission policy, however, the ratio of workers fell to 40 percent in 1965. Since then their number has increased, because the party is again emphasizing the recruitment of workers. In 1972, for example, almost 58 percent of the newly admitted party members were workers, and in 1977 the proportion was even higher, reaching nearly 72 percent of those newly admitted to membership.[61] The increase in the proportion of workers and the drop in that of peasants since 1965 also reflects the significant demographic changes that have taken place in Romania. As industrialization has proceeded there has been a considerable decline in the size of the work force engaged in agriculture: from 74.1 percent in 1950 to 56.5 percent in 1965 and 38.1 percent in 1975.[62] In the party this has been reflected in a decline in the proportion of peasants, from 33 percent in 1964 to the present level of less than 20 percent.

The drive to bring technicians, teachers, and the better-educated elements of Romanian society into the party was pursued with more vigor in the late 1960s, as the party showed growing concern with the impact upon the economy of the scientific-technological revolution. The result is that between the end of 1969 and the end of 1971 the proportion of academicians, doctors of science, and university teaching staffs in the party rose from 25 to 60 percent. By the latter date it was also reported that 47 percent of the primary and secondary school teachers, 52 percent of the engineers, 41 percent of the physicians, and 75 percent of those active in culture and the arts were party members.[63]

In addition to its continuous concern with social structure the party has also periodically voiced concern about the proportion of women. At the third party congress in 1960 Gheorghiu-Dej reported that only 17 percent of party members were women, and insisted that more be recruited. This theme was reiterated at the April 1962 CC plenum at which requirements for party membership were relaxed.[64] The results, however, were limited. By the time of the ninth party congress in 1965 the percentage of women had risen only to 21. At the National Party Conference in July 1972 Ceausescu again said that "more attention should be given to admitting women into the party, and to promoting them to various party and state functions," and the conference's resolution on party activity echoed this sentiment.[65] Some progress was registered with the election of 20 women as full and alternate CC members—half the number of new members elected at the conference. During 1972 almost 30 percent of new members admitted to the party were women, and at year's end they made up almost 24 percent of the total membership. In 1977, 37 percent of new members were women, but their proportion of the total reached only 26 percent.[66]

This same topic was given greater emphasis at the CC plenum in June 1973. On that occasion a special resolution on women was approved, and two full and two alternate women members were elected to the RCP CC Executive Committee. One of the full members was Ceausescu's wife, Elena, who was elevated to CC membership only in July 1972 and who became a member of the Political Executive Committee's Permanent Bureau (Politburo) in 1977. Mrs. Ceausescu appears to be a primary motivating force behind the drive to give greater recognition to women.

As was made clear in Ceausescu's speech to the June 1973 CC plenum, one of the primary considerations behind the effort to give women a greater role in the party is the role they play in the economy.[67] In 1974 some 45 percent of the employed ("active") population were women; they made up one-third of the workers in industry, almost 60 percent of those employed in agriculture, 47 percent of those in telecommunications, 62 percent of those in education and culture, and 72 percent of those working in the health and social services sector.[68] Thus women are a major portion of the total work force, and must be mobilized if the party's ambitious economic goals are to be met. Women also represent one of the most readily available but untapped industrial labor resources that Ceausescu would like to exploit more fully as the labor market becomes increasingly tight. Under these circumstances, increasing the number of women in the party and giving them greater responsibility are important in drawing them into more active economic participation. Also related to this policy is the simultaneous upgrading of the National Council of Women (the women's mass organization) by appointing a full member of the Political Executive Committee (Lina Ciobanu) to head it and making her an ex officio member of the Council of Ministers.

Another compositional consideration is the nationality structure of the party. Before 1944 the RCP had a particular appeal for non-Romanians, and they must have made up a large proportion of its membership. Even after it was legalized in 1944 the party must have retained a certain appeal for non-Romanians, particularly for Hungarians and Jews. Because of this the party has been somewhat sensitive about publicizing its ethnic composition in earlier periods. Of the delegates to the second RWP congress in 1955, 80 percent were Romanians and 20 percent other nationalities,[69] and there is no indication that the ethnic composition of the party as a whole differed substantially from these figures. It is quite probable that the non-Romanian fifth of the party was made up primarily of Hungarians and Jews, since in 1962 a CC resolution recommended admitting more ethnic Germans.[70] Lingering doubts about the loyalty of the Germans, reflected in the policy of seizing their property and other measures taken against them after World War II, must have hampered their admission to membership before that time.

As the party began its important expansion after 1962 and sought through its policies and propaganda to Romanianize its image, the proportion of Romanians grew while that of the minorities declined. It is doubtful whether loyal non-Romanians were expelled from the party on grounds of nationality, but new members were primarily Romanian. Since then the party has carefully maintained a nationality composition that is equivalent to that of the entire country.[71] By the ninth party congress in 1965, 87 percent of members were Romanian, over 9 percent were Hungarian, and over 3 percent were German, Serb, and other nationalities.[72]

The age structure of the party has been affected by the different admission policies followed at various times. Expansion of party membership has lowered the average age, because a large proportion of new party members are younger people. In 1974, for example, it was reported that over the previous five years some 60 percent of new party members were admitted directly from the Union of Communist Youth.[73] This suggests not only a high proportion of youth among newly admitted party members, but also a tendency to admit such young people as have been properly socialized in regard to the party's goals and policies. Table 4 indicates changes in the age structure of the party between 1962 and 1973. By 1962 the limited admis-

TABLE 4

Age Structure of the Rumanian Communist Party, 1962–1973
(*in percent*)

	1962	1965	1969	1973
Over Age 40	41	36	40	44
Under Age 40	59	64	60	56

SOURCE: *Scinteia*, May 17, 1962, July 20, 1965, and August 7, 1969, and *World Marxist Review* no. 5 (May), 1973, pp. 128–29.

sion policy had resulted in the aging of the party, but the influx of new members between 1962 and 1965 tended to slow down this trend. As admissions have stabilized since 1965, however, the age structure has shifted toward the older groups again. As it now stands, the party is somewhat "younger" than the population in general. On the basis of 1974 population estimates, 47 percent of the adult population (those over 20 years of age) are between the ages of 20 and 39, and 53 percent are over age 40.[74]

The controlled growth of party membership after 1955 was also accompanied by successful efforts to ensure the proper indoctrination of its members. While in the early years membership growth far outstripped the party's limited ability to provide training, after 1955 this ability was more commensurate with the task of educating new members. At the second party congress in 1955 Gheorghiu-Dej reported that fewer than 100,000 of the nearly 600,000 party members had completed party school courses lasting at least three months, although 500,000 party members and nonparty activists had studied Marxism-Leninism. Ten years later (in 1965, after the party ranks had been augmented by an influx of new members during the previous three years) it was reported that over 90 percent of the membership had graduated from central and regional party schools,[75] indicating both the considerably increased capacity of the party to indoctrinate new members, and the success of its institutionalization.

The frequent shortcomings discussed in party publications, however, reflect the continuing difficulties of the task.[76] The party education of the aktif has been fairly successful at least in quantitative terms, as is indicated by the report that in 1970, 69 percent of the members of county party bureaus and 46 percent of members of town and municipal party committees had graduated from or were attending party higher schools, while 84 percent of county, municipal, and town committee activists had graduated from one- to three-year party schools.[77] Despite these obvious statistical successes, the party continues to emphasize the need for continued political training and the importance of raising the level of political education.[78]

Although the number of party organizations has increased considerably, from less than 30,000 basic organizations in 1955 to more than 59,000 in 1977,[79] so has the number of loyal, indoctrinated cadres capable of satisfactorily leading these party units, permitting the expansion to proceed with relatively little difficulty. In 1965 it was reported that more than 76 percent of all party activists had been doing party work for more than five years, and by 1970 it was reported that 23 percent of them had served ten to fifteen years and 40 percent over fifteen years;[80] on the basis of this loyal aktif the party has created the conditions for stable continuation of the institution.

4
The Character
of the Party Elite

The focus in the last chapter was on the organization and its membership; this chapter will also deal with organizational development, but the focus will be on the party elite and the changes that have taken place in it as the RCP has become increasingly institutionalized. Just as the requirements for party membership became more stringent as the party underwent institutional development, so the qualifications required of those chosen for positions of leadership have become more demanding over time. This has been particularly true in regard to the length of party membership required before selection to party office, and the number of lower-level party offices held before designation to higher-level posts. This process at the elite level complemented what was taking place at the level of ordinary party membership; in the case of the RCP, however, boundary establishment was made more explicit and enforced much earlier with regard to the party membership than it was with regard to the party elite.[1]

Changing Requirements for Party Leadership Posts

Between 1944 and 1948, as the party went through a period of turbulent growth, the number of experienced party leaders was inadequate, and many younger, less-qualified individuals were drawn into leadership posts. As the party membership leveled off and then dropped substantially between 1948 and 1953, the requirements for leading positions were raised and much greater concern was devoted to the selection of party officials. Initially these requirements were not precisely spelled out, although general statements were made regarding the need to secure competent and experienced party officials; particular emphasis was laid on organizational work, shortcomings were enumerated and criticized, and cadre selection was an important concern.[2]

Until specific requirements regarding previous party experience were laid down in 1974, it was natural that as individuals with more experience became available they were promoted to leadership positions. Thus over time the average length of party membership, previous experience in party offices, and the age of those chosen for leading positions, all increased. Table 5 shows the trends among full and alternate members of the Politburos chosen in 1945, 1948, 1955, and 1960 and the full members of the

TABLE 5

Previous Party Experience and Age of
Party Leadership, 1945–1974

Leadership[a] Elected in	Total No. Elected	Average Party Membership		Average Full CC Membership[b]		Average Age	
		Years	Unknown	Years	Unknown	Years	Unknown
1945	7	17	1	—	0	41	0
1948	18	23	7[c]	3	5[c]	45	3
1955	15	23	2	9	0	47	1
1960	13	30	2	14	0	51	1
1965	15	29	3	16	0	53	1
1969	21	29	1	12	0	53	1
1974	23	33	6	13	0	54	3

NOTES ON SOURCES:

The data available on the Romanian party elite are very limited and it is consequently extremely difficult to analyze in much depth the characteristics of these individuals. There is, however, somewhat more material on the most prominent of the leadership, and therefore only the individuals who are members of the highest party bodies are analyzed. In the tables on the party leadership that follow, the analysis covers the full and alternate members of the Politburo elected at the National Party Congress of October 1945 and the party congresses of 1948, 1955, and 1960, and the full (but not alternate) members of the Executive Committee chosen at the party congresses of 1965 and 1969 and of the Political Executive Committee elected at the party congress in 1974. The biographical background data are drawn from the files of the Research and Analysis Department of Radio Free Europe, Munich, West Germany; these data are gleaned primarily from material published in Romania since 1951, but some information published in Western Europe and the United States is included when based on reliable public sources.

(a) Full and candidate members of the Politburo (or Presidium) elected in 1945, 1948, and 1960; full members of the Executive Committee (or Political Executive Committee) elected in 1965, 1969, and 1974.

(b) Length of full CC membership applies only to the period beginning in 1945 since data on the earlier period are incomplete. This tends to minimize length of CC membership in the earlier years (1945 and 1948 in particular) but it has less effect on the later years.

(c) The five Social Democrats who became members of the leadership at the founding of the RWP in 1948 are not included in the figures for that year on length of party membership and length of full CC membership because data on their previous leadership in the Social Democratic Party are not readily available and they are less relevant here.

Executive Committee chosen in 1965, 1969, and 1974. Data that would permit carrying out a similar analysis of the CC or other party leadership bodies are not available, but there is no indication that the trends in these bodies differ in organizations at other levels, and in fact the few indications that we have tend to confirm this.[3]

In examining the figures in table 5 it should be kept in mind that 1965 marks a change in the party leadership: Gheorghiu-Dej died and Ceausescu was elected head of the party. The organization chosen at the party congress in that year marked the end of the Gheorghiu-Dej era, but Ceausescu was not yet in a position to bring his own younger followers into positions on the Executive Committee until later. Thus the slight decline in average length of party membership, full CC membership, and age that took place after 1965 is a reflection of this change in leadership. It is significant, however, that the figures again crept up after 1969.

The process of instituting increasingly stringent requirements for holding leading positions was made explicit in party regulations adopted at the eleventh party congress in November 1974. Amendments to the party statute adopted on that occasion specified how long an individual must have been a party member and/or engaged in party activity before he could be elected to certain party posts. At the basic organization level, to be elected a secretary an individual must now have been a party member for four years, and to be a member of the bureau three years' membership is required. To hold such positions in the committees of communes, enterprises, agricultural units, and so on, the corresponding figures are six and four years, respectively. At the municipal and town party organization level secretaries are required to have been party members for six years and to have served for four years in leading positions in the party or mass organizations at the next lower level. Those selected as members of municipal and town committees must have been party members for five years. To be chosen secretary of a county party committee or of the Bucharest municipal committee requires eight years of party membership and five years of party activity at appropriate levels. Members of party committees at this level are required to be party members for at least six years. Members of the CC and the Central Auditing Commission are required to be party members for at least twelve years and to have been active for six years in leading organizations of the party, mass organizations, enterprises, and so on. Even delegates to the party congresses must have been members for six years, although those who have served four years in leading positions in the party's various youth organizations may be chosen after only three years of membership.[4]

Although these explicit and more stringent requirements were supported by the party leader, there were two curious episodes during the eleventh party congress (at which they were approved) that suggest a certain degree of opposition to them. The first of these was the proposal that party leader Ceausescu be elected secretary general for life, made by Gheorghe Cioara, head of the Bucharest party organization and a close associate of the party leader. As soon as Cioara had made his proposal, Ceausescu took the floor to express his appreciation of the "special personal trust" the proposal reflected, but modestly proposed that the congress not consider the suggestion.[5] Why the proposal was made and then dropped was never explained, but it may have been related to the newly specified requirements for party office.[6]

The second unusual incident occurred during the debate on the amendments to the party statute on the final day of the congress. After the proposed amendments had been read, Petre Blajovici, party first secretary of Bihor county and an alternate member of the CC Executive Committee (who—significantly—was not reelected to the latter position at the congress), called attention to the complex tasks faced by party officials and proposed "that the statute specify the age up to which a communist can be proposed for and elected to leading party organs on all levels, including the Central Committee." The Blajovici proposal was obviously designed to nullify the effects of the newly proposed requirements for election to party posts. Ceausescu himself responded to Blajovici and, while agreeing that the article regarding the age structure of party bodies was not satisfactory, argued that setting an age limit was also unsatisfactory since it failed to take into consideration individual differences. Ceausescu proposed that the CC be empowered to reword the article in question to reflect concern for the participation of younger cadres in party organizations, and the congress agreed to this.[7]

Since the original draft of the proposed amendments was not published, only the final version of the statement on age composition is available. This sheds little light on the problem, however, since it is vague enough to permit considerable latitude with regard to the age of those designated to leading party bodies. It specifies:

> On electing party bodies, from the bureau of the basic organization to the Central Committee, care must be taken that some members of these bodies be newly elected, and that new cadres who came to prominence during the struggle to translate into action the general political line of the party, the Program of the Romanian Communist Party, be promoted.

Corresponding age ratios shall be ensured between members of the party bodies by consistently encouraging the promotion of young cadres—in addition to broadly experienced cadres—representing all points of view.[8]

While the new wording commits the party to recognize younger party members in filling party positions, it does not go as far as Blajovici wished in limiting the number of older party members who may hold higher positions. The question of age was a key theme throughout the congress. Ceausescu's rejection of life tenure as party leader became the focal point in discussions of the issue, and provided an argument with which to counter the idea, prevalent among older party activists, that they had a perpetual right to be reelected to higher party positions. Miu Dobrescu, an alternate member of the Executive Committee, suggested that since Ceausescu had rejected election for life "other top party officials should also draw the appropriate conclusions."[9] CC Secretary Gheorghe Pana expressed agreement with Dobrescu's assessment and reiterated that "comrades in the party leadership have not been elected for life—as some of them have been given to understand." Pana also called upon the congress's Commission on Proposing Candidates to "make proper nominations" bearing this in mind.[10]

These comments reflected the existence of underlying problems related to the generation gap between older and younger party officials, one of the key elements of which was the increasing tendency to name those with greater seniority in the organization to leading positions. Despite the vague pledge to consider younger cadres (who nevertheless must meet the established minimum requirements), the age battle was won by the forces favoring promotion of individuals with longer exposure to the conditioning influences of party membership and work in lower levels of the organization.

Another aspect of the boundary maintenance question is the rate of turnover in the leadership, which has gradually declined as the leadership has stabilized. Table 6 gives data on the turnover of full and alternate members of the CC, and there is reason to believe that the picture is similar at other levels of the party apparatus. A number of things are particularly noteworthy with regard to the data in this table. The proportion of full CC members elected at the previous congress who are reelected at the following congress has risen to about 57 percent, where it has remained since 1960. The proportion of former alternate CC members elected to full membership has continued to increase, while the proportion of members without previous CC membership ("new" members) has shown a sharp decline. Among the alternate CC members, however, a very large proportion are new entrants into the party leadership. It appears that more and more often

TABLE 6

New and Re-elected Central Committee Members, 1945–1974

Central Committee Elected in	Full CC Members							Alternate CC Members						
	Total	Previously Full No.	%	Previously Alternate No.	%	New No.	%	Total	Previously Full No.	%	Previously Alternate No.	%	New No.	%
1945	27	—		—		—		None	—		—		—	
1948	41	19	46.3	—		22	53.7	16	1	6.3	—		15	93.8
1955	60	20	33.3	6	10.0	34	56.7	35	4	11.4	5	14.3	26	74.3
1960	79	45	57.0	14	17.7	20	23.3	31	0	—	9	29.0	22	71.0
1965	121	70	57.9	14	11.6	37	30.6	75	0	—	7	9.3	68	90.7
1969	165	92	55.8	27	16.4	46	27.9	120	2	1.7	13	10.8	105	87.5
1974	205	118	57.5	44	21.5	43	21.0	156	2	1.3	24	15.4	130	83.3

SOURCES: *Scînteia*, October 26, 1945, February 25, 1948, July 24, 1965, August 13, 1969, and November 29, 1974; *Congresul al II-lea al P.M.R.* (Bucharest: Editura de stat pentru literatura politica, 1956); *Congresul al III-lea al P.M.R.* (Bucharest: Editura politica, 1960).

entrance into full CC membership must be preceded by alternate membership. This trend would be even more obvious if we included data on those elected to full and alternate membership between party congresses. (As was noted earlier, the change of party head in 1965 is in part responsible for the fact that figures for that year deviate somewhat from the long-term trends; in that year the CC increased in size by more than a third and Ceausescu was able to add a number of new names to its roster.) Thus the figures on turnover in CC membership further confirm that the party experience of leaders is increasing over time.

Gheorghiu-Dej's Measures
to Increase Elite Coherence

One problem that particularly plagued the RCP during its early years was the lack of elite coherence. Any organization marked by vertical and horizontal differentiation faces this problem of coherence,[11] and it was one of the major sources of internal disunity in the RCP during the period of rapid growth between 1944 and 1948. Party organizations mushroomed throughout the country and various functional committees and subunits were set up to deal with specific groups and problems. The lack of established procedures and rules, and the leadership's lack of experience in dealing with such problems, naturally resulted in disunity and organizational incoherence.

Further complicating the problem was the subservience of the RCP to the Soviet Union during this initial period. Huntington has noted that coherence and autonomy "are often closely linked together;"[12] the dependence of the Romanian party upon the Soviet Union, and the links between members of the RCP elite and the Soviet leadership, certainly intensified the party's disunity.

Another factor that contributed to the lack of cohesion in the party was the more critical need for organs of coercion during the initial period. The process of seizing power required a powerful security, police, and military apparatus to deal with organized and individual forms of opposition to the new regime, and the extensive economic and social transformations that were being carried out during the early period of the party's rule also necessitated emphasis on coercion. The urgent need to create a reliable, responsible security force resulted in priority being given to that task; the lack of unity in the party was considered a problem of lesser priority.

This powerful force, though, became itself a source of disunity. It is indicative in this regard that when the "verification" campaign was carried out in 1948–1950 to reduce and purify the party ranks, the security and military organizations played a key role. In 1967, in the course of discrediting a rival (Alexandru Draghici), Secretary General Ceausescu recalled that "in the past" (though not in recent years), instead of having party organizations themselves deal with internal differences and mistakes, "they were sometimes referred to the security organizations, thus creating conditions for interference in the life of the party and seriously undermining its authority and leading role."[13] Somewhat earlier, in an extensive criticism of Ana Pauker, Gheorghiu-Dej had said that the Ministry of the Interior, "which was actually not under the control of the party leadership, undertook to supervise party and state cadres, to intercept telephone calls, and did not except even the secretary general of the party."[14] Thus the existence of a responsible and cohesive security apparatus in many ways hampered the development of coherence within the party.

Some of the insights that have been supplied regarding the inner workings of the party elite in this early period clearly indicate the lack of cohesion. Most of these revelations were made at the November 30–December 5, 1961, CC plenum at which Pauker, Luca, and other purged members of the leadership were linked with Stalinist and antiparty elements in the Soviet Union. Gheorghiu-Dej, for example, claimed that Pauker, Luca, and Georgescu, who together with himself constituted the CC secretariat, had "acted as a separate group above and beyond the elected organs, ignoring the Central Committee and the secretariat (which they dominated) and replacing the Politburo, which functioned almost as a committee." Not only did the group take over policy functions, but according to Ceausescu they did not even bother to hold formal meetings. In 1947 the CC met only once, and even the secretariat held only a single official meeting. On the same occasion Draghici described the situation in these terms: "The factionalist groups [Pauker, Luca, and others] turned the ministries they controlled into veritable fiefs, isolating them from the party and removing them from its control."[15] One of the principal reasons why these individuals could exercise such authority during this period, according to Ceausescu, was their claim to have connections with Stalin or other Soviet leaders. While these statements of Gheorghiu-Dej and others were clearly intended to absolve themselves of any Stalinist taint, their charges had to have some element of truth if they were to convince the members of the CC. Thus they do provide insight into the party's operations in the period before 1952, and carry a ring of authenticity that reflects the serious lack of cohesion that plagued the party during this time.

Gheorghiu-Dej and the rest of the party leadership were aware of this disunity within the party, but the problem was not really attacked with vigor until after control of Romania had been fully secured. The creation of the RWP in 1948 marked the beginning of the phase in which the emphasis was placed on organizational consolidation. The verification campaign was paralleled by a concerted campaign to strengthen the organizational discipline of the party. (Party discipline was a frequent demand in the CC resolutions and documents issued during this period.)[16] A CC plenum in early 1950 took perhaps the most important steps in this regard by deciding to establish a separate Orgburo, which was given the responsibility of supervising party organizational work. It was empowered to make decisions for the CC on organizational questions, to streamline the bureaucracy and eliminate red tape, and to discipline those who failed to observe party policies or discipline.[17] Other CC sessions dealing with this problem followed, and measures were adopted to further strengthen and emphasize discipline.[18]

One of the most important factors in establishing the cohesion of the party was the purge of three powerful figures, Pauker, Luca, and Georgescu, in 1952. It is significant that it should have taken place just then. By that year the more or less successful verification campaign had succeeded in establishing greater organizational unity, and in fact steps were under way to again open the party ranks to new members. The drive to strengthen party discipline was also achieving results, and Gheorghiu-Dej had largely succeeded in imposing his authority over the organization. Thus the party secretary general's move against his three most prominent rivals for power coincided with the strengthening of his domestic position in the party and his growing encroachment upon their individual fiefdoms. And while their links with individual Soviet leaders had previously given Pauker, Luca, and Georgescu considerable strength and encouraged a degree of disunity in the party elite, changes in Soviet ruling circles at that time favored Gheorghiu-Dej's action against the group. Stalin was preparing a purge in the Soviet Union, and in fact an anti-Semitic campaign had already been launched in Eastern Europe. This put Pauker, who was Jewish, on the defensive, and left Gheorghiu-Dej largely a free hand to deal with his opponents.[19]

With the elimination of his three rivals Gheorghiu-Dej was clearly the preeminent figure in the Romanian party. Increasing organizational coherence coupled with the successful purge of his leading rivals permitted him to impose a degree of unity upon the party that it had not previously known. This is not to suggest that the secretary general thereafter enjoyed unquestioned dominance of the party. In fact in 1957, in the wake of the de-Stalinization campaign initiated by Soviet party leader Nikita Khrushchev, Iosif Chisinevschi and Miron Constantinescu challenged Gheorghiu-Dej, but they lost and were themselves purged. Ceausescu, too, when he assumed the leadership of the party, faced challenges from some of the old guard as well as from Draghici, who was of his own political generation. These challenges were successfully met in large part thanks to the unity of the party organization, which provided Ceausescu with the support of a cohesive institutional base.[20]

Ceausescu's Practice of Rotating Cadres and the Problem of Coherence

While Gheorghiu-Dej had imposed a degree of unity on the party by establishing stricter organizational discipline and eliminating his most powerful rivals, the problems of coherence that face any large institution were certainly not completely resolved. The growth in the size of the party, and the increasing complexity of its tasks consequent to the modernization of Romanian society and development of the country's economy, have perpetuated the problem of coherence. In a complex organization with numerous functional and territorial subunits there is always a danger that party officials may become so identified with a particular subunit that they overlook the goals of the organization as a whole. One way of dealing with this problem is to encourage members of the elite to hold office in a variety of subunits; "thus horizontal mobility acts to reduce subunit provincialism and to coordinate subunit diversity."[21]

Although periodically transferring individuals to different positions increases the coherence of the party organization, an autocratic party leader also finds it useful in preventing potential opponents from developing strong bases of support, in a ministry or party subunit, from which to challenge the incumbent; such transfers also create a degree of uncertainty that helps the leader to maintain his position.

In spite of the fact there is little to indicate that Gheorghiu-Dej deliberately encouraged diversified careers for party officials in order to increase organizational coherence, examination of the careers of those officials who rose to positions of importance in the party hierarchy under his leadership does show considerable diversity. Even those who tended to concentrate in certain general areas were exposed to a number of different aspects of the activity these areas involved. Ceausescu, for example, followed a career primarily within the party, but in the period before 1944 he held leading positions in the Union of Communist Youth and later he was a regional party official, served in the party organizations of the armed forces, and ultimately became a CC secretary involved in organizational work. His career pattern is narrower than most because during his government experience (minister of agriculture from 1948 to 1950 and deputy minister of the armed forces from 1950 to 1952) he was principally concerned with party organizations in these two sensitive areas. While his career involved a number of different positions,[22] most other individuals had as great or even greater variety of experience under Gheorghiu-Dej.

But where Gheorghiu-Dej can be said to have encouraged such complex careers, the practice has been further expanded and institutionalized during Ceausescu's tenure in office. The principle has been designated by Ceausescu as "rotation of cadres." It was not until almost six years after he assumed office, however, that he began to refine the concept and enshrine it in theoretical terms. At a CC plenum in February 1971 he emphasized the importance of giving party officials experience in both government and the economy. If party activists were to be equipped to deal with complex and rapidly changing developments, he maintained, they must periodically go through a process of recycling, and rather than sitting passively through lectures they should be sent to work in production. This was to apply to "cadres from the lower levels up to that of the Council of Ministers and the Executive Committee."[23] The desirability of "giving party leaders experience" at the local level and in nonparty organizations was emphasized at the February 1971 CC session, when a number of prominent central party officials were rotated into positions in county party committees and mass organizations. Just over a year later Ceausescu again stressed the need for this type of rotation. He proposed to another plenary session that provisions be included in the party statute to the effect "that periodically comrades should occupy different positions—party activists should work in state offices and state activists should work in party offices."[24] At this session additional personnel changes were made in keeping with this view.

At the July 1972 National Party Conference the principle of rotation of cadres was included in the amended party statute: "In assigning cadres the principle of rotating them between party and state work will be borne in mind, so that they may acquire many-sided experience, so that they will be able to understand and resolve with increasing efficiency the complex problems of social life and the scientific management of society."[25]

There is good reason to believe that Ceausescu's espousal of the principle of rotation was motivated by the resistance he encountered to his policies. Vested interests and entrenched bureaucrats were less than responsive to certain of his policy initiatives. After his selection as head of the party in 1965 it was roughly four years before he could consolidate his position, but by the tenth party congress in August 1969 he had successfully managed to do so. As he turned then to the task of putting into practice his ideas in regard to domestic policy, however, he found that there was some reluctance to implement his suggestions. This is not to imply that there was an opposition faction within the leadership (there is no evidence that one existed), but Ceausescu clearly had to cope with disagreement, inertia, resistance to policy, and reluctance to implement directives. This was apparent in a speech he delivered just a few weeks after he had introduced the idea of rotation, in which he criticized the unwillingness of all kinds of officials to carry out economic changes announced some time previously.[26] Delays in finalizing the provisions of the 1971–1975 economic plan were also apparently attributable to a certain degree of resistance. Similar problems were encountered in the cultural field; writers, for example, were reluctant to accept the more restrictive cultural policy that Ceausescu sought to impose after 1968.

A complementary attempt to deal with the problem of compliance was represented by the ideological campaign inaugurated by Ceausescu in the summer of 1971. Although other considerations were also motivating factors, the concern with improving the manner in which policy was implemented was a major element. The frequently repeated call for a strengthening of the leading role of the party, and the emphasis on the fact that all party members must actively implement the party line, were part of the effort to break down resistance to Ceausescu's programs. In his speech to a CC plenum convened in July 1971 to consider his cultural-ideological proposals, he criticized the "attitude of smugness, of petit-bourgeois tolerance, of lack of firmness that has appeared in many places," and called for the introduction of the party spirit, the combative, firm spirit of the working class "into all our ideological activity; there can be no deviation from the policy of the party, from Marxist-Leninist principles." He was also critical of those in responsible positions whose attitude was expressed in the sentence: "This is my territory, and none can interfere," to which he responded: "No field of activity is anyone's personal property. Anyone who works in a ministry, a union, a trade union, is placed there by the party, by the working class, and if he does not fulfill the mission entrusted to him he must be removed and replaced by someone who is capable of carrying out the party's policy."[27]

Although the ideological campaign, when it was introduced in 1971, was intended among other things to improve implementation of party policy, in time other considerations came to be of greater importance. But the rotation of cadres seems to have been established as a permanent principle of personnel policy. The degree to which it is practiced and the frequency with which it is resorted to suggest that Ceausescu considers it an important means of maintaining coherence in the party.

The Consequences of Elite Institutionalization

The process of institutionalization that has taken place with regard to the leadership of the RCP has been of significant benefit to the party, but it has also brought with it certain problems. Since requirements for holding leading positions were codified, and even before specific criteria were set, the length of party membership, the variety and length of previous experience at lower levels, and the age of those serving in the leadership have all increased. The dynamics of this process within the RCP are reminiscent of what has taken place in other communist parties in Eastern Europe and the Soviet Union.[28]

Among the important results of the process is the conditioning undergone by the party leaders. It has been suggested that "the amount and manner of time spent in achieving office by aspiring elites serve to socialize them and generate qualities useful to the organization."[29] Thus the longer they serve and the more varied their experience with various subunits of the institution, the better conditioned such elites will be to serve institutional goals, values, and procedures. Thus individuals with longer party membership and greater leadership experience at lower levels are much less likely to become dissidents within the organization or lead break-away factions.[30]

Another consequence of this aspect of the institutionalization process is the greater tendency toward conservatism and continuity in the organization. Anthony Downs has argued that "conservers" in a bureaucracy are those who desire to maintain organizational continuity. He finds two factors to be relevant to this attitude: age and length of tenure in a position. The older an individual is, and the longer he remains in a given position, the more likely he is to become a conserver, since incumbents are more likely than new elites to continue past policies.[31] Thus the decreasing rate of turnover and the increasing age in the RCP CC and other leading institutions suggest greater organizational continuity and conservatism.

Probably the most serious difficulty inherent in the institutionalization process is the possibility that tensions will arise through frustration of lower level officials who must wait for longer periods of time before moving up in the hierarchy. Although only in the most extreme cases could this result in creation of a potential base of support for an individual or group seeking to subvert or replace the ruling leadership, it still probably results in exasperation.[32] One additional benefit of giving aspiring party cadres experience in various subunits of the organization, therefore, would be to reduce the frustrations caused by slow upward mobility through a variety of experience at lower levels. Thus Ceausescu's principle of "rotation of cadres" may have the side effect of providing greater lateral mobility as a substitute for vertical mobility, in addition to the beneficial role it plays in increasing coherence among the elite and strengthening the position of the party leader vis-à-vis his subordinates.

5

Party and Society:
Emerging Patterns of Authority

The relationship between the RCP and Romanian society has changed considerably since the party began its ascent to power in 1944, and the evolution of this relationship has been generally consistent with that considered typical of communist states. Alfred G. Meyer suggests three stages through which communist political systems pass as they establish authority over society; Huntington has described three stages through which "established one-party systems" evolve; and Jowitt has posited three "elite designated core tasks and stages of development" for Leninist regimes.[1] Although the theoretical differences between these analyses are significant, the basic framework is similar. During the first revolutionary period the principal task is to transform the previous society. This is followed by a period of system-building, or consolidation of the revolutionary regime, which in turn is succeeded by a system-management phase in which the principal task is to integrate the regime with other nonparty sectors of society. As Meyer has noted, while there are many similarities among communist systems in the first two stages, in the third stage communist countries that have achieved a high level of industrialization and modernization tend to exhibit more profound national differences.[2]

The Romanian party came to power largely as a consequence of Soviet assistance (it was, in Meyer's terminology, a "contrived revolution")[3] and thus the party could not successfully exploit the situation by establishing a charismatic relationship with society, as was the case with other communist regimes such as Russia, China, Yugoslavia, which came to power under genuine revolutionary circumstances. Furthermore, the role, membership, and policies of the party conferred little authority on it in interwar Romania; thus it came to power lacking the popular acceptance and links with the masses that normally accompany a revolutionary takeover. Nevertheless, its task was similar to that faced by communist parties elsewhere—to transform society by eliminating the opposition elites' capacity to resist and by restructuring authority relationships.

Meyer argues that communist leaderships experience a dramatic loss of authority after coming to power,[4] but since the RCP had only limited authority to begin with it suffered only a limited loss. At the same time the party chose not to cultivate legitimacy but gave priority to achieving rapid and comprehensive industrialization; though the party sought to secure a degree of popular support, it was unwilling to win support at the price of compromising its basic ideas for the transformation of the political and economic system. This determination, coupled with Soviet support, permitted the party to utilize coercion and violence in achieving its goals.[5]

During the second stage, of system-building or consolidation, the RCP's concern was to establish its authority vis-à-vis society; but this also involved an effort "to depersonalize the party's contacts with the society and to maximize obedience within the party."[6] Although the principal instruments available in this process include rewards, coercion, organization, and persuasion,[7] the Romanian party tended to use coercion and organization. The fact that Romania was underdeveloped economically limited the availability of rewards, particularly since the emphasis on industrialization required minimizing consumption. At this time the RCP followed what Peter C. Ludz called a "marginal psychology"; that is, the party elite was anxious to preserve a certain distance from its rank and file as well as from society as a whole.[8] This period (1948–1955) was marked by the RCP's successful drive to raise the level of party institutionalization, and by continuing stress on rapid, comprehensive industrialization.[9]

The third stage in the evolution of the party-society relationship, which the RCP now appears to have entered, is that of adaptation or inclusion. Given the emergence in Romania of only certain of the characteristics generally ascribed to this phase, it is apparent that only the first steps have been taken thus far.[10] Of the changes that have begun to take place in the party's relationship with society, three seem to be particularly apparent and important. First, there are indications that the party is willing to permit the development of certain group interests, and to see its role as the resolver of conflicting interests; second, owing to successful industrial development and modernization, a new figure, the political manager, appears to be emerging; and third, there are indications that the party has taken steps to expand popular political involvement and to shift its authority relationship with society from one "based on domination to one emphasizing manipulation," from "a sociopolitical order based almost exclusively on command and violence to one in which leadership skills of manipulation and persuasion are more significant than in the past."[11] Because this shift in the party-society relationship has largely been evident since Ceausescu assumed the leadership of the party in 1965, the changes have been identified with his rule and stamped with the idiosyncrasies of his style.

The Recognition of Conflicting Interests

The recognition of group interests is one of the important factors in the process of altering the relationship between an authoritarian regime and society. The emergence of cohesive groups that recognize the existence of their own interests (this process is a slow and limited one) does not imply atrophy of the party but merely a different role for it. In the absence of an effective representative body and of independent and competing parties, the single party "must serve as a broker of competing group interests."[12] But these developments in no way imply the approach of pluralism.

Since at least the early 1970s the Romanian party has cautiously admitted—and accepted—the existence of conflicting group interests, but its degree of acceptance has not approached that found in Hungary, Czechoslovakia in 1968, or Yugoslavia.[13] Perhaps the most detailed statement of the Romanian position was made by Secretary General Ceausescu in October 1976:

> Proceeding from the fact that the class struggle has been the driving force in the development of societies thus far, we must find out how it will manifest itself in the future. It is necessary to examine, in the spirit of our revolutionary outlook, the extent to which aspects or forms of the class struggle can still occur in our society. It is obvious that we no longer have antagonistic social classes; however, social classes and categories continue to exist. It is true that they are friendly classes, animated by the desire to jointly build the new social system; but it would be wrong to overlook the fact that contradictions and differences nevertheless exist between social classes and groups in our society.
>
> There are certain contradictions between peasants and workers, between village and town, and between various other social categories, concerning the type and conditions of work, the awareness level, incomes, and so forth. It is obvious that these differences must give rise to contradictions. These contradictions could develop and become antagonistic if they are not well understood and if no action is taken to eliminate the causes that generate them.

That is why we pay particular attention to the harmonious development of the entire economy—industry and agriculture, the two basic branches of the production of material goods. As a matter of fact, I believe that it is obvious to all those studying social development on the basis of dialectical materialism that, even in socialism, a certain contradiction is manifest between industry and agriculture and that the neglect of one or the other has great repercussions on the whole society. The neglect of either industry or agriculture avenges itself and eventually leads to contradictions and to the appearance of great difficulties in social development.[14]

Among the principal causes of such "contradictions" that Ceausescu cited was the existence of wage disparities, and he called for their eventual elimination.[15] At the same time, however, he admitted that the communist principle of remuneration—"from each according to his ability, to each according to his need"—could be put into practice only in the more distant future, and that for the present bourgeois differentiation of incomes would be necessary.

The Romanians have come to use the phrase "nonantagonistic contradictions" as the euphemism for conflicting group interests. It occurs frequently, and a book that gives prominence to the issue has been published for the benefit of those involved in explaining official ideology. The author not only discusses the existence of the phenomenon but also argues that conflicting group interests are inevitable: "It is often asserted that the political leadership of socialist society must avoid or prevent the appearance of contradictions. To me this statement does not seem logical since, being objective, contradictions can be neither avoided nor prevented."[16]

Only in the last decade, however, has the RCP come to admit that conflicting group interests exist. Prior to that time the official interpretation was that the party's accession to power had resulted in the elimination of all antagonistic and exploiting classes, and that the interests of workers, peasants, and the intelligentsia were identical. The cautious official recognition of different group interests thus represents an important change in the party's view of its relationship to and role vis-à-vis society.

The program adopted at the eleventh party congress in November 1974, and intended as the guideline for the party through the end of this century, stated that "contradictions in various fields of social life will continue to be noted" throughout the next quarter century; nevertheless, "fundamental class contradictions do not exist and cannot emerge in this country." Although different social classes exist, their relationships are harmonious and all are striving to contribute to the construction of a "comprehensively developed socialist society" in Romania. The program, however, specifies that "the party will endeavor to solve these contradictions in good time, before they develop or affect the general process of socialism."[17] Thus the party is to be the arbiter. In the long run, the basically harmonious interests of society are supposed to prevail and a truly classless society, lacking even "nonantagonistic contradictions," is supposed to emerge.

The Emergence of the Political Manager

A second important aspect of the adaptation or inclusion phase in the evolution of the party's authority arises from its success in industrial development and economic modernization. Some observers have argued that this economic progress produces conflict between party apparatchik and economic technocrat, between red and expert, with the former claiming precedence on the basis of political reliability and ideological orthodoxy, and the latter claiming it by virtue of technological expertise.[18] Jowitt, on the other hand, argues that during this phase of the evolution of party authority the important factor is not the dichotomy between apparatchik and technocrat but the emergence of the political manager, distinguished by both technical expertise or experience, and "manipulative skills in sociopolitical settings."[19] In terms of how the RCP has approached the problem, it is certainly Jowitt's political manager that is the ideal.

For Romania, as well as for the rest of Eastern Europe, the evidence suggests that the requirements of economic development have not been the most direct or predominant cause of change in the political leadership. Of course the need for specialized knowledge has been evident, and the party has used various means to secure the required expertise: personnel associated directly with economic and cultural organizations have been brought into the party elite; members of the political elite have been assigned to specialized sectors, thus deepening their involvement and providing them with experience in technical areas; and individuals with training or early career experience in specialized fields have been recruited into the political elite. Nevertheless, the introduction of personnel with specialized knowledge has been carried out without substantially altering the predominance of the political elite.[20]

But the growing sophistication of the economy and the increasing complexity of society—both consequences of the party's policy of furthering economic development—have made the need for technical expertise increasingly evident to the party leadership. What they desire is a dialectical synthesis of expertise and *partiinost* ("party spirit"). Paul Niculescu, at the time responsible for ideology in the RCP leadership, propounded this concept most explicitly in an article in the party's theoretical journal, *Lupta de Clasa*. "The man of the multilaterally developed society must possess a broad cultural horizon and a high level of specialized knowledge, particularly technical-scientific competence." But, on the other hand, "specialized knowledge is not sufficient in itself and does not spontaneously lead to a scientific concept of the world." Niculescu was particularly critical of those who failed to recognize the importance of ideological, in addition to technical, training:

> Man in our society must not be thought of as a simple specialist, a competent but apolitical technician. In a socialist society the level of cultural and technical-scientific knowledge cannot be looked upon separately from the degree of political training.[21]

To achieve the ideal combination of revolutionary enthusiasm and technical competence, the party has taken a dual approach. First, there has been a deliberate effort to co-opt into the party the technical intelligentsia and those holding responsible positions in the management of the economy. This process has been particularly evident under Ceausescu, but to some extent it was taking place even under Gheorghiu-Dej. A statement issued at a plenum of the party CC in April 1965 declared that "in recent years valuable scientific and cultural workers, engineers and technicians, scientific research workers, and writers and artists have been admitted to the party—a development of outstanding importance in enabling party organizations to solve production problems."[22]

That the attempt to draw technocrats into the party ranks was successful is apparent from the statistics on membership. By the end of 1971, 60 percent of the academicians, doctors of science, and university teaching staffs in the country were party members, as were 52 percent of the engineers.[23] There are no directly comparable figures available on the increase of technical personnel among the party membership, but in his report to the third party congress in 1960 Gheorghiu-Dej said that 11.1 percent (93,000) of the full and candidate members of the party were intellectuals, and that of this number 31 percent (28,280) were engineers and technicians working in agricultural and industrial production.[24] The latter figure is less than 6 percent of the total number of engineers, technicians, and skilled (nonworker) personnel employed in the Romanian economy in 1960.[25] The success of the party in gaining members among this group should not, however, be interpreted to mean that the party has fallen under their control. While their influence has increased, the organization is still dominated by the hard core of full-time party officials.

The second approach taken by the party to achieve this ideal combination of technical skills and political commitment is to develop technical competence among its activists. In a speech in Bucharest on the occasion of the Lenin Centenary, Ceausescu emphasized the importance of nonideological knowledge.[26] The attempt to raise the educational level of party cadres has been one of his most pressing concerns, and measures have been taken to emphasize the importance of education and managerial skills. In June 1967 it was revealed that some 85 secretaries of regional and town party committees had recently been dismissed for incompetence, and the editorial in *Lupta de Clasa* that mentioned this stressed that professional training was an "essential condition" in appointing people to responsible positions, and implied that present leaders of enterprises, party activists, and executives of mass organizations who "lagged behind the level of scientific organization required in our day by a modern economy" might also be dismissed.[27]

Among the most vigorous efforts in this respect was a series of measures announced by Ceausescu at a CC plenum in February 1971. Specialized three- to four-week training programs were set up under direction of the party, involving 15,000 party workers over the following year and a half. The course content clearly emphasized nonideological areas of study: cybernetics, the utilization of electronic calculators, modern economic analysis, scientific principles of management, as well as subjects related to the particular concerns of the cadres in question. In addition to this initial course the party workers were to be required to undergo educational recycling every few years.[28] Ceausescu also told the plenum that in addition to planned courses the education of cadres "presupposes the intensification of individual study. . . . Learning is a necessity and an obligation for each activist." Lest there be any misunderstanding of the party's serious intention to raise the educational level of its members, the secretary general declared, "No one will be promoted in the future, either in production or in political and social life, unless he makes a point of constantly increasing his knowledge, unless he masters all that is new in his field of activity."[29]

That this view has not changed substantially is apparent from a more recent observation by the party leader: "It should be clear to everyone that specialists must have a thorough political and ideological background"; and in a speech to county party leaders he noted that "professional and political" qualifications of party and state cadres must be raised.[30]

Ceausescu's speeches and the party documents continue to call for a combination of technical competence and revolutionary élan. In a speech at the Stefan Gheorghiu Party Academy in 1976 he said that henceforth party activists would be required to increase their knowledge of the economy by actively participating in the organization and actual practice of management while they were still students at the party academy. At the same time, he said, it is hoped that narrowing the gap between manual and intellectual labor will result in greater social homogenization and the molding of a new man "armed with the most advanced achievements of modern science and technology and a keen socialist awareness." But the task of molding this new man is far from completed, despite the fact that it is considered "the party's most significant and most noble goal, to which greater efforts than previously must be devoted."[31]

Combining Party and State

In Romania the evolution of the political manager, or at least the attempt to develop this ideal type, has also been accompanied by an effort to increase efficiency and improve management by combining party and state functions. In the process by which the CPSU came to power in Russia it was necessary to retain the state-economic bureaucracy because the party lacked members with the necessary skills. At the same time, since this bureaucracy was not committed to the revolutionary cause the party felt it necessary to create a parallel apparatus composed of political officials to oversee the implementation of policy by these suspect technocrats. Thus in the Soviet Union a system of parallel hierarchies was developed, and this was transplanted to Eastern Europe along with other features of the Soviet system when the communist parties were installed in power after 1945. With the passing of the precommunist technocratic elite and the rise of those trained since the parties have come to power, and with the institutionalization of the communist system, the logic of the dual hierarchy has become increasingly questionable, however.

As the ideal of the political manager began to be accepted in Romania, Ceausescu formulated and began implementing the concept of *impletirea* ("blending" or "intertwining") party and state. The concept is closely related to the idea of developing the political manager—a person with technical expertise or experience, political commitment to the party, and managerial skills. As explained by the party leader at the National Party Conference in July 1972, "The enhanced role of the state in the organized directing of all compartments of economic and social activity calls for more detailed specification of the forms of organization and of management methods." Thus,

> I have in mind a certain blending of party and state activities, while drawing clear-cut limits in order to avoid overlappings and parallelism. Undoubtedly, in the long run we shall witness an ever closer blending of the activities of the party, state, and other social bodies, this being the law-like process of socialist and communist development.[32]

This concept has received considerable attention as a theoretical innovation.[33] Two separate organizational approaches have been followed in blending party and state. The first takes into account the "plurality of party and state offices"; individuals simultaneously hold related party and government positions. This may not seem particularly unusual, since in all communist states leading government officials are members of the party Politburo, or at least of its CC. The Romanian approach is unique, however, in that these positions are explicitly linked. For example, the heads of the county, municipal, and town party committees are at the same time heads of the people's councils (local government units) at the corresponding level. Making the holders of certain party posts ex officio holders of important government positions gives the party officials, who in practice dominated the government apparatus when the posts were separate, a greater degree of legitimacy and a broader base from which to function. In part, the policy seems to represent an attempt to put important leaders into positions where they can deal directly with areas of concern, and to eliminate one layer in the bureaucracy between those who make top-level decisions and those who implement them. Rather than carrying out their responsibilities indirectly by overseeing other individuals who are government ministers, these party leaders hold the government positions and assume direct responsibility themselves.

The principle of "plurality of offices" evolved gradually, beginning in 1967 with the decision of the National Party Conference that year that the party head should also be chief of state. While this decision was an important further step in Ceausescu's consolidation of power, it was also related to the introduction of the general concept. Just two months later, in the context of a territorial reorganization, it was decided that county party first secretaries were to head the county government organizations as well. The system was further extended in 1972 when heads of lower-level party organizations assumed leadership of the corresponding government units, and other local party officials similarly became local government leaders.

Romanian assessments of the implementation of the "plurality of offices" concept have been generally positive. A certain degree of duplication has been eliminated, leaders holding dual posts have had increased resources available for implementing policy, and work style has improved. At the same time, however, there has been some criticism that party leaders have tended to ignore "propaganda-educational functions" (persuasion) because more immediate, "coercive" means of implementing decisions are directly available to party officials through their state positions. Furthermore, some individuals have focused on only one of their positions (usually the party post) and neglected duties connected with the other. Still, there are no indications of any plan to abandon or significantly alter this organizational approach.[34]

The second concept being implemented in the blending of party and state is the "plurality of attribution" of organizations, or "organizations with a dual [party-state] nature"; that is, certain bodies are subordinate to both higher party and higher state organizations.[35] The Council on Socialist Culture and Education, for example, is subordinate to the RCP CC, but it is also considered a government body subordinate to the Council of Ministers. Not only have such new institutions been created with dual party-state subordination but also older ones have been altered to conform to this new concept. Perhaps the most significant and interesting was the Ministry of National Defense. When it was reorganized in 1972, the new law specified that the ministry was to "implement *party* [emphasis added] and state policy on national defense." Furthermore it was stated that the ministry would act under "the direction and guidance of the party Central Committee," but it would also be responsible to the Council of Ministers "as a central organ of state administration."[36]

While "plurality of offices" tends to reduce parallelism and duplication by giving one individual both party and state responsibility for the same tasks, "plurality of subordination" appears to create confusion regarding lines of authority. The former approach seems to be a rational organizational measure, while the latter is probably more related to Ceausescu's desire to increase his personal authority and involvement in government administration. Although the Romanians have argued that blending party and state functions in no way changes the separate identity and distinct responsibilities of party and state, the line between the two is likely to become further blurred. Coupled with other changes in the party (such as the expansion of membership to the point that one in five adults is now a party member), this blurring of party-state boundaries has contributed to the legitimization of the party, helped expand its base, and improved its relationship with Romanian society.[37]

The Shift toward Greater Political Participation

A third aspect of the adaptation phase in the evolution of party authority is the tendency to foster greater mass participation. Meyer sees this as a shift along the continuum "from authoritarian to participative, from command and dictatorship to self-government and autonomy."[38] In Jowitt's terms there is a "shift from a regime-society relationship based on domination to one emphasizing manipulation," that is, "a shift from a sociopolitical order based almost exclusively on command and violence to one in which leadership skills of manipulation and persuasion are more significant."[39]

Meyer's "participation" and Jowitt's "manipulation" are perhaps less dissimilar than may appear at first, and both deal with the same phenomenon. Thomas A. Baylis notes that participation may be "influential" or "manipulative": "In the first case participation means the channel through which the ordinary citizen exerts some real influence over decisions affecting his round of life; in the second, participation is an instrument through which a regime enlists support for itself and forges social solidarity by creating a sense of involvement."[40] At the same time, however, participatory institutions are used by all modern governments for manipulative purposes, and in all societies the population has at least some influence over decisions. Also, manipulative forms are capable of being transformed into influential forms.[41] Thus the two do not represent a dichotomy, but rather two ends of a spectrum, with both elements present to some degree in most societies.

This has certainly been true with regard to political participation in Romania. While the manipulative element has been the more prominent, both the degree of genuine participation and the party's concern with the concept of participation are considerably greater than was the case earlier. This change dates from the early 1960s, when one of its first indications was the substantial expansion in the membership of the RCP noted in chapter 3. Gheorghiu-Dej was involved in its early phases, but the process has expanded considerably under the leadership of Ceausescu and many of the features of the new emphasis on participation are associated with him.

The phrase used in Romania to describe the process is "socialist democracy," a term that has been appearing with increasing frequency in recent years. Although it has been discussed in theoretical journals for some time, it was given its most official exposition at the National Party Conference in July 1972, in Ceausescu's speech to the conference and in a resolution subsequently adopted by the gathering. "Socialist democracy" differs considerably from Western ideas of democracy (with which the party was not necessarily concerned), its primary aim being to mobilize mass support for its own goals while at the same time keeping party officials sensitive to popular feeling. As explained by Ceausescu and the conference resolution, socialist democracy involves "deliberate and planned management of socio-economic activity and of all society," with emphasis on the leading role of the party and the principles of "democratic centralism." The resolution noted that "an important role in developing socialist democracy, in mobilizing the masses, in building a comprehensively developed socialist society, is played by mass and civic organizations."[42] The same view was propounded in the program adopted by the eleventh party congress; the section devoted to socialist democracy was very similar to the National Party Conference's resolution on this topic two years earlier.[43]

Ceausescu has been personally identified with this effort to expand the appearance, and in some cases the reality, of popular participation through maintaining what he terms "a permanent dialogue with the people." His frequent inspection tours of industrial, agricultural, and retail sales units in various parts of the country have become a distinctive feature of his activity. These visits give the party leader an opportunity to see personally the implementation of policy at the grass-roots level, and to feel for himself the sentiment of the people; they also give him an opportunity to instruct and direct local officials.

Although maintaining contact with the people has always been important to Ceausescu, this has been particularly emphasized during times of stress or national crisis. On occasions when external pressure has been exerted on Romania (such as after the Soviet-led invasion of Czechoslovakia in 1968, and during the period of Soviet pressure on Romania following Ceausescu's visit to Peking in the summer of 1971) he has visited ethnic Hungarian areas in Transylvania. During natural calamities (such as the floods of 1970 and 1975 and the earthquake of 1977) he has toured stricken areas giving instructions and encouragement. Among the more spectacular periods of such activity, however, was immediately after the Polish workers' protests over food price increases in December 1970. A *Scinteia* editorial noted that, during the first 30 working days of 1971, the party secretary general visited "some 45 industrial enterprises and agricultural units." The editorial observed that "consulting" with the masses "permits the party to work out a scientific and realistic policy based on an exact, undistorted assessment of the state of affairs, examined directly at the very source."[44]

Ceausescu periodically lectures his subordinates on the value and necessity of establishing such contact with the masses. He told a CC session devoted to problems of local party organizations that "radical changes" must be made at all levels of activity. "Closer consultation between the top level and the basic units and the resolving of problems together with the masses is an important task, incumbent upon both the Central Committee secretariat and the Executive Committee. On this depends the solution of the major problems we face."[45]

Despite his frequent expressions about the necessity of establishing a dialogue between the leadership and the masses, Ceausescu's visits are hardly calculated to permit a real exchange of views. If the visit is spontaneous and unplanned, as apparently some of his visits to the Bucharest markets have been, the brief exchanges that take place hardly rise above the level of an exchange of pleasantries. A more serious obstacle to dialogue with the population, however, is the careful preparation that goes into any visit by Ceausescu. When the party leader visits a provincial city or a major industrial enterprise, the local leaders make sure that everything is prearranged. The children who present flowers are drilled in advance; the worker who will "spontaneously" express the factory's appreciation of the leader's visit is chosen and prepares his comments; even the apparently spontaneous shouting that greets Ceausescu when he arrives is rehearsed beforehand.[46] The visits to farms and factories tend to be ceremonial inspections rather than opportunities for meaningful discussion. During a tour in September 1972, he met coal miners from the Jiu Valley, who apparently did not follow the prearranged script and "did not hesitate" to express their dissatisfaction with living and working conditions.[47] After hearing the complaints, the party leader issued directives for remedying some of the difficulties, but just a few days later in Cluj he criticized the fact that he had received complaints from the population.[48] A reflection of Ceausescu's attitude can be seen in the fact that, after the incidents in the Jiu Valley and in Cluj, contact with the workers and the population in general was almost eliminated from his itineraries, and Ceausescu spent his inspection tours dealing with officials from Bucharest and the leaders of the local party, government, and economic units, though on occasion he did meet with "representatives" of the workers.

Despite the fact that his contacts with the people are carefully staged affairs during which there is little opportunity for the party leader really to communicate with the masses, these visits serve some useful purposes. But regardless of what he learns, his visits contribute importantly to the image he seeks to create: that of a leader concerned for the welfare of his people who acquaints himself with conditions everywhere. Since any visit includes giving instructions to the local leaders, Ceausescu also develops his image as a leader who issues directives and closely follows developments throughout the country. Since he has shown his concern for the population by his contacts with the masses, when problems do arise it is the subordinates, not the party leader, who are blamed.

Another interesting recent indication of the party's increasing efforts to involve the population in political and economic life was the adoption of specific procedures to deal with petitions and suggestions. A CC plenum in July 1976 criticized past lack of receptivity and excessive delays in this regard. Specific time limits within which such proposals must be considered were fixed for all levels, and it was specified that citizens are entitled to interviews with party and government leaders. Furthermore, certain kinds of suggestions were to be publicized in the mass media as well. County party first secretaries and other party officials were directed to assume particular responsibility for these petitions and suggestions.[49]

The kinds of suggestions to be dealt with, however, were limited to practical proposals for increasing economic efficiency and reaching economic goals, and statements of support and expressions of adherence to the party's policies. It is significant that when this issue was first raised in a session of the Political Executive Committee a few months before the CC decision, personal concerns and complaints were specifically included, but they were not mentioned in the final document.[50]

The 1976 CC resolution did not really represent a new departure, since a Council of Ministers' decision relating to this topic had been adopted ten years earlier.[51] The CC decision did, however, reiterate and reemphasize the party's concern in this regard. That this was useful is indicated by a *Scinteia* article on abuses by county officials reported by citizens and confirmed by official investigation; but after a year no disciplinary action had yet been taken.[52] Obviously conditioning old mentalities to deal with new realities is a difficult task.

Multiple Candidates in State Elections

Among the most interesting and significant aspects of the expansion of socialist democracy was the decision to permit multiple candidacies for elected positions in government legislative bodies.[53] This decision was taken well in advance of the election in which it was first tried and was carefully planned and executed. The resolution on socialist democracy of the National Party Conference in July 1972 specified that in keeping with "the need for the people to participate more broadly in the country's management," the election system should be improved to ensure "that in the future several candidates run for each position as deputy to the Grand National Assembly or the people's councils, either by constituency or directly on county, municipal, or communal slates which list more candidates than positions to be filled." The 1974 party congress reaffirmed that position in the party program that it adopted.[54]

Permitting multiple candidacies was not intended to offer a choice between the party's programs and other alternatives, but merely between individuals who would be responsible for certain aspects of implementing and legitimizing that program. Nevertheless, this procedure does give some sense of participation in the choice of individuals who hold elective posts, even though that choice is limited. Furthermore, candidates who face competition at the polls are more likely to be sensitive to the expectations and interests of those who elect them.

The changes in electoral procedure for the 1975 elections were contained in a new electoral law that specified "several candidates can be nominated for each electoral constituency" for the Grand National Assembly and people's councils. While this was more explicit than previous legislation, earlier regulations also permitted multiple candidacies.[55] These provisions, however, had not been utilized in practice since the 1940s. The new law balanced explicit provisions for multiple candidacies with somewhat more restrictive rules governing nomination, specifying that candidates could be nominated only by the party-led Front of Socialist Unity. The law, in another measure to increase the sense of participation, reduced the term of office of people's council representatives (the local government legislative bodies) from five to two and one-half years, although the number of deputies to the people's councils and the national parliament was reduced.

That the party's intentions were serious became apparent when the nomination process was completed, although there was some scaling down from the originally announced proposal that there be more than one candidate for each position.[56] Under the direction of the Front of Socialist Unity some 36,900 meetings, attended by 6,000,000 people, were held throughout Romania for the purpose of nominating candidates. There were two candidates for 139 (40 percent) of the 349 seats in the Grand National Assembly, and some 90,858 individuals were nominated for the 51,411 places on the people's councils (approximately seven candidates for every four seats).[57]

Data on the nearly 91,000 candidates for the people's councils is not available, but there is considerable material on the national assembly candidates. It is difficult to determine the extent to which the people's council election procedures were comparable to those for the assembly, but there is no reason to assume that any different policies were followed.

An examination of the candidates nominated for the Grand National Assembly suggests a high degree of centralized control. In no instance of a multiple candidacy were the individuals running against each other leading figures in the party or the government, though in some cases full and candidate members of the CC faced competition. There were no opponents running against nominees who were members of the party's Political Executive Committee or of the Council of Ministers, county party first secretaries, or CC members who held posts in the central party bureaucracy.

The candidates who did face opposition were not only less prominent individuals, but they were also very carefully balanced against their opponents according to a number of very specific criteria. In fact, the degree to which this was true of all multiple candidates is the most convincing evidence that the nomination process was subject to careful and close central direction. In almost all cases the two candidates held positions that were equivalent. There were a few instances of a director running against the deputy director of a factory, but in most cases it was an enterprise manager versus the manager of another enterprise, foreman versus foreman, and school principal versus school principal. Not only were the positions of opposing candidates roughly equivalent, but they were usually employed in the same field. There were no instances of a factory manager running against a school teacher, for example. In part this can be attributed to the fact that there is a degree of demographic and occupational homogeneity in the constituencies (some are predominantly rural while others are industrial), but this alone cannot explain the careful matching. In one Iasi constituency, for example, both candidates were from the field of culture; one was the manager of the Junimea Publishing House and the other was chairman of the Iasi branch of the Union of Plastic Artists. In another constituency in the same county, one candidate was prorector of the Iasi Institute of Polytechnics and the other prorector of the A. I. Cuza Institute. This practice was carried to the point where candidates were balanced by sex and apparently even by nationality; women ran against women, men against men, and members of the same ethnic minority faced each other.

This degree of control over the nominating process permitted the party to maintain the proper balance of various groups in the national assembly without having to intervene in the actual election.

In cases where two candidates facing each other were unequal in prominence, the most important person usually won. There were enough exceptions to this generalization, however, to indicate that the party apparently did not intervene to affect the outcome. Having carefully managed the nomination process to ensure that all candidates were acceptable, the party then gave the voters the opportunity to express their preference. There were four interesting races in which the candidate with clearly better party credentials lost, which tends to confirm this view. The most interesting of these was the contest in which Suzana Gadea, an alternate member of the RCP CC and prorector of the Bucharest Polytechnical Institute, lost to Zoe Dumitrescu-Busulenga, a professor at Bucharest University. It is significant that Gadea was reelected to alternate membership in the CC at the eleventh party congress just four months before the national assembly election while Dumitrescu-Busulenga was dropped from full CC membership on that occasion. Furthermore, Gadea was named minister of education some months later and in order for her to assume that position a by-election was held in which she ran unopposed for a national assembly seat.

The March 1975 elections were the first instance of multiple candidacies on a large scale in communist Romania, but as we have noted competition existed only between relatively less important individuals. Nevertheless, the freedom of choice actually allowed went well beyond that currently permitted in other Warsaw Pact states. In Hungary, for example, where the practice of having multiple candidacies began in 1967, the number of candidates for the National Assembly who faced opposition reached a high of 14 percent in 1971, and declined to less than 10 percent in the 1975 elections. In the Soviet elections in June 1975 none of the candidates running for positions in the Supreme Soviet, the republican soviets, or local councils faced opposition.

The significance of multiple candidacies in the 1975 Romanian election will depend on what happens in subsequent contests. The careful effort to balance the candidates and the fact that there were some apparent upsets suggest that voters did indeed have a real influence on the outcome. At the same time, the party has sought to increase participation by using faster turnover to increase the number of individuals who hold office. The party has advocated "the periodic transfer of people holding various party and government posts . . . in order to gradually renew the leading cadres and to combat stagnation and outdated methods."[58] A reflection of this principle is the fact that of the deputies elected to the Grand National Assembly in March 1975, some 225 (or 64 percent) were not members of the previous parliament. This high figure is even more striking considering that the number of deputies was reduced from 465 to 349.

While continuing multiple candidacies for government legislative bodies and changing the individual office holders frequently may help to give a sense of increased participation, this procedure is unlikely to make the elected officials responsive to their constituents. Although membership in the national assembly and the people's councils is largely an honorary function, it does carry with it a certain prestige that makes serving desirable. In cases of multiple candidacies for a single seat some effort will have to be made to appeal to the interests of the constituents, but the critical problem is being nominated or renominated. Thus, the anointing by the party hierarchy is still more important than the support of the voters. It seems likely that once-elected officials will still be more sensitive to pressure from above since renomination under party auspices, rather than reelection, is the more serious problem. Finally, leading officials, who are sure of renomination and are less likely to face competition, are least likely to be responsive to popular will.

Renewed Emphasis on Ideological Mobilization

Despite these indications that the RCP is shifting its relationship with Romanian society from one based on domination to one based on manipulation,[59] the party has not been unanimous in its views of their long-term consequences and, in some cases, even of their short-term desirability. Also, ingrained relationships and patterns of interaction have not been easily abandoned in the face of new and untried ones. Among the most interesting remnants of earlier times is the continuation or reappearance of mobilization in supposedly "post-mobilization" regimes.[60] As Jowitt points out, however, there are important differences between mobilization in regimes that are in the consolidation stage and those that have initiated the task of integrating the party with the wider society.[61] In fact he suggests that mobilization is an attempt to deal with problems that have both brought about and been intensified by the party's efforts to alter its relationship with society. Among such developments that face the RCP are the growing heterogeneity of society, the emergence of group interests (which the party has been willing to deal with more openly), and the rise of new social strata (in particular the technical intelligentsia), which demand a greater role. Perhaps the most important problem for the party is how to maintain its institutional identity, while at the same time expanding its boundaries to include other elites in the political process.

The response of the Romanian and other East European regimes— particularly since the early 1970s—has been to give greater attention to ideology. Although these internal developments have been an important factor in the return to ideological mobilization, a significant external stimulus was increased contact with Western societies, encouraged by East-West detente and institutionalized in the Final Act of the 1975 Helsinki Conference on Security and Cooperation in Europe.[62] Though similar problems have faced all European communist parties, the RCP has given greater attention to ideology than the others. (Romania has also shown a willingness since 1971 to cooperate with its Warsaw Pact allies on ideological questions—a cooperativeness that has not been exhibited in other areas.)

The first wave of this renewed campaign came in July 1971, with the publication of Ceausescu's seventeen-point program calling for intensification of ideological, cultural, and educational activity along Marxist lines; it culminated the following November with a CC plenum devoted to the topic. The second wave came during 1976, with a year-long buildup for the Congress on Political Education and Socialist Culture, which was followed by the party's Action Program on ideological, political, cultural, and educational work.[63]

Speeches and articles during the campaigns indicate that there were a number of factors behind it. One motivating aspect was the expectation that renewed emphasis on ideology would yield concrete results in terms of economic efficiency and output. It is probably no coincidence that major ideological drives were made in 1971 and 1976, each the first year of a five-year-plan period. Having set ambitious economic targets, the party undoubtedly felt that a massive effort was required to induce the population to reach them. After stating that economic efficiency, labor productivity, and product quality were matters deserving "great attention," Ceausescu told a group of ideological officials: "It is obvious that political and ideological activity must attach primary importance to these basic and essential problems for our country's development in the next stage."[64]

The approach of the party in utilizing ideology and education for the benefit of the economy has been twofold. First, the work ethic is to be firmly established. This involves eradicating negative attitudes toward work, such as laziness, avoidance of manual labor, procrastination, poor-quality workmanship, slovenliness, and bureaucracy. Second, closer links must be established between education and research on the one hand and production on the other; education must be geared to satisfying the manpower and technological requirements of the economy. The main problem the RCP is attempting to deal with in its educational and ideological program is the growing demand for skilled labor. The emphasis on the work ethic and the glorification of labor are intended to encourage more people to participate in the economy, and the educational system is charged with providing them with the required skills. The concern with raising labor productivity, also a key aspect of the ideological-educational programs, is prompted by the need to reduce the demand for manpower by increasing the efficiency both of those currently employed and of new entrants into the labor market.

Economics was undoubtedly a major reason for the ideological mobilization, but a second important consideration was concern about the younger generation; youth organizations and the educational system have been criticized for ideological shortcomings. This was a topic referred to particularly often in 1971 but frequently since that time as well; the motivation behind the concern is complex. In the first place, young people represent the key to the future and their political socialization is essential if party authority in Romania is to remain firmly established. A second aspect is related to the desire to increase the participation of youth in the work force and upgrade the skills and interest of young workers in order to increase labor productivity. This is not conditioned solely by the need for additional workers, however. Those whose energies are not expended on socially useful work are much more vulnerable to undesirable influences and have time to develop and cultivate "decadent Western tastes." Thus emphasis on productive labor and political education are two sides of the same coin.

Another important group involved in the ideological campaign is the cultural elite. The party's primary concern here is to win the support of writers, musicians, and artists for party policies, and to utilize their talents in the mobilization of the masses. Huntington considers the reemergence of a critical intelligentsia apart and alienated from the institutional structures of power to be an important aspect of the adaptation phase.[65] The Romanian cultural elite—in particular some of the writers—have shown the potential to assume such a role. The ideological campaign is an important aspect of the effort to maintain party control over this group.

The call for politically committed creative works was heard frequently in the past, but it was made with increasing insistence after the 1971 campaign, and since the rash of ideological activities in 1976 it has been voiced still more urgently. In essence, it is primarily a demand that art contribute to the party's goal of mobilizing the masses. This Ceausescu made clear in his speech to the cultural congress: "The working people need a truly revolutionary art . . . that is permeated by a strong mobilizing attitude and militates fervently for the improvement of society and of man."[66]

To insure the impact of a committed creative elite upon the masses, the 1976 ideological campaign stressed two elements. First, inspiration must be drawn from the masses. "The working people want to recognize their own moral image in artistic and literary creations."[67] The second means of harnessing the creative elite to the party's mobilizing campaign and at the same time strengthening the party's hand is having them participate in amateur cultural groups. Perhaps the best illustration of the mass concept in ideology and culture was the national festival given the designation "Hymn to Romania," which began in October 1976 and reached its climax in June 1977, as the centennial of Romanian independence was being celebrated. The various cultural activities inspired by the festival took place on judet, interjudet, and republic-wide levels, and henceforth such festivals are to be held every second year.

The response of the Romanian cultural elite to the program can hardly be described as enthusiastic, although party control of the cultural press has restricted the potential forum for dissent. Few if any artistic works that both possess aesthetic merit and give evidence of revolutionary commitment have appeared. In fact, there were clear signs (such as discussions in the cultural press) that the new directives on cultural policy, particularly with regard to popular music and the theater, resulted in declining audience interest.

The scope of the latest ideological mobilization in Romania is broader than that in any other East European state. In certain respects it harks back to the Stalinist methods of the early 1950s, with the focus on ideological incentives for economic performance as perhaps the most striking parallel. At the same time, however, there are important distinctions from this earlier time. Among the most obvious is the current effort to achieve greater productivity and higher quality, while quantitative increases are relatively less important. But since three decades of communist-directed modernization have produced a much more sophisticated and complex economic system, thus making earlier methods of management and incentives unsuited to current conditions, it is questionable that ideological incentives can achieve the economic goals that the party seeks without material rewards.[68]

6

Changing Attitudes toward the National Heritage and the Nation

One key aspect of the adaptation, system management, or inclusion phase of the development of party authority has to do with the attitude toward nationalism and the national heritage. It has been noted that during this phase the regime adopts the practice of "enlisting and mobilizing existing groups, structures, and cultures, including those surviving from precommunist periods, not abolishing them."[1] Thus the inherited national cultures are no longer seen as being inimical to the party's interests, and national distinctions are permitted to develop without the restrictions imposed previously. Also, in this phase the party is more likely to adopt a more positive attitude toward the nation-state.[2]

While this process of giving greater value to the national heritage and greater ideological worth to the nation has been apparent throughout Eastern Europe in the last decade, it has achieved greater momentum and gone much further in Romania than elsewhere; it has been marked particularly by an attempt to identify the RCP with the Romanian national heritage, and the fact that the role of the nation has been given great ideological significance.

Identifying the RCP with Romanian History

In Romania (as elsewhere in Eastern Europe) the communist party based its legitimacy primarily on ideological grounds. It embodied the interests of the working class and the peasantry (which in time would be transformed into workers); when national interests or national sentiment came in question, the argument was advanced that what was shown by the working class was true national sentiment or patriotism, which differed qualitatively from the nationalism of the bourgeoisie. Given the class-conflict emphasis in the ideology of the late 1940s and 1950s "bourgeois nationalism" had its antithesis in "socialist patriotism." The former was exploitative and selfish, but nevertheless predominated under the capitalist system; the latter was generous and positive but only came to the fore as a consequence of the rise of the RCP. In the early years the international aspect of socialist patriotism was also given considerable emphasis: "The workers' movement is international in its very substance. This fundamental characteristic is expressed by proletarian internationalism, by the ideology and policy of international solidarity of all workers." Communism "by its definition and nature is an international notion, and it cannot be imagined otherwise."[3]

As the party began to move from the consolidation to the inclusion phase, there was a noticeable shift in the treatment of nationalism; this change in concept was also related to the evident change in the RCP's relationship with the Soviet party in the early 1960s. Among the most obvious aspects were the following: greater emphasis on the positive values of national sentiment coupled with a decline in the stress on the class character of nationalism, and a significant decline in the emphasis given to the international aspects of communism; the party and the working class were no longer seen as the bearers of a kind of antithetical national sentiment that was to replace bourgeois class nationalism, and the party was conceived of as the culmination of the whole process of Romanian history. This shift became obvious in the years 1964–1966, and was documented in articles that appeared in the organ of the RCP Central Committee's Institute of Party History.[4] The emphasis and concern clearly shifted from narrow studies of party or working class activity to the much broader themes of national history, which are nevertheless interpreted in an appropriate ideological framework.

In the past the party's coming to power was seen as the successful culmination of a succession of revolts of the exploited masses against their rulers, but the advent of communist power is now interpreted as the culmination of the nation's history, and the entire population is given a progressive role. While this new thrust in the treatment of Romanian history has been increasingly evident since the mid-1960s, it was given its most official and explicit formulation in the party program adopted at the eleventh party congress in November 1974. The program's first section provides the historical context, which begins not with Marx and Engels but with the Dacians of some two thousand years ago and the romantic Romanian nationalist interpretation of the formation of the nation. There is a nod toward ideology ("The entire history of the Romanian people reads like a history of ceaseless class struggle, of a struggle waged by the masses to promote social freedom and justice, to safeguard their national identity and independence, to achieve progress and civilization"), but there is also much stronger emphasis on the historical unity of the population, which is somewhat inconsistent with a narrow ideological interpretation ("A united Romanian national state" came about through "the struggle waged by the broad masses, the workers, the peasantry, the intellectuals, by advanced circles of the bourgeoisie and major social classes and strata; it was the work of all people of the entire nation"). Clearly, however, the advent of a communist regime is the culmination of the national history:

> The period [following the coup d'etat of August 23, 1944] marked the start of a new history for our fatherland, the history of the fulfillment of ideals of social and national justice for which countless generations of our forefathers had struggled—the history of the complete achievement of Romania's national independence and sovereignty and of the Romanian people's sacred right to be masters in their own country.[5]

Even on the centenary of Romanian independence, greatly as the achievement of full independence in 1877 was hailed, the drive for national self-expression that began in the mists of Dacian antiquity was described as culminating in the coming to power of the RCP.[6]

In the process of linking itself with the national history, the RCP has also sought to portray itself (and the working class movement before 1921) as having supported the major national aspirations, including national unification, independence, state integrity, and sovereignty. This has created certain problems, since the party's policies and activities during the 1930s were clearly contrary to what most Romanians considered the national interest. Among the most sensitive of the issues was the question of the right of self-determination, including succession, which the party endorsed in its platform on the national question.[7] In the late 1940s and the 1950s the party was less concerned to identify itself with the national tradition, and consequently historians were not permitted to discuss Bessarabia (the most sensitive of the national issues).[8] Thus, when the party started to align itself with the national tradition, its policies in the interwar period and its treatment of history in the 1950s presented a significant problem.

The way in which the dilemma was resolved was a measure of the strength of the RCP's commitment to linking itself with the national history. In effect the party repudiated certain interwar policies, and the significance of this action is emphasized by the communist concern to show the historical correctness of the party line. The first hints that the RCP had decided to repudiate its previous position appeared in history texts published in the early 1960s in which the Soviet or tsarist annexations of Bessarabia were described in brief but negative terms, in contrast to the previous brief positive assessments. In 1964 a collection of Karl Marx manuscripts was published in Romania in which the communist prophet clearly accepted the Romanian claim to Bessarabia.[9]

The most official, straightforward, and definitive statement rejecting the party's interwar national policies came in a speech by Secretary General Ceausescu on the 45th anniversary of the RCP's founding. He criticized the resolutions of the third, fourth, and fifth party congresses (held during the interwar years) in which "Romania was called a 'typical multinational state' created on the basis of occupation of foreign territories," and stated that contrary to the party's stand during that period Romania was "a unitary state." In order to absolve the RCP of responsibility, Ceausescu described these policies as "a consequence of the practices of the Comintern, which laid down directives that ignored the concrete situation in our country, and gave tactical orientations and indications that did not correspond to the economic, sociopolitical, and national conditions prevailing in Romania."[10] This approach had the advantage of repudiating the party's past policies while at the same time shifting the blame to the USSR, further emphasizing certain points regarding interparty relations that the RCP had made previously.

The line established in this speech has remained the party's official stand, but the degree to which it is emphasized is essentially a function of the state of Soviet-Romanian relations. During the flare-up between Soviet and Romanian historians in 1975–1976 the theme was repeated again with considerable force. In a speech to the Congress on Political Education and Socialist Culture in June 1976 Ceausescu was even more explicit in his criticism of the historiography of the 1950s:

> Serious mistakes were committed in the interpretation of our country's history, of the formation of the Romanian people and language, and of the nation itself. . . . As is also well known, for a considerable time the progressive experience and traditions of our country were not utilized in education and cultural life; instead, foreign systems and methods were mechanically copied.[11]

At this time those of the party's interwar policies that were contrary to Romanian national interests were again criticized (the Comintern again being cited as the culprit) and the party's support for national unification was stressed.[12]

One of the more curious aspects of this attempt to link the RCP with the Romanian heritage is the effort to interpret various episodes of the national past in the context of contemporary concerns; history is not regarded as providing means of understanding the past, but is used to illustrate those things the party considers more important at present. One of the most interesting examples of this is the identification of various past leaders with Ceausescu. For example, Prince Michael the Brave, who united the Romanian principalities briefly at the end of the sixteenth century, was first "demythologized" by communist historians, but as the party began to stress nationalism he was again made the object of officially approved myths. He is now pictured as a progressive prince whose foreign policy is remarkably similar to that of Ceausescu. Even the controversial and complex Vlad the Impaler (1431–1476), who was the prototype of Bram Stoker's Dracula, has been reappraised as a progressive prince who followed a foreign policy similar to that pursued by the RCP.[13]

New Importance for the Role of the Nation

The nation and its role have been given a much more important place than was the case earlier under the party in Romania, or than is now the case elsewhere in Eastern Europe. Orthodox Marxist ideology tends to deprecate the nation as a social category associated with the bourgeoisie, which is generally irrelevant for the proletariat, whose class interests transcend narrow national limits. Although this view is rather quickly dashed on the rocks of reality, communist parties have generally played down the importance of the nation in their ideology.

With the advent of Bolshevik power in Russia and the adoption of Stalin's policy of "socialism in one country," support for the Soviet Union as the motherland of socialism became the touchstone of internationalism, at least for parties on good terms with the CPSU. This was further emphasized with the establishment of the Stalinist *Gleichschaltung* in Eastern Europe after World War II. But as the Romanian party began to identify itself with national tradition and to follow a more independent course in its foreign policy in the early 1960s, new emphasis on the importance of the nation was a logical concomitant. Among the early assertions of this was the statement of newly chosen party leader Ceausescu at the ninth RCP congress in July 1965: "For a long time to come the nation and the state will continue to be the basis of the development of socialist society. The development of the nation, the consolidation of the socialist state, comply with the objective requirements of social life."[14]

Generally speaking, the RCP's attitude toward the nation has two major elements. First, the nation "fulfills its role as a powerful factor in achieving progress and civilization in the world."[15] Furthermore, this progressive role is not destined to pass with the advent of socialism; it will continue to be a positive factor well into the communist future. The reason for this is that under the party the nation has been raised to a higher level of development and it is now described as a "socialist nation, . . . incomparably more powerful and more homogeneous than bourgeois society."[16] This effort to endow the nation with theoretical respectability has occupied a number of Romanian researchers for some time.[17]

A second premise in the RCP's thinking with regard to the role of the nation is that "communist parties, in countries where they have become ruling parties, must be the most faithful representatives of national interests."[18] Each party must consider first the specific needs of its own country and adopt the strategy and tactics appropriate to its own conditions. Although this conclusion logically follows the contention regarding the persistence and progressive nature of the nation, in actual fact it followed differences with the Soviet Union over concrete policy questions, which led to the elaborate theoretical framework created to justify autonomous action on the part of the RCP. The right of each party to pursue its own policies independently has since that time been among the most consistent themes in RCP statements.[19]

Reasons behind the Party's National Policy

Three reasons stand out as influencing the RCP's decision to follow a policy of identifying itself with Romanian historical tradition and upgrading the role of the nation in ideological terms. First of all, this policy was intended to secure a measure of popular support for the party; second, it was related to the conflict with the Soviet Union over economic policy and the right to pursue a degree of autonomy in foreign affairs; and third, it was seen as a useful means to achieve party goals by inspiring greater popular effort to achieve economic progress.

Among the more important elements in the party's strategy for pursuing a better relationship with the population was the decision to strengthen party links with the Romanian national heritage, thus seeking to minimize its image as an alien, Soviet-imposed regime, and to emphasize its indigenous Romanian roots. Because Romanian consciousness is very much a product of a sense of history and national identity, this became a key element in the process of garnering popular support. This effort, however, has been complicated by the fact that in this century Romanian nationalism has taken on a strongly anti-Russian element.

The Romanian attitude toward the tsarist empire in the nineteenth century was a complicated one. Although the Russians seized Bessarabia in 1812 (and reacquired the southern section of it in 1878, after having lost it in the Crimean War) and tended to interfere in the internal affairs of the principalities, the Orthodox Russians were nevertheless regarded as a shield, protecting the Romanian Orthodox faithful against the Muslim Sublime Porte, who was anxious to retain his hold over Romania, and against the Roman Catholic Hapsburg emperor, who sought to suppress Romanian nationalism in Transylvania. Thus, while Russia was not Romania's best ally, it was better than the other powers who exercised influence in the area.

After old Romania was joined to Transylvania and Bessarabia in 1918, however, the unified country found the new Soviet Union to be the most consistent and hostile critic of its territorial integrity. The hostility between the two countries was by no means lessened when the Soviet Union demanded and received Bessarabia in 1940, and the reconquest of the contested area by Soviet troops in 1944 did not improve matters. Anti-Russian sentiment was further intensified by the Soviet occupation and the imposition of the communist regime.

Thus, in order to gain credibility for its new national orientation, the Romanian party had to display an anti-Russian attitude but at the same time avoid provoking any response by the Soviets that might have included the use of force. In the early 1960s the party's efforts to strengthen its links with Romanian history included veiled anti-Soviet moves: playing down the Soviet role in Romania's liberation during World War II; dropping Russian-language requirements from school curricula; changing the names of streets, theaters, and institutions from Russian or Soviet to Romanian ones. Perhaps among the most daring undertakings was the decision to permit historians to revive—though cautiously—the Romanian view of the Bessarabian question.[20] Although these steps have introduced certain problems into Soviet-Romanian relations, they have been very successful in linking the party with Romanian history.

As mentioned above, the second reason behind this national policy arises out of Romania's relationship with the Soviet Union. Jowitt suggests that the interrelation of beliefs and attitudes is an important aspect of this process.[21] As the members of the RCP elite came to accept the concepts of diversity and sovereignty in relations with the Soviet Union, they also began to adopt a more positive attitude toward the idea of the nation, and their belief was strengthened by the conflict with the USSR over economic and other issues in the early 1960s. Thus autonomy in foreign affairs and conflict with Moscow were justified and reinforced by a policy of upgrading the role of the nation and linking the party to national values; as such, the two policies were interdependent.

A third element was the role the party assigned to national awareness and patriotism in inspiring the masses to the fulfillment of its goals; through this policy the RCP sought to bolster its authority and strengthen its legitimacy, in order to secure greater popular support for its goals. That this was indeed a factor in the RCP's espousal of nationalism was evident from the many comments uttered by the party leaders during the mid-1960s, and its existence has been pointed up with particular openness since the ideological campaign of 1976. The resolution adopted at the Congress on Political Education and Socialist Culture in June of that year stated that "the education of all working people, regardless of nationality, and primarily of our youth, in a spirit of love for country and of revolutionary and socialist patriotism" was a matter of "central concern." History was described as a "powerful element in patriotic education and advanced thinking":

> By cultivating gratitude to and appreciation of our forefathers—who defended our people's national existence at the cost of great sacrifice and raised the banner of the struggle for freedom and independence and national and social justice—education must instill in the people's minds a feeling of responsibility for our forefathers' inheritance and a determination to continue to carry the beacon of progress and civilization in Romania under new historical conditions.[22]

The didactic use of history and the emphasis on patriotic education have been considered particularly useful in achieving the party's primary objective: the industrialization of the country. Ceausescu has made no secret of this ultimate goal: "Being a patriot, loving one's fatherland, means doing everything possible to increase the national wealth and socialist property, sparing no effort in carrying out the communist party's policy, which is fully in keeping with the vital interests of the entire nation."[23] In other words, patriotism is something that leads people to sacrifice for the good of the nation; since it motivates the population to carry out party policy, it is to be encouraged. This was put even more clearly by the party leader in response to a West German journalist's question about the contemporary importance of cultivating historical traditions. Ceausescu maintained that it is "an important factor in creatively and actively stimulating the building of a better and more equitable world. . . . The study of history is closely connected with the development of the forces of production, with the peoples' struggle for national and social liberation, with their efforts to achieve progress."[24]

Thus the party has sought, by inculcating patriotism and respect for national traditions, to win increased support and credibility. By linking itself to the national tradition and acquiring a degree of credibility as a defender of the national interests it seeks to gain legitimacy and strengthen its base of support among the population.

The Impact on the National Minorities

One important additional factor that has complicated the RCP's effort to link itself with the Romanian heritage and upgrade the role of the nation is the existence of a substantial minority population. Although the proportion of non-Romanians has declined considerably since the interwar period, when they made up almost 30 percent of the population, at the time of the 1977 census there was still a minority population of some 12 percent. Hungarians make up the largest group, representing almost 8 percent of the total population, followed by the Germans with almost 2 percent. There are also sizable groups of Gypsies, Ukrainians, and Serbs, and a scattering of other nationalities. The party's emphasis on Romanian history and the Romanian nation is a particularly sensitive issue among the Hungarians, since Transylvania is an area to which both Romania and Hungary lay claim, and one that has played a prominent role in the history of both countries and peoples. The conflicting historical claims regarding the area thus pose a problem for the RCP when it embraces Romanian national history, and there are similar sensitive issues involving the Germans and other minorities, though these are perhaps less acute.[25]

In the first years after the RCP came to power, the minorities, with the exception of the Germans, were generally well treated.[26] While no part of the population was accorded extensive rights, the minorities enjoyed the same treatment as Romanians and enjoyed in addition extensive linguistic and cultural rights. But this minority policy was less a function of enlightened leadership than of tactical considerations; it was Soviet strategy in Romania to utilize non-Romanian ethnic elements to maintain control of the country. In Bulgaria, Czechoslovakia, and to some extent Poland, the Soviets benefited from local nationalism and pan-Slav sentiment, but among Romanians anti-Russian feelings had been intensified by the annexation of Bessarabia by the Soviet Union during the Second World War. The RCP, though, included a sizeable non-Romanian membership; leaders from this group would be less able to win popular support, and thus would be more dependent on Soviet power and more amenable to Soviet control.

All minorities were not treated equally, however. The Germans were initially under suspicion because some had supported Hitler's Third Reich, and restrictive measures in many cases were applied to the minority as a whole rather than only to those guilty of collaboration. Restrictions against the Germans were then gradually done away with between 1948 and 1956.[27] The Jewish population, which lost most of its civil rights and much of its property under the Antonescu regime, was initially well-treated by the RCP, but with Stalin's growing anti-Semitism after the war, the Jewish population eventually faced greater limitations and discrimination.[28]

The most favored of the minorities were the Hungarians, who were permitted their own political organization, though it (like all other institutions) was brought under the party's control as the RCP consolidated its hold. The most important symbol of the Hungarian minority's favored status was the creation in the 1952 Romanian constitution of the Hungarian Autonomous Region. The region was in the heart of Transylvania, some distance from the border with Hungary, but it included a substantial and compact Hungarian population, which made up three-quarters of the total population of the region. Although the Hungarian Autonomous Region functioned just like all other local administrative districts, the fact that most of its government and party officials were Hungarian and that it was designated a Hungarian region was important to the minority.

The generally favorable treatment of minorities during this early period was not a universally accepted policy within the party, however. Lucretiu Patrascanu, one of the party's early leaders and the minister of justice from 1944 to 1948, apparently favored a more Romanian national approach. When he was purged in 1948, a resolution of the RCP Central Committee noted that "the struggle against the anti-Marxist national-chauvinism of Patrascanu has helped to establish fraternal relations between the Romanian people and the other nationalities living on the same territory."[29] Though charges against purge victims were frequently distorted and magnified, there had to have been some truth to the claim for it to have any credibility. Patrascanu's nationalism was also echoed by other Romanians in the party who were anxious to improve the mass appeal of communism.

The year 1956 marked a turning point in the treatment of the minorities in general, and of the Hungarian minority in particular. The Hungarian revolution indicated the difficulty and cost of maintaining communist parties in power in Eastern Europe principally by means of Soviet power. After 1956 there was greater emphasis on each party developing closer links with the local population and reducing the alienation between party and population. It was in this context that the Romanian party first began to turn toward a more national orientation and began to minimize the non-Romanian aspects of its past. Gheorghiu-Dej was helped by the fact that Jewish Ana Pauker and Hungarian Vasile Luca with many of their non-Romanian associates had been purged in 1952 and that many of the followers of Gheorghiu-Dej who benefited from his success were ethnic Romanians. Another key factor in the changed policy was reflected in the attitude toward the minorities. The impact of the Hungarian revolution upon the Hungarians in Transylvania demonstrated their isolation from Romanian life and emphasized their links with Hungary. This led Gheorghiu-Dej to conclude that the minority must be integrated into Romania and its links with Hungary weakened.[30]

Not long after the Hungarian revolt, the Romanian party initiated a policy of integrating the Hungarian and other minorities into Romanian society. Since intellectuals and students had been most influenced by events in Hungary, these groups were the first to be affected. The first anniversary of the Hungarian revolution was turned into an occasion for leading Hungarian intellectuals to denounce nationalism among their minority and to pledge loyalty to Romania. The minorities—and the Hungarians in particular—had been entitled to education in their mother tongue, for the most part in separate schools; increasingly after 1956 these schools were integrated with Romanian institutions, and though some classes were taught in Hungarian or German, all students were required to learn Romanian. The most serious blow to the Hungarian intellectuals, and another indication of the general trend, was the merger of the Hungarian-language Bolyai University in Cluj (the Hungarian cultural center of Transylvania) with the Romanian-language Babes University in the same city. Hungarian-language instruction declined gradually after the two institutions were consolidated, and the administration was increasingly dominated by ethnic Romanians.

Another symbolic gesture was made in 1960 with the alteration of the boundaries of the Hungarian Autonomous Region. The two most heavily Hungarian districts were added to a nearby region having a predominantly

Romanian ethnic population, and new territory with a proportionately smaller Hungarian population was added to the Autonomous Region. The percentage of Hungarians in the region declined from 77 percent to 62 percent, while the proportion of Romanians increased from 20 to 35 percent. A further symbolic gesture was the addition of the Romanian place name "Mures" to the region's official name, making it the Mures Autonomous Hungarian Region. At the same time Romanians began to assume a greater role in the administration of the area.

Until his death in 1965, Gheorghiu-Dej continued to follow the minority policy that emerged in the aftermath of the Hungarian revolution. Although there were no further demonstrative actions such as the merging of the universities in Cluj or the gerrymandering of the Hungarian Autonomous Region, Romanian nationalism increased under official guidance, and on occasion it was permitted to assume anti-Hungarian form. The advent of Ceausescu's leadership did not mark any basic change in minority policy; links between the Hungarian minority and Hungary were restricted and emphasis continued to be placed on the integration of all minorities into Romanian society. He was, however, more willing than Gheorghiu-Dej to permit the use of the Hungarian language and the development of Hungarian culture, as long as it was clearly established that the minorities are Romanian citizens and their first loyalty must be to Romania. It was significant that among the first visits Ceausescu made after assuming the party leadership were to areas with substantial Hungarian populations.

Although Ceausescu has been willing to permit the nationalities to exercise cultural and linguistic rights, he has also continued the effort to break down the sense of minority isolation. Under his leadership the Mures Autonomous Hungarian Region was completely eliminated. This was carefully carried out in the context of a general country-wide administrative reorganization, but the fact that no autonomous region was designated can be attributed to the desire to emphasize that minorities are an integral part of the Romanian state. Though this step had symbolic significance to the Hungarian population, the territorial changes were carefully carried out to avoid difficulties with the minority or with the Hungarian government, which had become involved in matters affecting treatment of the minority in Romania. Two of the new counties had a substantial Hungarian population (88 percent and 79 percent) while several others were between one-quarter and one-half Hungarian.

One of Ceausescu's major aims has been to render the Hungarian and other minorities less useful in Soviet attempts to pressure Bucharest. The

Soviet-led invasion of Czechoslovakia, which Romania roundly condemned, was the first test of that policy. The Soviet Union and Hungary were extremely critical of Romania's stand on Czechoslovakia, and the visit to Bucharest of a Hungarian Politburo member and specialist on nationalities questions just five days after the invasion suggested that the minority question was used to threaten the Romanians. The RCP leadership immediately embarked on a series of steps to mobilize minority support for the Romanian regime, including a quick tour of the Hungarian areas by Ceausescu. Within a few months the party established a new national front organization as part of a campaign for national unity; among the important groups included in the front were organizations of the national minorities, which were set up both country-wide and in each county with a large minority population. Influential party officials with minority background assumed the leading roles in these organizations.[31] Also in the aftermath of the Czechoslovak crisis, books, newspapers, periodicals, and radio and television in minority languages became more readily available.

In 1971 the same problem again arose. Soviet displeasure with a Ceausescu visit to China was demonstrated with a campaign of pressure against Romania, an important element of which was criticism by party officials in Hungary of the treatment of the Hungarian minority in Romania. This was the first time this very sensitive issue was raised so publicly and authoritatively. Obviously it was done at Soviet instigation, although the Hungarians may well have had their own reasons for doing so. The Romanians responded with a vigorous counteroffensive, which included personal attacks on the Hungarian spokesman, and a campaign to mobilize the minorities; party leaders visited minority areas, improvements were announced in the cultural and educational field, and statements of support from non-Romanians were given publicity.[32] That storm was successfully weathered, but the potential for the Soviet Union to utilize the minorities for internal disruption remains.

More recent indications of problems involving the minorities have come from within Romania and do not appear to have been instigated by the Soviets. A Hungarian who previously held important positions in the RCP wrote three letters to top party officials expressing dissatisfaction with the treatment of Hungarians. The letters, which received considerable attention in the Western press, provoked other critical responses from Hungarians in Romania, as well as an official countercampaign designed to show that the minorities are being treated well.[33]

While the Hungarian minority has been most concerned with issues involving cultural and linguistic rights, and ties with Hungary, the major issue for ethnic Germans has been the right to emigrate to West Germany. After Bonn and Bucharest established diplomatic relations in 1967 it became somewhat easier for ethnic Germans to join family members in the West, as the German government quietly pressured Romania to permit greater numbers to leave and Romania sought to maintain good relations in view of German economic assistance. Between emigration and intermarriage, the German community in Romania has dwindled to the point that its continued separate existence is open to question. The party's emphasis on Romanian nationalism has no doubt intensified the pressures among Germans to emigrate or assimilate. At the same time, however, the ethnic Germans include a high proportion of skilled workers; their loss to the Romanian economy would be serious, particularly since labor has become increasingly scarce with continuing industrialization. To counter the pressures for emigration, the party has launched periodic campaigns to discourage the Germans from leaving, and bureaucratic obstacles have made the process of receiving permission to depart lengthy and uncertain.[34]

For the Jewish community, emigration to Israel was a major issue, but since World War II the Romanian regime has quietly permitted a large portion of the Jewish population to leave. Though some 30,000 to 70,000 Jews remain in Romania (of a postwar population of half a million), many of those still there are integrated well into Romanian society, or are older people who do not wish to start life again elsewhere. Since Romanian nationalism in the past has been associated with anti-Semitism, its revival under RCP auspices increases the uncertainty for the Jewish community.

The desire to integrate the minorities more closely into a unified Romanian state does create certain inconsistencies, involving the theoretical view of the continuation (even under socialism) of the "nation," which is not always synonymous with the "state." If "nations" continue to exist, so will minorities. In a speech at the Congress on Political Education and Socialist Culture in June 1976, Ceausescu seemed to suggest that the national differences within states would disappear more quickly than those between states. On the one hand he stressed that "the role of the nation is not diminishing, let alone disappearing," under socialism, but he went on to say that the nationalities question must be viewed in terms of the nation-state: the party must "guarantee all conditions for the expression of nationhood and the existence of nationalities, and at the same time bring national positions closer to one another and make the differences gradually disappear under communism, so as to form a nation of working people, an aware and fully united nation building its own history and its own free and communist future."[35]

Some of the complexities of this problem have been evident in the emphasis on patriotic education that has been part of the 1976 ideological campaign. Ceausescu's ideological addresses and the party's ideological documents have always included frequent and favorable references to the "coinhabiting nationalities." Emphasis has also been placed on the beneficial reciprocal influence exerted by "the indigenous population and the peoples who have passed our way or who settled side by side with the Romanians," and on the harmonious relationship between them. Despite favorable references to the minorities and pledges to perpetuate their national rights, however, Ceausescu made at least two comments that may have raised eyebrows. Once he stated that migration of "certain Asiatic peoples [Hungarians? Slavs?] to Europe ... greatly hampered social progress in this area," and on another occasion he observed that the coinhabiting nationalities "did not bring with them a higher civilization" but found in Romania an advanced one that "constituted a primary factor in their development."[36] Though coupled with positive statements, such sentiments, plus the emphasis on *Romanian* history, are no doubt seen by the minorities as an effort to erode their separate identity. This feeling may well be reinforced by a directive in the 1976 ideological action program: "More attention will have to be paid to having children of the coinhabiting nationalities master both the Romanian language and their mother tongue, to educating them in a spirit of fraternity and unity, of love for the common fatherland—socialist Romania."[37]

That the party faces a real dilemma as a result of the decision to strengthen its ties with the Romanian heritage is clear. On the one hand its efforts to link the minorities with the Romanian tradition are unlikely to find a responsive chord, since the latter have their own strong and different historical traditions.[38] On the other hand the party does not wish to alienate the minorities by pushing integration too hard. The Hungarians in Transylvania are regarded as a weak link in the Romanian national chain. This is evident from the fact that in any national crisis or in case of the application of external pressure, the loyalty of the Hungarian minority is an issue that is immediately raised.

7

The International
Policy of the Party

$\mathbf{A}$mong the most important aspects of the evolution and Romanianization of the RCP has been its changing relationship with the Soviet party and state. In fact, foreign policy has been Romania's main claim to uniqueness and the major reason it has achieved international recognition in the postwar era. For the past two decades the RCP leadership has carefully pursued Romania's own national interests in international affairs and gradually expanded autonomy from the Soviet Union. They have managed to avoid Soviet military intervention while at the same time pursuing policies that have differed in important regards from those of Moscow. Romania remains a member of the Soviet-dominated military and economic blocs (the Warsaw Pact, and the Council for Mutual Economic Assistance, or Comecon), but the Romanians have developed their international contacts across a broad front, maintaining good relations with countries that have a wide variety of internal political and economic systems and quite different foreign policies.

Western observers frequently refer to the country's "independent" foreign policy or speak of "independent" Romania, but using this term to describe Romanian foreign policy is misleading. "Independent" means not dependent, not in subordination to or subject to external control or rule. Although Romania has frequently differed with the Soviet Union on some foreign policy issues, it still recognizes and acts within limits set by Moscow, the transgression of which would provoke armed Soviet intervention. "Autonomy" is a more accurate and suitable term to describe Romania's foreign policy, as it denotes the right of self-government, of making one's own laws and administering one's own affairs. Although "independent" and "autonomous" are sometimes used as synonyms, the two have rather different connotations. "Independence" is usually declared unilaterally (no state has declared "autonomy"), and frequently it must be won by forcible rejection of a subordinate relationship. "Autonomy," on the other hand, is usually granted or permitted by a hierarchically superior political unit. Independence is an absolute condition, whereas autonomy is frequently qualified or limited in scope (American counties, for example, have a degree of "local autonomy" and American trust territories enjoy "administrative autonomy"). In the case of Romanian foreign policy, "autonomy" is clearly a more accurate descriptive term than "independence."

The Nature of the Soviet-Romanian Relationship

The forbearance shown by the Soviet Union toward Romania's foreign policy deviance has not been a function of enlightened self-interest on the part of the CPSU leadership and still less an acknowledgment of Romania's right to conduct its own foreign affairs as it sees fit. Probably the most important factor in Soviet restraint has been the RCP leadership's acute sensitivity to the limits of Soviet indulgence.

The RCP's policies have thus far threatened only the first of what Fritz Ermarth has termed the three "fundamental dimensions" of Soviet policy in Eastern Europe: "internationalism" (the relationship among communist states), "security" (the preservation of the prevailing East-West balance of political power), and "legitimacy" (maintaining the communist parties' monopoly of power within the individual countries of Eastern Europe).[1] Unlike the situation that developed in Czechoslovakia in 1968, the Romanian party's internal power monopoly has not been jeopardized by its domestic or foreign policies. The Romanians have also been careful to give no indication that they would harm core Soviet security interests. Though Romanian leaders have called for the dissolution of all military blocs and limited participation in Warsaw Pact exercises, they periodically reaffirm the intention to fulfill all obligations assumed under the Warsaw Treaty and the bilateral treaties that link the country with each of its Warsaw Pact allies. Further limiting any Soviet sense of threat in this regard is Romania's good fortune in not having a common border with any member country of the North Atlantic alliance.

Only in the area of relations between communist states and parties have the Romanians challenged Moscow, but their position has been strengthened because they have not been alone. Although the other Warsaw Pact states have generally accepted Soviet primacy and followed its lead in inter-state and interparty relations, many parties beyond the Soviet sphere, including the Chinese, Yugoslav, Cuban, and several of the non-ruling ones (the Italian, Spanish, Japanese, and, at times, the French), have taken positions on interparty relations that are similar to the RCP's stand on "internationalism."

As long as the Romanian challenge is confined to only one of the three dimensions of Soviet policy toward Eastern Europe, the Soviet leaders are unlikely to conclude that military intervention is either necessary or worth the political cost. The RCP leadership, which has shown itself to be highly sensitive to these Soviet concerns as it has expanded its own foreign policy autonomy, is unlikely to depart from the basic policy it has so skillfully pursued for two decades.

The Soviet impact on the RCP and its policies is complex. The existence of the Soviet Union, and its decision to exercise hegemony in Eastern Europe, remains probably the major element in the RCP's hold on power despite its growing popular acceptance. This is not to imply that if Soviet interest or influence in Eastern Europe were suddenly withdrawn the RCP would be toppled or replaced. But the Soviet presence is a key factor in the popular recognition that there is no real alternative to communist party rule in Romania; without the Soviet threat the party might still be able to maintain control, but it would most likely be a significantly altered party with a much different relationship to Romanian society. The Soviet Union is frequently (though never explicitly) invoked to secure support for certain less popular policies or personnel decisions taken by the RCP; yet the Soviet Sword of Damocles permits the party to pursue such policies while nevertheless successfully calling for national and party unity.

The Soviet Union also remains a factor in the legitimation of the Romanian party. Despite the successful effort to link the party with the Romanian national heritage and identify it with the national interests, its legitimacy is still grounded in ideology. It is difficult to embrace Lenin's ideology without admitting a special position for the CPSU, which is his institutional heir. Despite the RCP's assertion that each party must serve the interests of its own working class, its persistent effort to cultivate links with other communist and left-wing parties reflects the continuing importance of internationalism in establishing the legitimacy of communist rule in Romania.

The attempt to validate its nationally oriented policies on an international level has occasionally found the RCP with strange bedfellows. The West European parties that have been most adamant in affirming the right of each party independently to pursue policies calculated to serve the interests of its national constituency have also rejected the Soviet approach on domestic issues, which, despite their foreign policy differences with the USSR, the Romanians have followed. Thus, the RCP has often defended the right of any party to pursue policies it alone determines, but at the same time has criticized some of the specific policies these parties have adopted.

An interesting example was the Romanian reaction to the French Communist Party's decision to abandon the concept of the dictatorship of the proletariat in February 1976. Ceausescu criticized the French decision and declared that in Romania conditions were different and the concept remained valid. The portions of the speech of the French party leader Georges Marchais defending that decision were selectively edited out of the excerpts of his speech initially published by the Romanian press. After a two-week delay, however, the full text of Marchais' controversial statements on the dictatorship of the proletariat was published in Romania.[2] On another similar occasion, the RCP defended Spanish Communist Party leader Santiago Carrillo after a Soviet journal virulently criticized him. An editorial in the party daily noted the duty and responsibility of each party to work out its policies, taking into consideration the country's "specific peculiarities, and the economic, social, political, and historical factors," but it pointed out that the East European parties came to power in circumstances quite different than those prevailing in Western Europe; hence the RCP should not necessarily pursue the same policies.[3]

The limits within which Romanian foreign policy makers must operate are not explicitly defined, thus there is continuing Soviet pressure to narrow the scope for autonomous action and continuing Romanian probing to expand those limits. Four important factors affect the Soviet reaction and are crucial in determining Romanian success in any particular case. The first of these is the nature and seriousness of the specific challenge as seen from Moscow. In some cases a particular Romanian action may turn out to have more serious consequences than initially assessed. The Soviet Union apparently did not consider the Romanian decision to establish diplomatic relations with West Germany in 1967 to be a serious problem, but the violent East German reaction convinced Moscow that the implications could be far more serious. Thus the step-by-step approach of the Romanians in establishing their autonomy has been an important factor in their success.

A second factor is the character of the Soviet leadership at the time they face a challenge. The stability or instability of the Politburo, and the impact of controversial domestic decisions upon personal relationships, are important considerations affecting the ability of the Soviet leaders to agree upon vigorous action or acquiesce through inaction. Khrushchev's growing problems with his Politburo colleagues in 1963 and 1964 was probably important to the Romanian success in stymying his Comecon integration proposals and in permitting the Romanians to attempt their mediation efforts between the Soviet and Chinese parties in early 1964. Unfortunately, however, our knowledge of the Soviet decision-making process is very limited, making analysis of this crucial element particularly difficult.

Third, the international setting can both inhibit or encourage a Romanian challenge or Soviet response. The visit of Henry Kissinger to Peking in the summer of 1971, which started the Chinese-American rapprochement and opened the way for President Nixon to visit China, was a major factor in provoking a stronger Soviet reaction to Ceausescu's visit to Peking that same summer. On the other hand, the improvement of U.S.-Soviet relations and the convening of the Soviet-inspired Conference on Security and Cooperation in Europe in the early 1970s led Soviet leaders to exercise more caution in responding to Romanian challenges in order to avoid upsetting the course of detente.

The fourth factor is the ability of Romania to maintain its challenge and withstand the Soviet response. The relevant considerations include the RCP leadership's cohesion and agreement on the particular issue, national unity and support for the leadership, support from other countries and parties, and, most important, the capability to resist. Romanian leaders have enhanced their capacity to resist by announcing that they would use, and by taking action to insure the use of, military force against any armed foreign threat to the country's sovereignty. Furthermore, they have benefited from the Romanian oil reserves, which have contributed to making the country less subject to external economic pressures. The most serious Soviet-Romanian confrontation thus far came at the time of the Soviet invasion of Czechoslovakia in 1968, when it was clear that the Romanian leadership and population were united in opposition. While the Romanian military would have been no match for the Soviet army, the fact that it was mobilized showed the Romanian intention to resist, which would have made Soviet intervention more costly in political and military terms than it had been in Czechoslovakia. The international reaction to the Czechoslovakian events and the diplomatic support expressed for Romania were also factors that influenced the Soviet leadership's decision not to take military action against Romania at that time.

These four are not the only elements that may influence the outcome of a Romanian-Soviet contest, but they are the most important. The interrelationship between them is obvious, but so also is the inability to determine the relative importance of any one in a particular case because of limited information on the inner workings of the Soviet and Romanian leaderships. Nevertheless, in reviewing the course of Soviet-Romanian relations these elements should be kept in mind.

Foreign Policy and Popular Support

Its autonomous foreign policy has been a significant factor in the RCP's rapprochement with the Romanian population; thus the popular impact of a particular foreign policy action is an important consideration in the foreign policy decision-making process. It also imposes certain limitations that must be considered by the leadership; as the party has acquired a measure of popular support for its anti-Russian actions, its flexibility in dealing with the Soviets has been correspondingly curtailed.

The anti-Russian sentiment associated with Romanian nationalism, for example, has complicated the RCP's relationship with the Soviet Union. Among the earliest indications of the more national orientation of the RCP, and an initial indication of the emergence of problems with the Soviet Union, was a series of very popular measures to deemphasize Soviet and Russian ties. In the early 1960s, the Russian or Soviet names of streets, squares, and theaters were changed back to prewar Romanian titles, or they were given new ones based on Romania's national past. The study of the Russian language was dropped as a compulsory subject in schools, and institutes for friendship with the Soviet Union or for the study of Russian language and literature were downgraded or quietly phased out. In the early 1960s these derussification measures caused a sensation, although the party implemented them quietly and without fanfare. The Soviet reaction, of course, was negative, but the steps were symbolic rather than substantive and by themselves did not represent a fundamental challenge to Soviet interests.

One significant issue with strong anti-Russian overtones is the public reassertion of the Romanian claim to Bessarabia. The party revives this matter when it wishes to emphasize its links with the national heritage or to rally popular support for some particular purpose. In many ways polemics over Bessarabia have become something of a barometer of the state of Soviet-Romanian ties. When relations between the two countries are good, the historical debates over Bessarabia are downgraded; when relations deteriorate, the scholarly polemic intensifies.[4] But the popular anti-Russian/ anti-Soviet aspect of Romanian nationalism does create certain problems for the RCP, because that sentiment cannot be manipulated as easily as the Bessarabian polemics, which can be turned on or off at will.

For Ceausescu confrontations with the Soviet Union have certain advantages on the domestic front. His popular support, which has varied considerably during the fifteen years he has led Romania, reached its apogee in the aftermath of his stern denunciation of the Soviet-led invasion of Czechoslovakia in 1968, but began to wane quickly as he continued to call for sacrifice in order to build the country's economy rather than increasing the standard of living. Further contributing to the decline in his support has been mismanagement, most evident in his reluctance to implement economic reforms that might have permitted better utilization of the economic ties with the West. Ceausescu's autocratic and somewhat capricious leadership style, as well as tolerance for incompetence, cronyism, and nepotism have further contributed to the alienation. A confrontation with the Soviet Union—Romania's traditional foe and the principal threat to its autonomy— always galvanizes patriotic sentiment; these occasions are used to play up nationalist themes and turn popular attention away from domestic problems.

But while a confrontation with the Soviet Union results in increased popular support for the RCP and its leader, it is unlikely that this lasts much beyond the end of the crisis. The daily problems and frustrations of coping with the low standard of living are a much more important and immediate source of popular attitudes toward the government and party than periodic conflicts with the Soviet Union. In the long run, tension between a popular, autonomous foreign policy and a repressive, less popular domestic policy may be the factor that will determine Romania's ability to maintain its international position.

Expanding the Scope of Autonomy in the 1960s

The origin and timing of Romanian foreign policy differences with the Soviet Union remain a matter of controversy. Some observers suggest that as early as 1955 Romania's leaders were cautiously pursuing "national policies" first formulated a decade earlier, others point to 1958 as the beginning, while still others have suggested 1962 as the critical year.[5] The earliest suggested date is clearly erroneous, while the latter ones are more a disagreement over the point at which the gradually evolving divergencies can be said to represent real differences. The economic issues that led to conflict with the Soviet Union only began to emerge in the late 1950s, when Romanian policies were not initially perceived as being contradictory to Soviet goals. By the early 1960s, however, the policies of the Soviet and Romanian parties clearly diverged and the differences became public.

Khrushchev's advocacy of a supranational planning agency for Comecon in 1962 became the initial focal point of controversy, with Romania opposing the Soviet leader's concept on economic, political, and national grounds. Although Khrushchev's proposal was abandoned at the Comecon summit in July 1963, Romanians were sensitive about such ideas for some time, as was evidenced by the vigorous Romanian reaction to an article by Soviet geographer E. B. Valev arguing the rationality of creating an economically integrated area consisting of parts of the Ukraine, Romania, and Bulgaria.[6]

From economic issues, differences with the Soviet Union widened to include key interparty issues. The Romanian interest in China began in 1963 after the Comecon integration dispute had been resolved in Romania's favor. Ostensibly acting in the interest of communist unity, the RCP assumed for itself the role of mediator between Moscow and Peking, a role that it still continues to play to some extent. The more fundamental reason for active Romanian intervention in Sino-Soviet relations, however, appears to have been concern to delay a Soviet showdown with China, toward which Khrushchev seemed to be moving.[7] The unsuccessful early 1964 mediation effort of a high level RCP delegation to Moscow and Peking precipitated the now famous Central Committee Statement of April 1964, in which the RCP presented its most authoritative statement asserting the sovereignty and independence of each party, and the principle of noninterference in the internal affairs of other parties. The explicit statement of these principles of interparty relations contradicted Soviet practice and became a factor in further increasing tension with Moscow.[8]

The changing of the guard in both Moscow and Bucharest (Khrushchev was deposed in October 1964 and Gheorghiu-Dej died in March 1965) ushered in a brief period of calm, but by late 1965 there were again indications of tension between the two countries, regarding the Warsaw Pact. The new Soviet leader Leonid Brezhnev sought to strengthen the alliance's supranational character, while the Romanians presented counterproposals designed to weaken the dominant Soviet role in the military bloc.[9] In the course of this controversy, Romania's objections to joint military maneuvers on its soil were established, and since that time Romanian participation in joint Warsaw Pact maneuvers has been limited. On occasion, staff officers of other countries have been permitted in Romania for joint exercises, and Romanian staff officers have participated in such training operations in other Warsaw Pact countries, but no Romanian combat troops and equipment have been involved outside its borders and no foreign troops have entered Romania.

Perhaps the climax of this period of controversy came on the 45th anniversary of the founding of the RCP in May 1966, when in a commemorative speech Ceausescu criticized Soviet domination of the party during the interwar period, and made thinly veiled references to the historic Romanian claim to Bessarabia.[10] Brezhnev made a quick unscheduled visit to Bucharest, during which both sides apparently agreed to soft-pedal their differences; both the Soviets and Romanians quietly dropped their proposals on the Warsaw Pact, and Soviet-Romanian tensions abated somewhat.

The year 1967 marked the further broadening of Romanian foreign policy autonomy as differences with Moscow were extended to issues outside the sphere of the "socialist camp." First, Romania established diplomatic relations with West Germany in response to overtures from the Kiesinger-Brandt government, which came to power in Bonn at the end of 1966. This Romanian move provoked a particularly vigorous response from the East German government and resulted in a major Soviet diplomatic campaign to coordinate the policies of all Warsaw Pact states toward West Germany and other Western states. Second, Romania adopted a policy of strict neutrality following the Arab-Israeli war in June 1967, whereas the Soviet Union and its loyalist Warsaw Pact allies all severed diplomatic relations with Israel and took a strong pro-Arab stand. Differences between the Soviet and Romanian parties continued over the advisability of holding a world communist conference, with the Romanians arguing that if one were held, China must be invited and the rules of the conference should not permit criticism of any party, present or absent.

The Soviet-led invasion of Czechoslovakia in August 1968 provoked the most serious crisis in Soviet-Romanian relations. Just days before Soviet troops and tanks rolled into Prague, Ceausescu visited the Czechoslovak capital to sign a renewed treaty of friendship and alliance—a particularly demonstrative act of support for the Dubcek regime, since the Romanians had been refusing to sign a similar new agreement with the Soviet Union. Romania was not invited by the Soviets to participate in the interparty conferences that preceded the military invasion, although all other Warsaw Pact members attended and the invasion was billed as an alliance action. Ceausescu denounced the invasion in the strongest terms, and, fearing the possibility of military moves against Romania, mobilized the armed forces and the population. Apparently blunt Soviet instructions led Ceausescu to cease criticism, though he refused to retract his earlier condemnation. The

Romanian leaders continued to make known their disapproval of the military action and their rejection of the "Brezhnev doctrine" invoked to justify the occupation of Czechoslovakia.[11]

Despite something of a retrenchment following the Czechoslovak invasion, it became evident in the summer of 1969 that Romania had not altered its basic foreign policy. At the Moscow world communist conference in June, Ceausescu continued to voice outspoken opposition to criticism of the absent Chinese, and he called for all parties to observe the Romanian principles for interparty relations enunciated in the April 1964 Statement.[12] Then in August 1969 U.S. President Richard Nixon received a spectacular welcome in Bucharest, which clearly angered the Soviets; they sent a significantly low-level delegation to the Romanian party congress a few weeks later, and apparently cancelled a scheduled visit to Bucharest by Brezhnev and/or Soviet Prime Minister Alexei Kosygin to sign a new friendship treaty.

These events established for Romania a degree of autonomy within the Warsaw Pact, despite Soviet efforts to prevent it. Symbolic acknowledgment and institutionalization of Romania's autonomous relationship was the signing of a new Soviet-Romanian Treaty of Friendship, Cooperation, and Mutual Assistance in July 1970.[13] That this action was not fully in keeping with Soviet desire was evident by the fact that Soviet party leader Brezhnev cancelled participation in the signing ceremony in Bucharest at the last minute (in keeping with strict protocol, Ceausescu was also conspicuously absent when the heads of government signed the document). The treaty replaced an earlier twenty-year treaty signed in 1948, which had automatically continued in force in 1968 when a new treaty was not signed. The provisions of the treaty with Romania differ in several important respects from the series of similar documents signed by the Soviet Union with all other members of the Warsaw Pact in the years between 1967 and 1970. In the treaty with Romania the USSR implicitly recognized Bucharest's special position and acknowledged its degree of foreign policy autonomy, but at the same time Romania acknowledged a continuing political and military relationship with the Soviet Union. This institutionalization of Romanian autonomy, however, has not meant that the Soviets have ceased their efforts to narrow the bounds within which the RCP must act, nor has it prevented the Romanians from seeking to expand the limits of permissible activity.

Difficulties Maintaining Autonomy in the 1970s

Romania's first steps toward autonomy in the 1960s were made at a time when the cold war still dominated Soviet-American relations, the East-West division in Europe was clearly marked, and both major powers sought to seduce wavering members of the opposing alliance. Soviet-Chinese differences were still treated as an interparty matter, and Peking was largely isolated from the rest of the world; this gave Romania an opportunity to expand its autonomy by adopting a policy of neutrality between the two. A further important influence on Romanian policy was the example and support of Yugoslavia.

The decade of the 1970s, however, was marked by changes in the international scene, which in turn affected the course of the RCP's foreign policy behavior.[14] The Soviet-American confrontation gave way to detente, and the Soviet Union and the East European states expanded political and economic relations with the Western states. When Romania was the only East European state working to further economic and political ties with the West, there was considerable support for its foreign policy. With improved East-West relations across the board, however, Romania's position was no longer unique and other considerations came to play a more important role in Western policies.

The Romanians expected the Conference on Security and Cooperation in Europe to result in legal and moral support for their foreign policy position, and in economic and political advantages through improved relations with the Western states.[15] While the 1975 Helsinki conference did create a better atmosphere in East-West relations, it did not prove to be as directly beneficial to Romania as was hoped. Furthermore, Western (and particularly U.S.) interest in humanitarian questions tended to emphasize Romania's common interests with the Soviet Union. In short, the Helsinki conference contributed to the gradual erosion of Western interest in Romania.

For a short time in 1970–1971, when Romania was searching for an alternative to the West as a political and economic counterweight to the USSR, China became a serious candidate for the role, but Soviet pressure against Romania in the summer of 1971, following Ceausescu's visit to Peking, made both Romanian and Chinese leaders aware that China had only limited ability to defend Romania against the USSR. Also, the Chinese seem to have concluded after President Nixon visited Peking in 1972 that they could influence international affairs and deal with the Soviet threat more effectively by establishing good relations with the United States, Japan, and other major nations, rather than by promoting the autonomy of Romania and its Balkan neighbors. This is not to suggest that Romania and China were no longer interested in maintaining good relations (high level delegations continue to be exchanged), but the aura of importance evident in the past faded.[16]

Yugoslavia's support also began to appear less certain, mainly for domestic political reasons. That country's unstable internal situation, primarily a consequence of its ethnic and ideological fragmentation, was exacerbated by Tito's advanced age. The post-Tito succession struggle, which was already underway in the early 1970s, resulted in Yugoslavia's being less secure domestically and less important internationally.

These changes in the international scene prompted a serious Romanian search for alternative sources of support, for new ways to maintain and perhaps expand the sphere for autonomous action. The most significant shift in Romanian policy was the decision to pursue closer relations with the developing countries.[17] Primary considerations were economic, as Romania's rapidly expanding industries needed foreign markets and raw materials. Romania declared itself a developing country in the early 1970s to gain special Common Market and UN trade preferences, and in 1976 Romania was accepted as a member of the UN's "Group of 77," which acts in the world body to further the interests of the developing states. Gradually Romania made a greater effort to identify with these countries politically. An important part of that attempt was played by Ceausescu, who personally visited a large number of Asian, African, and Latin American countries, and received their leaders in Bucharest.

Somewhat more ominous, from the Soviet perspective, was the Romanian effort to establish links with the nonaligned movement, in which Yugoslavia has played such a prominent role. Although its membership in the Warsaw Pact precluded its becoming a full member of the nonaligned group, Romania argued for "observer" status since its policies were directed toward overcoming bloc divisions. The nonaligned, however, decided that Romania might be an "invited guest" at its summit conference in Colombo in 1976, a step below observer status. The Romanians expressed pleasure at this recognition of their country's nonaligned foreign policies.

Once a certain degree of autonomy in a particular area has been established, it does not mean that the Soviets will continue to respect what Bucharest has won. On subsequent occasions Moscow has not been averse to raising issues previously resolved. Maintaining autonomy requires constant effort to fend off Soviet encroachments. The most recent Soviet-Romanian confrontation emphasized that point—most of the issues had been raised before.[18]

Taking advantage of the more assertive international posture of the post-Mao leadership in China, Ceausescu visited Peking in May 1978; Chinese Premier and party leader Hua Kuo-feng traveled to Bucharest the following

August. The Soviets were displeased with Ceausescu's visit, but Hua's trip to Bucharest and Belgrade three months later was considered an even more serious matter. Soviet fears were given timely and dramatic emphasis on the eve of Hua's arrival in Bucharest with the publication of an open letter to China from the Albanian party leadership. The letter asserted that in the past the Chinese repeatedly suggested the creation of a Belgrade-Bucharest-Tirana military axis in order to counterbalance Soviet expansionist designs in the Balkans.

Soviet anxiety over Chinese policies was a key factor in a renewed effort to strengthen the cohesion of the Warsaw Pact. At the November 1978 Warsaw Pact summit in Moscow, the Soviet Union proposed improved centralized military command, increased defense expenditures by all member states, coordinated support for Vietnam against China, and opposition to Egyptian-Israeli peace treaty efforts. Romania rejected each of these Soviet demands, and subsequently made public the differences that had come up in Moscow. This provoked indirect but clear attacks on the Romanian position by other East European leaders and a strong—though still indirect—criticism from Brezhnev himself.

The 1978 dispute with Moscow was an opportunity to gain international attention and to dramatize Romania's unique position vis-à-vis the Soviet Union, something that was more difficult to do in the 1970s than in the 1960s. Romania called forth support from various quarters: the "Eurocommunist" parties sent high officials to Bucharest, a Romanian deputy prime minister stopped in Peking, and U.S. President Jimmy Carter sent his treasury secretary to Romania to reaffirm "the importance we attach to Romania's independence and to U.S.-Romanian friendship."[19]

For both sides the experience was another of the familiar limit-testing exercises, in which both countries recognized the boundaries to their actions. The USSR was not successful in bringing Romania into closer cohesion with the rest of Soviet Eastern Europe, but at the same time Romania did not expand the boundaries within which it operates, though it did reaffirm what had been gained in the past. Neither side was willing to compromise its basic position, but neither was willing to risk pushing the differences to an open confrontation.

Although the Soviet Union and Romania periodically go through rituals of confrontation, the limits on both sides have remained quite stable for more than a decade. And though the post-Brezhnev succession crisis in the Soviet Union may provide an opportunity for Romania to expand the limits of its foreign policy autonomy, it is unlikely, even at a time when Soviet leaders are preoccupied with their own internal relationships, that Romania will be permitted substantially greater latitude than it now enjoys. Furthermore, it is not probable that the RCP would opt to sever all links with the Soviet Union even if that became a viable alternative.

If other factors do not change, the Romanian-Soviet relationship will most likely continue in much the same fashion that it has over the last decade. In international politics, however, stability seems to be the exception rather than the rule; uncertainties may very well alter this relationship, and unfortunately, change is likely to be to the detriment of Romanian autonomy. A major factor will be the course of events in Yugoslavia after the death of Marshal Tito. If Yugoslavia continues its independent nonaligned foreign policy, Romania's course will be relatively secure, but the growth of internal instability and centrifugal tendencies among the Yugoslav nationalities may well induce the Soviets to impose greater conformity in Romania, as part of a broader effort to influence Yugoslavian developments. Changing of the guard in the Bulgarian party leadership could reintroduce the factionalism that has been the mark of that party so often in the past, and if this rock of Soviet Balkan influence becomes shaky, Moscow may well feel a greater need to reimpose discipline upon Romania. Events in Turkey, Greece, or the eastern Mediterranean could also enhance the value to Moscow of Romanian conformity.

Changes in Romania, too, could affect the course of its foreign policy. Although the drive for autonomy from the USSR was well underway before Ceausescu became party leader in 1965, and appears to have firm support in the party hierarchy as well as in the rank and file, Ceausescu has closely identified himself with that policy. It may not receive the same emphasis or priority under a successor, whatever the cause and circumstances for a replacement. In addition, Ceausescu has been extremely skillful in managing the relationship with the Soviet Union and in developing Romania's ties with the industrialized countries and the Third World. Whether any leader who might follow him would be as adept at managing that policy is open to question.

It would seem that the most hopeful prospect for Romania is continuing the present relationship with the Soviet Union in much the same terms as have stabilized over the last decade. This would involve periods of confrontation with Moscow (as the Soviet leaders seek to narrow, and the Romanian leaders attempt to maintain or possibly expand, the bounds for autonomy), alternating with periods of normalization and reconciliation. The nature of U.S.-Soviet relations, events elsewhere in the Balkans, and international circumstances will continue to play a key role in setting the stage for future interaction. Unfortunately, the most important of these factors affecting the evolving relationship of the two countries are beyond the control of Romania. This, however, has always been the fate of smaller powers.

Conclusion

The RCP began as an insignificant movement on the periphery of Romanian politics, dominated by the Soviet Union, and with a membership that included a large proportion of minorities. It was hostile to Romanian national goals and insensitive to indigenous conditions as it came to be manipulated by the Soviets to serve their own interests. The outlawing of the party within a few years of its founding further hampered any efforts that might have been made to expand its base of support or alter its relationship with the Comintern. During the first quarter-century of its existence the RCP had little popular following and little incentive or capacity to change that situation.

The party's rise to power was largely a consequence of the dominant Soviet role in Romania following the Second World War. With Moscow's support and under its direction the RCP quickly became the sole organized political force in the country. The party's most pressing task was to deal with its own internal problems, caused by the growth in membership from a few thousand to over 1 million between the end of 1944 and early 1948. A massive effort was required to establish organizational coherence and create a responsive, disciplined cadre of members, but by the mid-1950s this had been accomplished for the most part. The party elite also underwent a parallel process of institutionalization.

Once the party had dealt with its internal problems, it could consider its relationship with Romanian society. Through longevity, the elimination of viable alternatives, and political and economic success, the RCP has achieved a fair degree of acceptance, legitimacy, and authority. This in turn has reinforced the party's efforts to alter its relationship with the society. In an attempt to increase the sense of popular participation, a number of measures have been taken, including expansion of party membership to include one out of every five adults. Though to some extent the steps taken have been more perceptual than real, there have been potentially significant developments, such as multiple candidacies for the election of representatives to national and local legislative bodies.

In this context the RCP has gone much further than any other East

European party to align itself with local national sentiment, though this has cost it some degree of minority support. Foreign policy autonomy from the Soviet Union has been skillfully expanded over the last two decades, and this has won the RCP considerable international recognition as well as contributed to its popular support.

The RCP has evolved from a minor political movement serving external interests and having few indigenous roots to the dominant political institution in Romania, possessing a substantial measure of authority and a distinctive Romanian coloration. This evolution is unique among the East European communist states.

Notes

Introduction: History as Science, Myth, and Ideology

1. *Praxis* (Zagreb), No. 3–4 (May–August 1972), p. 375.

2. *Fundamentals of Marxism-Leninism: Manual,* 2d rev. ed. (Moscow: Foreign Languages Publishing House, 1963), pp. 145, 146.

3. A discussion of the functions of history in the Soviet context, which is relevant for Romania as well as other communist party-states, is found in Nancy Whittier Heer, *Politics and History in the Soviet Union* (Cambridge, Mass.: The MIT Press, 1971), pp. 13–33 and 261–76.

4. *Scinteia,* June 9, 1976. See also Ceausescu's speech to that conference in ibid., June 3, 1976, and Gh. I. Ionita, "Rolul educative al istoriei," *Era socialista,* No. 11 (June), 1976, pp. 29–30, 35.

5. Among the most interesting examples is the festering controversy between the Soviet Union and Romania over the ethnicity of the inhabitants and the territorial possession of Bessarabia. For a discussion of the use of history in debating this topic, see Robert R. King, "Verschaerfter Disput um Bessarabien: Zur Auseinandersetzung zwischen rumaenischen und sowjetischen Historikern," *Osteuropa* 26, no. 12 (December 1976): 1079–87 and A670–76; and Robert R. King, *Minorities Under Communism: Nationalities as a Source of Tension among Balkan Communist States* (Cambridge, Mass.: Harvard University Press, 1973), pp. 220–41. This latter work, pp. 170–219, also provides examples of other such debates in Eastern Europe.

6. *Scinteia,* December 24, 1955.

7. Institutul de istorie a partidului de pe linga C.C. al P.M.R., *Lectii in adutorul celor care studiaza Istoria P.M.R.* (Bucharest: Editura politica, 1960).

8. *Scinteia,* December 7 and 13, 1961.

9. Ibid., October 29, 1965.

10. Ceausescu's speech was published in *Scinteia,* March 29, 1975. The idea was echoed by Ion Mitran, "Dinamism si combativitate in activitatea ideologica," *Era socialista,* no. 8 (April), 1975, pp. 7–10, and Valter Roman in *Contemporanul,* no. 24, June 13, 1975.

11. *Scinteia,* June 3, 1976.

12. The principal source of such articles has been the official journal of party history, *Analele Institutului de istorie a partidului de pe linga C.C. al P.M.R.* (1955–1966); *Analele Institutului de studii istorice si social-politice de pe linga C.C. al P.C.R.* (1966–1968); and *Anale de istorie* (since 1969). Occasionally some of the more significant of the articles to appear in the party journal or elsewhere have subsequently been published separately or in a collected volume on a specific topic. Informal attempts at a more comprehensive approach to the party history have been used by instructors but not distributed generally. An example of this is Titu Georgescu, *Prelegeri de istorie a Partidului Comunist Roman* (Bucharest: Tipografia Universitatii, 1976) published in mimeographed typescript by the Faculty of Philosophy of the University of Bucharest.

13. Gh. I. Ionita, "Cercetarea istoriei contemporane a Romaniei in ultimul sfert veac," *Anale de istorie* 15, no. 6 (November–December 1969): 38–51; and Stefan Musat, "Consideratii privind dezvoltarea istoriografiei miscarii muncitoresti si a P.C.R. dupa 23 August 1944," ibid. 18, no. 3 (May–June 1972): 11–31.

14. For details on these document collections, see the bibliographical note at the end of this volume.

15. Ionita, "Cercetarea istoriei contemporane."

16. Musat, "Consideratii privind dezvoltarea istoriografiei."

17. *Documente din istoria miscarii muncitoresti din Romania: 1916–1921* (Bucharest: Editura politica, 1966).

1: The Legacy of the Interwar Period

1. A number of works in English deal with the politics of interwar Romania. The most comprehensive is Henry L. Roberts, *Rumania: Political Problems of an Agrarian State* (New Haven, Conn.: Yale University Press, 1951). Other useful accounts that deal with some or all of this period are Stephen Fischer-Galati, *Twentieth Century Rumania* (New York: Columbia University Press, 1970), pp. 7–69; R. W. Seton-Watson, *A History of the Roumanians* (Cambridge: Cambridge University Press, 1934); Hugh Seton-Watson, *Eastern Europe Between the Wars, 1918–1941* (New York: Harper and Row, 1967); David Mitrany, *The Land and the Peasant in Rumania: The War and Agrarian Reform (1917–1921)* (London: Oxford University Press, 1930); Sherman D. Spector, *Rumania at the Paris Peace Conference: A Study of the Diplomacy of Ioan I. C. Bratianu* (New York: Bookman Associates, 1962); Ghita Ionescu, *Communism in Rumania, 1944–1962* (London: Oxford University Press, 1964), pp. 28–86; *Politics and Political Parties in Roumania* (London: International Reference Library Publishing Company, 1936); and Andreas Hillgruber, *Hitler, Koenig Carol und Marschall Antonescu* (Wiesbaden: Franz Steiner Verlag, 1954).

2. For the party's current interpretation of the significance of the founding of the Social Democratic Party, see Nicolae Copoiu, "1893: clasa muncitoare din Romania isi faureste propriul partid politic," *Era socialista*, no. 5 (March), 1973, pp. 21–23; Damian Hurezeanu, "Afirmarea clasei muncitoare pa arena vietii social-politice," ibid., no. 7 (April), 1973, pp. 6–9; and Nicolae Ceausescu's

speech on the 80th anniversary of the party's founding, in *Scinteia,* March 31, 1973.

3. The Romanian Communist Party has published a collection of articles from these journals in *Presa muncitoreasca si socialista din Romania* (Bucharest: Editura politica, 1964–1966), under the auspices of the Institutul de studii istorice si social-politice de pe linga C.C. al P.M.R. [P.C.R. after 1965]. Vol. 1 (in two parts) deals with the 1865–1900 period; vol. 2 covers the years 1900–1907.

4. One of the more interesting of these individuals was Constantin Stere. For an assessment of his influence on the Romanian Social Democrats in this early period, see Michael Kitch, "Constantin Stere and Rumanian Populism," *The Slavonic and East European Review* 53, no. 131 (April 1975): 248–71.

5. For biographical information on Dobrogeanu-Gherea and recent favorable assessments of his ideas, see I. Vitner, "C. D. Gherea," *Viata romanesca,* nos. 11 and 12 (November and December 1956); "C. Dobrogeanu-Gherea," *Studii,* no. 3, 1957; Nora Z. Munteanu, "Pro Constantin Dobrogeanu-Gherea," *Anale de istorie* 16, no. 2 (March–April 1970): 80–92; Stefan Voicu, "Constantin Dobrogeanu-Gherea," ibid. 16, no. 3 (May–June 1970): 3–18; Augustin Deac, "Constantin Dobrogeanu-Gherea, personalitate marcanta a miscarii muncitoresti internationale," ibid. 21, no. 5 (September–October 1975): 89–100; Z. Ornea, "1907—miscarea socialista si problema agrara," *Era socialista,* no. 3 (February), 1977, pp. 18–24; Damian Hurezeanu, "Gindirea lui C. Dobrogeanu-Gherea in 'Neoiobagia,' " *Anale de istorie* 16, no. 2 (March–April 1970): 64–79; idem, "C. Dobrogeanu-Gherea, un eminent teoreticial al socialismului in Romania," *Era socialista,* no. 10 (May), 1975, pp. 42–45; and the introduction (also by Hurezeanu) to the recently published collection of Dobrogeanu-Gherea's works, *C. Dobrogeanu-Gherea: Scrieri social politice* (Bucharest: Editura politica, 1968), pp. 5–62. An excellent treatment in English of his ideas and influence is Michael Kitch, "Constantin Dobrogeanu-Gherea and Rumanian Marxism," *The Slavonic and East European Reivew* 55, no. 1 (January 1977): 65–89.

Because Rakovsky was purged as a Trotskyite there has been considerable reluctance to treat him in Romanian publications. The best biography is J. A. Rothschild, "Rakovsky," *St. Anthony's Papers on Soviet Affairs,* no. 18, St. Anthony's College, Oxford, February 1955. An interesting account of his pre-Soviet experience and his association with the Romanian socialist movement is to be found in Gheorghe Cristescu, "Amintiri despre dr. Cristian Racovski," *Anale de istorie* 18, no. 1 (January–February 1972): 145–54.

6. There are rather pronounced differences of opinion on this question. In December 1918, for example, the Romanian government harshly put down a workers' demonstration in the square in front of the National Theater. *Scinteia,* December 13, 1966, claimed the demonstration was a deliberately organized action in which the Socialist Party played an important role, and that it had been called to protest against the government ban on the socialist newspaper *Socialismul.* Constantin Titel Petrescu, on the other hand, claims that the action had no revolutionary intent; it had come about by accident, and the leaders of the socialist movement had not known of it in advance. See *Socialismul in Romania* (Bucharest: Biblioteca socialista, 1944), p. 318.

7. See V. Liveanu, *1918: din istoria luptelor revolutionare din Rominia* (Bucharest: Editura politica, 1960), pp. 126–28, 169–91, 253–83, and 399–422; Robert Deutsch, "Despre activitate unor grupe revolutionare romanesti pe teritoriul Rusiei Sovietice, 1918–1921," *Analele inst. de istorie* 3, no. 5 (September-October 1957): 177–92; and V. Cherestesiu and N. Copoiu, "Participarea oamenilor muncii din Romania la apararea si sprijinirea marii revolutii socialiste din octombrie," ibid. 13, no. 4 (July–August 1967): 71–84. An excellent treatment of this period in English is Keith Hitchings, "The Russian Revolution and the Rumanian Socialist Movement," *Slavic Review* 27, no. 2 (June 1968): 268–89. Hitchins has also written two very good articles on the Romanian socialists during the period before the RCP was founded: "Rumanian Socialists and the Nationality Problem in Hungary, 1903–1918," *Slavic Review* 35, no. 1 (March 1976): 69–90, and "The Rumanian Socialists and the Hungarian Soviet Republic," in Andrew C. Janos and William B. Slottman, eds., *Revolution in Perspective: Essays on the Hungarian Soviet Republic of 1919* (Berkeley and Los Angeles: University of California Press, 1971), pp. 109–44.

8. The program was published in the socialist newspaper *Socialismul,* May 27, 1919, and it resembled the Socialist Party's draft program of December 1918. The text of the latter is to be found in *Documente din istoria Partidului Comunist din Romania,* 4 vols. (Bucharest: Editura pentru literatura politica, 1953), 1 (1917–1922): 77–83. (Citations from this collection of documents are given hereafter as *Documente,* with volume and page number.) This May program was harshly criticized by Grigory Zinoviev, chairman of the Comintern's executive committee (see his letter to the Romanian Socialist party published in *Die Kommunistische Internationale,* no. 16 [1921]:455–64). An interesting account of these events written from the Comintern point of view is K. Arbori-Ralli, "Die sozialistische Bewegung in Rumaenien," ibid., nos. 7–8 (November–December 1919): 80–92.

9. Reports on the executive committee sessions at which the Romanian party was discussed were published in *Die Kommunistische Internationale,* no. 15 (1921): 408–9 and 416–17.

10. "An die Mitglieder der Sozialistischen Partei Rumaeniens, an alle klassenbewussten Arbeiter," ibid., no. 16 (1921): 455–64.

11. Petrescu, *Socialismul in Romania,* pp. 358–60.

12. *Documente din istoria miscarii muncitoresti din Romania, 1916–1921* (Bucharest: Editura politica, 1966), p. 724; Ceausescu's remarks were made in his speech on the 45th anniversary of the founding of the party, and were printed in *Scinteia,* May 8, 1966.

    The creation of the RCP is one of the most frequent themes in contemporary party history. Two volumes commemorating the 50th anniversary of the party's founding probably reflect the current approach most accurately: Ion Popescu-Puturi and Augustin Deac, eds., *Crearea Partidului Comunist Roman (May 1921)* (Bucharest: Editura stiintifica, 1971); and Clara Cusnir-Mihailovici, Florea Dragne, and Gheorghe Unc, *Miscarea muncitoreasca din Romania, 1916–1921. Crearea Partidului Comunist Roman* (Bucharest: Editura politica, 1971). An account of the proceedings of the congress is to be found in Augustin Deac and Florea Dragne, "Lucarile Congresului I al Partidului Comunist Roman," *Analele inst. de istorie* 12, nos. 2–3 (March–June 1966): 83–98. A full bibliography is contained in *Bibliografia istorica a Romaniei* (Bucharest: Editura Academiei Republicii Socialiste Romania, 1970 and 1975), vol. 1, pp. 218–19 and vol. 4, pp. 282–84.

13. For the Romanian estimates see Constantin C. Giurescu and Dinu C. Giurescu, *Istoria Romanilor* (Bucharest: Editura albatros, 1971), p. 621; and Miron Constantinescu et al., *Istoria Romaniei* (Bucharest: Editura didactica si pedagogica, 1969), p. 462. The Soviet estimate is given in *Voprosy istorii*, no. 11 (1957), p. 83, as cited by George D. Jackson, Jr., in *Comintern and Peasant in East Europe, 1919–1930* (New York: Columbia University Press, 1966), p. 83.

14. *Piaty vsemirnyi kongress Kommunisticheskogo Internatsionala (17 iunia–8 iulia 1924 goda): Stenograficheskii otchet* (Moscow, 1925), vol. 2, p. 298.

15. Ibid.

16. *International Press Correspondence* 15, no. 52 (October 10, 1935): 1310. This periodical is hereafter cited as *IPC*.

17. Ibid. 16, no. 50 (November 7, 1936): 1371, and Roberts, *Rumania,* p. 243.

18. *Documente* II, p. 189.

19. *The Communist International Between the Fifth and Sixth World Congresses, 1924–1928* (London: Communist Party of Great Britain, 1928), pp. 251–52.

20. *IPC* 6, no. 18 (March 10, 1926): 271; *Documente* II, pp. 444–60.

21. *IPC* 10, no. 43 (September 18, 1930): 914–16.

22. For more on this front organization see Florea Dragne, "Activitatea Blocului muncitoresc-taranesc, organizatie revolutionara de masa creata si condusa de Partidul Comunist din Rominia," *Analele inst. de istorie* 8, no. 1 (January–February 1962): 49–75. Party strength was augmented by the creation of this and other front organizations; see "Cu privire la organizatiile de masa create, conduse, sau indrumate de P.C.R.," ibid. 10, no. 6 (November–December 1964): 115–34, and Gh. I. Ionita, "Organizatiile democratice create, indrumate si influentate de P.C.R.," ibid. 15, no. 1 (January–February 1969): 31–52.

23. Data on communist success in these three elections are to be found in Al. Badulescu, "Gegen eine Welt von Feinden," *Die Kommunistische Internationale* 10, no. 2 (January 9, 1929): 53–62; see also *IPC* 9, no. 2 (January 10, 1928): 26–27.

24. For an analysis of the 1931 elections see "Der Sieg des Arbeiter- und Bauernblocks bei den Wahlen in Rumaenien," *Die Kommunistische Internationale* 12, no. 20 (May 23, 1931): 881–89. A report on the invalidation of the election of the five bloc candidates is to be found in *IPC* 11, no. 33 (January 25, 1931): 594.

25. *IPC* 12, no. 33 (July 28, 1932): 679–80.

26. Roberts, *Rumania,* pp. 67–69. For a discussion of some of the reasons for Romania's economic problems, see John R. Lampe, "Varieties of Unsuccessful Industrialization: The Balkan States before 1914," *The Journal of Economic History* 35, no. 1 (March 1975): 56–85.

27. The figures for 1919 and 1929 are from *Industrial and Labor Information* (Geneva: International Labor Organization), 33, no. 8 (February 24, 1930): 265, as cited in Roberts, *Rumania,* p. 248. N. Ciordiu and I. Lupescu, in "Oglinda insufletitoare a unei glorioase istorii de lupta," *Analele inst. de istorie* 12, nos. 2–3 (March–June 1966), p. 188, state that trade union membership increased from 41,000 in 1934 to 80,000 in 1938. The problems and limited success of the trade union movement before 1924 are discussed in N. Ghiulea, "Labor Organizations in Roumania," *International Labour Review* 9, no. 1 (January 1924): 31–49.

28. *Documente* II, pp. 121–22. For an account of the unitary trade union movement, see N. Petreanu, "Sindicatele unitare si rolul lor in lupta P.C.R. pentru apararea intereselor celor ce muncesc si refacerea unitatii miscarii sindicale (1932–1929)," *Analele inst. de istorie* 9, no. 3 (May–June 1963): 73–92.

29. *Documente* II, pp. 248–61.

30. Ibid., pp. 309–11.

31. Ibid., pp. 410–13 and 419–21.

32. *The Communist International, 1924–1928,* p. 252.

33. For accounts of this congress, see V. Hurmuz, "Despre Congresul Sindicatelor unitare de la Timisoara (2–5 aprilie 1929)," *Analele Universitatii Bucharest. Seria stiinte sociale. Istorie* 9, no. 16 (1960): 179–97, and N. G. Munteanu, "Congresul Sindicatelor unitare din 1929," *Analele inst. de istorie* 5, no. 3 (May–June 1959): 110–26. Luca's role in the congress was recognized and praised by party spokesmen before 1952, but after he was purged all references to his role were dropped and in some cases his activity among the workers was criticized. Luca's own account of the congress, in a speech marking its twentieth anniversary, is to be found in his *Ueber den Kongress der Einheitsgewerkschafter in Temesvar* (Bucharest: Verlag der Rumaenischen Arbeiterpartei, 1949).

34. *IPC* 10, no. 43 (September 18, 1930): 914–16.

35. In fact, with regard to the 1933 railwaymen's strike and associated labor unrest, one contemporary report by the Romanian party representative at a plenary session of the Comintern executive committee noted that *"for the first time* [emphasis supplied] the Romanian Communist Party succeeded in organizing tremendous struggles of the workers." See *IPC* 14, no. 15 (March 5, 1934): 385.

36. Bela Kun, "Ein Beispiel wurde statuiert," *Die Kommunistische Internationale* 11, no. 31 (August 20, 1930): 1706–07.

37. Petre Beschenaru, "Ein klassisches Muster 'linken' Sektiertums," ibid. 11, no. 35 (September 17, 1930): 1915–16.

38. The Grivita strike is one incident in the party's prewar history that has been written about extensively. See, for example, V. Hurmuz and N. Lupu, "Procesul conducatorilor luptelor ceferistilor si petrolistilor din ianuarie–februarie 1933," *Analele inst. de istorie* 5, no. 3 (May–June 1959): 5–28; A. Deac, "Solidaritatea internationala a cerlor ce muncesc cu conducatorii eroicelor lupte ale ceferistilor si petrolistilor," ibid. 5, no. 3 (May–June 1959): 29–48; P. Constantinescu-Iasi, "Insemnatatea istorica a eroicelor lupte ale muncitorilor ceferisti si petrolisti din ianuarie–februarie 1933," *Studii* 16, no. 1 (1963): 19–44; A. Deac

and Gh. Matei, "Miscarea de solidaritate internationala cu luptele eroice ale ceferistilor si petrolistilor din 1933," *Analele inst. de istorie* 9, no. 1 (January–February 1963): 35–50; and Gheorghe Stoica, "Luptele din februarie 1933," in *Din istoria contemporana a Rominiei* (Bucharest: Editura stiintifica, 1965), pp. 13–39.

39. For data on Romania's peasant population see Jackson, *Comintern and Peasant*, pp. 7, 9, 12, and 237–40. The peasant problem is also discussed extensively in Roberts, *Rumania*; Mitrany, *The Land and the Peasant in Rumania*; and Philip Gabriel Eidelberg, *The Great Rumanian Peasant Revolt of 1907* (Leiden: E. J. Brill, 1974).

40. The first edition was published in Bucharest in 1910, the second by the Bucharest firm of Viata romaneasca, n.d.

41. In a speech on the 30th anniversary of the founding of the party in 1951, Gheorghe Gheorghiu-Dej said: "The [fifth] congress rejected the bourgeois-liberal theories of *Neoiobagia* as well as sectarian theses of the left." See his *Artikel und Reden: Auswahl aus den Jahren 1945–1952* (Berlin: Dietz Verlag, 1955), pp. 296–97, 308. Regarding the recent rehabilitation of Dobrogeanu-Gherea's theoretical ideas, see note 5 above.

42. Roberts, *Rumania*, p. 274–83, discusses the influence of Dobrogeanu-Gherea's thinking on the Social Democrats, and Jackson, *Comintern and Peasant*, pp. 247–65, considers its influence on the communist party.

43. *Documente din istoria miscarii muncitoresti*, pp. 656–69 and 669–75.

44. *Fourth Congress of the Communist International: Abridged Report of Meeting Held at Petrograd and Moscow, Nov 7–Dec. 3, 1922* (London: Communist Party of Great Britain, 1923), p. 199.

45. *Piaty vsemirnyi kongress Komunisticheskogo Internatsionala*, vol. 1, pp. 774–77.

46. See Jackson, *Comintern and Peasant*, pp. 252–54.

47. A. Martinov, "Problema revoliutsii v Rumynii," *Kommunisticheskii Internatsional*, no. 4 (April 1926), p. 65. This dispute is summarized in Jackson, *Comintern and Peasant*, pp. 255–56.

48. Ordon, "Bemerkungen ueber die Bauernbewegung in Europa," *Die Kommunistische Internationale* 8, no. 6 (February 8, 1927): 273–74. The Romanian party still admits the lack of success of its activity among the peasantry before 1928. See M. C. Stanescu, "Din activitatea P.C.R. privind problema taraneasca in anii 1922–1928," *Analele inst. de istorie* 11, no. 6 (November–December 1965): 150–64.

49. On these developments, see Roberts, *Rumania*, pp. 106–8 and 130–32.

50. Solomon Timov represented the right-wing faction within the RCP, and A. Mikhailov was his principal antagonist. The controversy was published in a number of journals over a period of some six months. For a detailed account of it and references to the journals in which it was published, see Jackson, *Comintern and Peasant*, pp. 257–63.

51. See the resolution adopted by the congress in *Documente din istoria Partidul Comunist din Romania, 1917–1944* (Bucharest: Editura pentru literatura politica,

1951), pp. 129–30, and Horn, "Ueber den 5. Parteitag der K. P. Rumaeniens," *Die Kommunistische Internationale* 13, no. 7 (April 10, 1932): 551–65.

52. Eugen Weber, "The Men of the Archangel," *Journal of Contemporary History* 1, no. 1 (1966): 105–22.

53. Ibid., p. 118.

54. Eugen Weber has written several excellent studies on Romanian fascism. In addition to "Men of the Archangel," cited above in note 52, see the chapter "Romania" in Hans Rogger and Eugen Weber, eds., *The European Right* (Berkeley and Los Angeles: University of California Press, 1966), and his *Varieties of Fascism* (Princeton, N. J.: Princeton University Press, 1964). Other studies include Nicholas M. Nagy-Talavera, *The Green Shirts and Others: A History of Fascism in Hungary and Rumania* (Stanford, California: Hoover Institution Press, 1970); Emanuel Turczynski, "The Background of Romanian Fascism," and Stephen Fischer-Galati, "Fascism in Romania," in Peter F. Sugar, ed., *Native Fascism in the Successor States, 1918–1945* (Santa Barbara, California: ABC-Clio, 1971), pp. 99–121.

55. Postwar Romanian historians and party officials have produced a large number of articles dealing with the antifascist struggle. Among the more interesting are the following: Ion Babici, *Solidaritate militanta antifascista, 1933–1939* (Bucharest: Editura politica, 1972); Petre Constantinescu-Iasi, "Professorii si miscarea antifascista din Romania," *Studii si articole de istorie,* no. 3 (1966), pp. 7–15; Gh. I. Ionita, *P.C.R. si masele populare (1934–1938)* (Bucharest: Editura stiintifica, 1971); Gh. I. Ionita, *Pentru front popular antifascist in Romania* (Bucharest: Editura politica, 1971); "Lupta P.C.R. impotriva fascizarii tarii, pentru crearea Frontului popular antifascist," *Analele inst. de istorie* 2, no. 5 (September–October 1956): 45–90; Olimpiu Matichescu, "40 de ani de la realizarea acordului antifascist de front popular de la Tebea," *Era socialista,* no. 23 (December), 1975, pp. 40–43; I. M. Oprea, "Masele muncitoare, forta principala in lupta impotriva fascismului in perioda 1934–1938," *Studii revista de istorie* 17, no. 4 (April 1964): 725–48; Stefan Voicu, "Pagini de lupta a Partidului Comunist Roman impotriva fascismului, pentru independenta si suveranitate nationala," *Lupta de clasa* 46, no. 6 (June 1966): 59–80; and a collective volume published by the party's historical institute, *Din lupta antifascista pentru independenta si suveranitatea Romaniei* (Bucharest: Editura militara, 1969).

56. Particularly since 1965 Romanian communist historians have attempted to reverse the tables on the Iron Guard by claiming that the RCP consistently supported Romanian national ideals while the Iron Guard was foreign and contrary to Romanian interests. The Guard is portrayed as "an instrument, a direct agency, of the Hitlerite policy in Romania," which "stood on a single fascist, pro-Hitlerite platform." The fascist movement was "a foreign body in the Romanian nation's moral-political structure," and was "flagrantly opposed and treasonous to the basic interests of the Romanian nation." For some of these themes, see the summary of a scholarly conference on Romanian fascism in *Scinteia,* March 17, 1971. See also Stefan Musat, "Coloana a V-a hitlerista in Romania," *Anale de istorie* 16, no. 6 (November–December 1970): 128–44, and

Mihai Fatu and Ion Spalatelu, *Garda de fier—organizatie terrorista de tip fascist* (Bucharest: Editura politica, 1971). The classical Marxian analysis of the Iron Guard is to be found in Lucretiu Patrascanu, *Sub trei dictaturi* (Bucharest: Editura politica, 1970), originally published in 1944.

57. The data on the ethnic composition of the Romanian population according to the results of the 1930 census are to be found in *Anuarul Statistic al Romaniei, 1937–1938* (Bucharest: Institutul Centrala de Statistica, 1939), pp. 58–63.

58. Louis Fischer, *Men and Politics: An Autobiography* (London: Jonathan Cape, 1941), pp. 130–32. Rakovsky's position on Bessarabia, about which he wrote on several occasions, is interestingly inconsistent. Prior to the Russian revolution he was a supporter of Romania's claim to Bessarabia (see his *Russie en Orient* [Varna, 1898] and his article in *Romania muncitoare,* February 3, 1913), but afterward he became an equally vigorous partisan of the Russian claim (see his *Roumanie et Bessarabie* [Paris: Librairie du Travail, 1925]).

59. At the time of the negotiations with Romania a number of articles appeared asserting the Soviet claim. See *IPC* 4, no. 21 (March 20, 1924): 183; ibid., 4, no. 23 (April 3, 1924): 207; and ibid. 4, no. 25 (April 17, 1924): 233.

60. *Piaty vsemirnyi kongress Kommunisticheskogo Internatsionala,* I, p. 598.

61. *Documente din istoria miscarii muncitoresti,* pp. 678–79.

62. The theses are to be found in *Die Kommunistische Internationale,* no. 13 (1920), pp. 127–35; the Zinoviev letter to the Balkan parties is also in ibid., no. 9 (1920), pp. 181–87.

63. This paragraph is based on an article by Sandor Korosi-Krizsan published in *Uj Latohatar* (Munich), July–August 1966. A somewhat briefer account is to be found in *East Europe* 15, no. 12 (December 1966): 13–15.

64. *Documente,* II, p. 257.

65. Ibid., p. 258.

66. *Piaty vsemirnyi kongress Kommunisticheskogo Internatsionala,* I, pp. 589–603, and II, pp. 123–31.

67. See "Die Beschlusse der VI Konferenz der Kommunistischen Balkan-Foderation," *Die Kommunistische Internationale* 5, no. 34–35 (1924), pp. 57–64. The section of this resolution devoted to the Romanian national question is essentially a repetition of the third RCP congress resolution on the topic. Another statement of the Comintern views on the national question in the Balkan states is contained in an article by Vasil Kolarov, "Die nationale Frage auf dem Balkan," ibid., pp. 53–57.

68. *Documente,* II, pp. 567, 592–95.

69. *Documente din istoria PCR, 1917–1944,* pp. 130–32.

70. *Socialismul,* June 7, 1931, as quoted in "Der Sieg des Arbeiter- und Bauernblocks bei den Wahlen in Rumaenien," *Die Kommunistische Internationale* 12, no. 20 (May 23, 1931): 336. *Socialismul* was the Socialist Party's organ. The date seems inconsistent, but it is as given in the original.

71. Ibid., p. 337.

72. R. V. Burks, *The Dynamics of Communism in Eastern Europe* (Princeton, N. J.: Princeton University Press, 1961), p. 163.

73. Jewish efforts to deal with this problem of identity frequently led to conflicting solutions within the same family. Ana Pauker, for example, became a committed communist while her brother became a Zionist and emigrated to Israel where he was an inspector in the Ministry of Education. See the interesting article about her in the *Jerusalem Post Magazine,* December 26, 1975.

74. Burks, *The Dynamics of Communism,* pp. 150–58, considers the Hungarians, as well as the Jews, to be "rejected people." But as Andrew Janos has observed, the Hungarians have a clear-cut national identity; they have not sought to escape ethnic identity but for the most part have deliberately opposed assimilation. Irredentism was a far more important factor in their adherence to the party. "Ethnicity, Communism, and Political Change in Eastern Europe," *World Politics* 23, no. 3 (April 1971): 498–99.

75. Nissan Oren, *Bulgarian Communism: The Road to Power* (New York and London: Columbia University Press, 1971), p. 139.

76. Charles Upson Clark, *Bessarabia: Russia and Roumania on the Black Sea* (New York: Dodd, Mead and Company, 1927), pp. 264–68, claims, on the basis of information supplied by the Romanian government, that the unsuccessful putsch by a communist group to seize the Bessarabian town of Tatar-Bunar was directed not by the RCP but by the Soviet party in Odessa.

77. On the Romanian and Bulgarian parties' relations over Dobruja, see Oren, *Bulgarian Communism,* pp. 138–43.

78. *Documente din istoria PCR, 1917–1944,* pp. 327–32.

79. Ionescu, *Communism in Rumania,* p. 60. Exactly when the shift in policy took place is not clear. Roberts (*Rumania,* p. 258) claims that in December 1939 Boris Stefanov "wrote an article in *The Communist International*" attacking the British and French for attempting to drag Romania into the imperialist war and instructing Romanian communists to work for the right of self-determination in the provinces of Bessarabia, Bukovina, Transylvania, and the Dobruja. Roberts does not, however, give a citation for this article. The English- and German-language versions of *The Communist International* did not publish any article by Stefanov in 1939 or 1940. The Russian-language version did have an article by him in 1939, but it appeared in the April, not the December, issue. A passing comment on the minority question merely noted that progressive forces should struggle for "equality of all Romanian nationalities with the Romanian people." B. Stefanov, "Polozhenie v Ruminii i zadachi kompartii," *Kommunisticheskii Internatsional,* no. 4 (April 1939), pp. 90–95. If Stefanov did indeed write the article suggested by Roberts, it would indicate that the change in national policy did not take place until after the Soviet annexation of Bessarabia.

80. *Documente din istoria P.C.R., 1917–1944,* pp. 338, 346–47.

2: The Path to Power

1. Chalmers Johnson, "Comparing Communist Nations," in Chalmers Johnson, ed., *Change in Communist Systems* (Stanford, California: Stanford University Press, 1970), pp. 31–32.

2. Robert Tucker includes it in his category of "imposed revolutions"; R. V. Burks called it a "baggage-train government" (i.e., one that was brought in along with the baggage of the Red Army); and Cyril Black calls it a "revolution from without." See Robert C. Tucker, "Paths of Communist Revolution, 1917–67," in Kurt London, ed., *The Soviet Union—A Half Century of Communism* (Baltimore: The Johns Hopkins Press, 1968), p. 29; Cyril E. Black, "The Anticipation of Communist Revolutions," in Cyril E. Black and Thomas P. Thornton, eds., *Communism and Revolution: The Strategic Uses of Political Violence* (Princeton, N. J.: Princeton University Press, 1964), pp. 417–18; and R. V. Burks, "Eastern Europe," ibid., pp. 88–89.

3. See Ion Vinte, "Partidul Comunist din Rominia in fruntea luptei pentru rasturnarea dictaturii fasciste," *Scinteia,* July 31, 1964; Dumitru Damaceanu, "Pregatirea militara a insurectiei armate sub conducerea Partidului Comunist din Rominia," ibid., August 9, 1964; Mihail Rosianu, "Cum a fost organizata evadarea tovarasului Gheorghe Gheorghiu-Dej din lagarul de la Tg. Jiu in august 1944," ibid., August 18, 1964; Vl. Zaharescu, "Intarirea partidului si a legaturilor lui cu masele," *Analele inst. de istorie* 8, no. 4 (July–August 1962): 3–19; "August 1944–Memorii," ibid. 13, no. 4 (July–August 1967): 85–97; "Insurectia armata din August 1944," *Lupta de clasa,* no. 8 (August 1964).

4. Gheorghe Zaharia, "Partidul Comunist Roman—forta conducatoare a insurectiei din august 1944," *Anale de istorie* 15, no. 4 (July–August 1969): 35–48, esp. p. 42.

5. *Scinteia,* May 9, 1961.

6. Gheorghe Gheorghiu-Dej, "Fuenf Jahre seit der Befreiung Rumaeniens," in his *Aufsaetze und Reden* (Bucharest: Editura politica, 1952), 3d edition, p. 337; *Scinteia,* August 23, 1955 and August 23, 1961.

7. "Victoria insurectiei populare de la 23 august 1944 . . . ," *Analele inst. de istorie* 2, no. 1 (November–December 1956): 68.

8. Emilian Ionescu, "Momente din timpul doboririi dictaturii militare-fasciste," ibid. 11, no. 6 (November–December 1965): 30–37.

9. Trian Udrea, "Insurectia nationala antifascista—factor hotaritor in schimbarea raportului de forte in viata politica a Romaniei," *Revista de istorie* 27, no. 8 (August 1974): 113–44, contains extensive bibliographical footnotes and is a useful guide to contemporary Romanian historical writing on the coup.

10. Among the Western accounts of the coup are those to be found in Arthur Gould Lee, *Crown Against Sickle* (London: Hutchinson and Company, 1950), in part based on materials supplied by Queen Helen, mother of King Michael; Reuben H. Markham, *Rumania Under the Soviet Yoke* (Boston: Meador Publish-

ing Company, 1949); Robert Bishop and E. S. Crayfield, *Russia Astride the Balkans* (New York: Robert M. McBride and Company, 1948); and Andreas Hillgruber, *Hitler, Koenig Carol und Marschall Antonescu: Die Deutsch-Rumaenischen Beziehungen, 1938–1944* (Wiesbaden: Franz Steiner Verlag, 1954).

Speech by Valter Roman at the November 30–December 5, 1961 CC plenum, published in *Scinteia,* December 12, 1961.

12. See Vinte, "PCR in fruntea luptei," as well as speeches delivered during the November 30–December 5, 1961 CC plenum and reported in *Scinteia,* December 10–19, 1961. The charges against Foris appear to be justification for his replacement by Gheorghiu-Dej, rather than detailed indictments. There had in fact been some good results during his term in office (see Ghita Ionescu, *Communism in Rumania, 1944–1962* [London: Oxford University Press, 1964], pp. 79–81), and after Gheorghiu-Dej's death he and a number of other purged party members were rehabilitated at a CC plenum in April 1968 (the relevant CC resolution was published in *Scinteia,* April 26, 1968). For further information about Foris, see N. I. Florea, "Stefan Foris," *Anale de istorie* 18, no. 3 (May–June 1972): 150–53.

13. Their success was meager, but there was some partisan activity in Moldavia in 1944 near areas held by Soviet troops and in the Carpathian Mountains. Patriotic struggle units were set up in that year and played some role after August 23. See Mihai Roller, "Despre actiunea grupului de partizani 'Carpati' in lunile iunie-august 1944," *Analele inst. de istorie* 3, no. 3 (May–June 1957): 123–30; Ion Popescu-Puturi, "Partidul Comunist Roman, organizatorul si conducatorul miscarii de rezistenta pentru eliberarea patriei de sub jungul fascist," *Studii revista de istorie* 12, no. 4 (April 1969): 617–31; and Dumitru Simulescu, "Formatiunile de lupta patriotice in insurectia populara antifascista," *Scinteia,* August 12, 1964. Bibliographies of Romanian writings on resistance are to be found in Valter Roman, et al., "Cercetarea istoriei miscarii de rezistenta antifascista din Romania," *Analele inst. de istorie* 11, no. 2 (March–April 1965): 23–38; Aurica Simion, "Contributii la istoriografia romaneasca privind perioada 1940–1944 din istoria patriei," *Anale de istorie* 20, no. 1 (January–February 1974): 17–36; and Maria Sanciuc and Maria Ion, "Rezistenta si insurectia nationala antifascista din Romania: Bibliografie istorica selective (1964–1974)," ibid. 20, no. 3 (May–June 1974): 156–63.

14. Fischer-Galati argues that a detailed operation had been mapped out, which was to result in the "outright assumption of political power in Rumania" through "the instrumentality of the communist contingent comprising the so-called Tudor Vladimirescu Brigade." He claims that "the plan also contemplated the 'liquidation' of the Rumanian communists incarcerated by the Antonescu regime, so as to prevent the formation of any coalition government prior to the arrival of the Red Army and of the 'Moscow' communists headed by Ana Pauker, Vasile Luca, and other Rumanian expatriots." "The Communist Takeover of Rumania: A Function of Soviet Power," in Thomas T. Hammond, ed., *The Anatomy of Communist Takeovers* (New Haven: Yale University Press, 1975), p. 310. The evidence Fischer-Galati cites (Ionescu, *Communism in*

Rumania, pp. 79–81 and his own *The New Rumania* [Cambridge, Mass.: MIT Press, 1967], pp. 16–25), however, fails to confirm this claim, particularly the plans for the liquidation of the party leadership within Romania. In view of the USSR's failure to act during the Warsaw Uprising, one can argue that if similar resistance had been offered in Romania the USSR's response would also have been similar, but it is difficult to go further than that on the basis of available evidence. The Soviets' approach to the postwar role of the communist party in Germany seems to have been quite flexible; while various alternatives were considered and certain preparations were made, there was a considerable amount of adapting to changing circumstances (see Wolfgang Leonhard, *Die Revolution entlaesst ihre Kinder* [Cologne: Kiepenheuer und Witsch, 1955]). There is no evidence that there was a "linear plan" for the takeover in Romania that "would have been simple and direct and probably would have served as a prototype for seizures of power in other countries about to be liberated by the Soviet Union." Fischer-Galati, "The Communist Takeover," pp. 310–11.

15. See Frederic C. Nano, "The First Soviet Double-Cross: A Chapter in the Secret History of World War II," *Journal of Central European Affairs* 12, no. 3 (1952): 236–58; and Alexander Cretzianu, *The Lost Opportunity* (London: Jonathan Cape, 1957).

16. Fischer-Galati, *The New Rumania,* pp. 17–43 provides a useful analysis of how Gheorghiu-Dej successfully used this asset to establish his leading position in the party and to isolate and remove various opponents or competitors, including Patrascanu, Pauker, and Luca.

17. *Scinteia,* December 7, 1961.

18. Ibid., December 10, 1961.

19. Ambassador Harriman to the Secretary of State, September 15, 1944, *Foreign Relations of the United States, 1944,* vol 4 (Washington: U.S. Government Printing Office, 1966), pp. 234–35.

20. On U.S. policy toward Romania in this period, see Gabriel Kolko, *The Politics of War: The World and United States Foreign Policy, 1943–1945* (New York: Random House, 1968), pp. 128–31, 156–58, 404–6, 579–81; Lynn Etheridge Davis, *The Cold War Begins: Soviet-American Conflict over Eastern Europe* (Princeton, N. J.: Princeton University Press, 1974), especially pp. 255–66 and 273–87; Geir Lundestad, *The American Non-policy Towards Eastern Europe, 1943–1947* (Tromso-Oslo-Bergen: Universitetsforlaget; and New York: Humanities Press, 1975), especially pp. 225–56; and *Foreign Relations of the United States, 1944,* vol. 4; *1945,* vol. 5; and *1946,* vol. 6.

21. *The East European Revolution,* 3d Edition (New York: Praeger, 1956), pp. 167–71.

22. More detailed accounts of the RCP's rise to power are found in ibid., pp. 202–11; Ionescu, *Communism in Rumania;* Alexandre Cretzianu, ed., *Captive Rumania* (New York: Praeger, 1956); Stephen Fischer-Galati, ed., *Romania* (New York: Praeger, 1957), and his *The New Rumania;* E. D. Tappe, "Roumania," in R. R. Betts, ed., *Central and South East Europe, 1945–1948* (London: Royal Institute of

International Affairs, 1950); Elizabeth Barker, *Truce in the Balkans* (London: Percival Marshall, 1948); and the works cited in note 10 above.

23. In the Second Vienna Award of August 1940 the German and Italian governments decreed that the northern half of Transylvania should be ceded to Hungary. The Romanian armistice agreement, however, stipulated that "Transylvania (or the greater part thereof) should be returned to Rumania." See Robert R. King, *Minorities Under Communism: Nationalities as a Source of Tension Among Balkan Communist States* (Cambridge, Mass.: Harvard University Press, 1973), pp. 35–44.

24. For more background on this change in policy and the reasons for it, see Zbigniew K. Brzezinski, *The Soviet Bloc: Unity and Conflict* (Cambridge, Mass.: Harvard University Press, 1967), pp. 41–83.

25. For an excellent account of the RCP's approach to the writers during this period, see Anneli Ute Gabanyi, *Partei und Literatur in Rumaenien seit 1945* (Munich: R. Oldenbourg Verlag, 1975), pp. 11–39.

26. Kenneth Jowitt has convincingly argued this point in his *Revolutionary Breakthroughs and National Development: The Case of Romania, 1944–1965* (Berkeley and Los Angeles: University of California Press, 1971); see especially pp. 114–30.

27. Fischer-Galati, "The Communist Takeover," pp. 310, 320.

28. *The New Rumania,* pp. vii, 20–21.

29. Jowitt, *Revolutionary Breakthroughs,* pp. 198–228; see also J. F. Brown, "Rumania Steps Outs of Line," *Survey* 49 (October 1963): 19–35, and "Eastern Europe," ibid. 54 (January 1965): 65–89.

3: Institutional Transformation

1. Nelson W. Polsby, "The Institutionalization of the U.S. House of Representatives," *American Political Science Review* 62, no. 1 (March 1968): 144. The argument for the importance of institutionalization is perhaps best presented by Samuel P. Huntington, "Political Development and Political Decay," *World Politics* 17, no. 3 (April 1965): 386–430, and idem, *Political Order in Changing Societies* (New Haven: Yale University Press, 1968), pp. 12–24.

2. On this aspect of institutionalization, see Polsby, "Institutionalization of the U.S. House," and E. Spencer Wellhofer, "Dimensions of Party Development: A Study in Organizational Dynamics," *The Journal of Politics* 34, no. 1 (February 1972): 153–82.

3. Philip Selznick, *The Organizational Weapon: A Study of Bolshevik Strategy and Tactics* (New York: McGraw-Hill, 1952), pp. 17–73.

4. Wolfgang Leonhard, *Die Revolution entlaesst ihre Kinder* (Cologne: Kiepenheir und Witsch, 1955) provides an interesting autobiographical account that illustrates the importance of ideology in boundary establishment.

5. Gheorghe Gheorghiu-Dej, "Fuer die Reinheit der Partei," *Fuer dauerhaften Frieden, fuer Voksdemokratie,* June 23, 1950, in *Artikel und Reden* (Berlin: Dietz Verlag, 1955), pp. 260–61.

6. See Huntington, "Political Development and Political Decay," pp. 399–401; Polsby, "Institutionalization of the U.S. House," and Wellhofer, "Dimensions of Party Development."

7. This aspect is discussed in Huntington, "Political Development and Political Decay," pp. 403–5. For an excellent analysis of the problem of coherence-disunity in the Romanian party, see Kenneth Jowitt, *Revolutionary Breakthroughs and National Development: The Case of Romania, 1944–1965* (Berkeley and Los Angeles: University of California Press, 1971), pp. 131–49.

8. "Political Development and Political Decay," p. 403.

9. Ibid. On this point see Jowitt, *Revolutionary Breakthroughs,* p. 132 ff.

10. The spelling was *Scanteia* until April 1954 when orthographic changes were made in the Romanian language. Since that time it has been spelled *Scinteia.* For the sake of convenience and to avoid confusion, the current spelling is used throughout this study.

11. Office of Strategic Services, Research and Analysis Branch, "Current Party Politics in Rumania," R & A No. 2727, December 6, 1944, p. 15.

12. Two articles are particularly informative with regard to this early period of party development, although they present a rather idealized picture: Gheorghe Tutui, "Dezvoltarea Partidului Comunist Roman in anii 1944–1948," *Anale de istorie* 16, no. 6 (November–December 1970): 3–15; and by the same author, "Partidul Comunist Roman [PCR] in primul an dupa victorie insurectiei nationale antifasciste armate din august 1944," ibid. 19, no. 4 (July–August 1973): 33–47. Unless another source is cited, the statistical data on party membership and organization in this section are from these two articles.

13. On the reforms see Henry L. Roberts, *Rumania: Political Problems of an Agrarian State* (New Haven: Yale University Press, 1951), pp. 292–99.

14. The speakers who dealt particularly with these issues at the plenum were Gheorghe Gheorghiu-Dej, Nicolae Ceausescu, Alexandru Draghici, and Dumitriu Coliu. See *Scinteia,* December 7, 13, and 19, 1961.

15. *Artikel und Reden,* pp. 255–62.

16. The initial charges against Luca, Pauker, and Georgescu were made in a letter from the CC published in *Scinteia,* June 3, 1952. CC Secretary Alexandru Moghioros also reviewed the charges in an article for the Cominform journal, *For a Lasting Peace, for a People's Democracy* 23, no. 187 (June 6, 1952). See also *Documents Concerning Right Deviation in Rumanian Workers' Party* (Bucharest: Romanian Workers' Party Publishing House, 1952) and *Rezolutii si hotariri ale CC al PMR,* vol. 2, 1951–1953 (Bucharest: Editura pentru literatura politica, 1954), pp. 188–208. Pauker's role in recruitment in the early period was not mentioned at all in these criticisms. In a major speech at the end of June 1952, Gheorghiu-Dej reviewed the failings of Pauker, Luca, and Georgescu (*Scinteia,* June 29, 1952), but again no mention was made of Pauker's connection with recruitment. The first (and incidental) mention of her culpability in this regard seems to have appeared in an editorial in *Scinteia,* December 14, 1952. She was again criticized by Gheorghiu-Dej at the second RWP congress in 1955, but the detailed criticisms were not voiced until 1961.

17. Petru Russindilar, "Insemnatatea alegerilor sindicale din 1946 in cadrul luptei pentru consolidarea Frontului Unic Muncitoresc," *Anale de istorie* 18, no. 6 (November–December 1972): 108–16; see also Gh. Tutui, "Alegerile sindicale din anul 1946—moment important in lupta pentru unitatea deplina a clasei muncitoare," *Analele inst. de istorie* 9, no. 3 (May–June 1963): 59–72.

18. Tutui, "PCR in primul an," pp. 40–42.

19. Roberts, *Rumania,* p. 261; OSS, R & A Branch, "Current Party Politics in Rumania," p. 7.

20. Tutui, "PCR in primul an," p. 46.

21. "Partidul Comunist Roman—conducatorul revolutiei democrat-populare (1944–1947)," *Anale de istorie* 18, no. 2 (March–April 1972): 112.

22. Gh. Tutui and V. G. Ionescu, "Faurirea Partidului Muncitoresc Romin, victorie deplina si definitiva a leninismului in miscarea muncitoreasca din Rominia," *Analele inst. de istorie* 9, no. 1 (January–February 1963): 65.

23. On this conference and its significance see Constantin Barbulescu, "Conferinta Nationala a P.C.R. din octombrie 1945—eveniment important in dezvoltarea partidului si a tarii," *Anale de istorie* 16, no. 5 (September–October 1970): 80–92, and Gheorghe Surpat, "Transformarile revolutionare de dupa 23 august 1944, in lumina documentelor Conferintei Nationale a P.C.R. din octombrie 1945," ibid. 21, no. 5 (September–October 1975): 13–24.

24. Gheorghiu-Dej's comments on organizational matters on this occasion are to be found in *Artikel und Reden,* pp. 34–36 and 79–81, and in *Scinteia,* October 31, and November 1, 2, and 3, 1945.

25. These national problems were at least partially attributable to the RCP's interwar policies in regard to the national question. As noted in chapter 1, the party advocated self-determination, including the right of secession, for minority populations during most of that period. That this was primarily a tactic to weaken the bourgeois Romanian state, as Soviet Comintern officials stated when the policy was forced upon the RCP in 1923, was confirmed by the policy followed after the RCP gained power. There seem to have been some initial attempts by Hungarian communists and leftists to establish some kind of autonomy in Transylvania, but they were quickly reintegrated into Romania. *Foreign Relations of the United States, 1945,* vol. 5 (Washington, D.C.: U.S. Government Printing Office, 1968), p. 471. For some comments on this problem see R. V. Burks, *The Dynamics of Communism in Eastern Europe* (Princeton, N. J.: Princeton University Press, 1961), pp. 155–57.

26. See Zina Brincu, "Zece ani de la infiintarea scolii superioare de partid 'Stefan Gheorghiu,' " *Analele inst. de istorie* 2, no. 1 (January–February 1956): 20–28; "P.C.R.—conducatorul luptei maselor populare pentru consolidarea si dezvoltarea regimului democrat popular (6 martie 1945–30 decembrie 1947)," ibid. 3, no. 1 (January–February 1957): 97–102; and Tutui, "Dezvoltarea PCR, 1944–1948," pp. 10–15.

27. See C. Olteanu, "Masurile politice si organizatorice stabilite de plenara C.C. al P.C.R. din ianuarie 1947 si insemnatatea lor pentru imbunatatirea muncii de

partid si intarirea legaturilor lui cu masele," ibid. 9, no. 5 (September–October 1963): 29–42.

28. The German Communist Party carried out the merger in the Soviet occupation zone in the spring of 1946 for reasons related to the specific conditions there. In the remainder of Eastern Europe, the communist-socialist mergers all came in 1948, after the founding of the Cominform. Zbigniew K. Brzezinski, *The Soviet Bloc: Unity and Conflict,* rev. ed. (Cambridge, Mass.: Harvard University Press, 1967), pp. 84–85.

29. On the founding of the RWP, see Tutui and Ionescu, "Faurirea PMR"; C. Barbulescu, "Partidul unic muncitoresc—expresie a desavirsirii unitatii politice, ideologice, si organizatorice a clasei muncitoare din Romania," *Anale inst. de istorie* 14, no. 1 (January–February 1968): 16–26; and L. Tismaneanu, "Zece ani de la Congresul I al Partidului Muncitoresc Romin," ibid. 4, no. 1 (January–February 1958): 55–72.

30. *Rezolutii si hotariri ale CC al PMR* (Bucharest: Editura pentru literatura politica, 1952), vol. 1 (1948–1950), pp. 5–10; Gheorghiu-Dej, *Artikel und Reden,* pp. 126–34.

31. *Scinteia,* October 10, 1947.

32. Ibid., October 8, 1947, and December 13, 1961.

33. Gheorghiu-Dej, *Artikel und Reden,* pp. 127–28.

34. *Congresul al II-lea al Partidului Muncitoresc Romin* (Bucharest: Editura de stat pentru literatura politica, 1956), pp. 128–29.

35. Report of the Credentials Commission, ibid., p. 327.

36. Gheorghiu-Dej, *Artikel und Reden,* p. 131.

37. *Rezolutii si hotariri,* I, pp. 239–52.

38. Ghita Ionescu, *Communism in Rumania, 1944–1962* (London: Oxford University Press, 1964), pp. 204–5.

39. *Scinteia,* December 13, 1961.

40. *Rezolutii si hotariri,* I, pp. 250–51.

41. The Credentials Commission report to the second RWP congress said admissions had been suspended between 1948 and 1952 (*Congresul al II-lea al PMR,* p. 337). An instruction from the CC dated March 8, 1952, restated the conditions for admission to the party and specified in precise terms the procedures that were to be followed (*Rezolutii si hotariri,* II, pp. 168–87). An editorial in *Scinteia* (December 14, 1952) on the admission of new candidates enjoined strict enforcement of membership requirements.

42. *Scinteia,* September 6, 1957. Despite this report, however, other data (see table 2) indicated little change in the percentage of workers from the end of the verification campaign in 1950 until 1955.

43. The Romanian party was not unique in experiencing a period of exceptionally rapid increase in membership followed by an extensive purge. The same pattern was followed in the other East European countries in the period immediately after World War II, and the Soviet party also went through a similar

pattern after its own seizure of power. T. H. Rigby, *Communist Party Membership in the U.S.S.R., 1917–1967* (Princeton, N.J.: Princeton University Press, 1968), pp. 88–109; and Brzezinski, *The Soviet Bloc,* pp. 84–97.

44. *Rezolutii si hotariri,* I, pp. 69–83.
45. Ibid., pp. 149–67.
46. Ibid., II, pp. 451–70.
47. Ibid., I, pp. 124–25.
48. Ibid., pp. 256–67.
49. Ibid., II, pp. 437–48.
50. Ibid., I, p. 248.
51. *Congresul al II-lea al PMR,* p. 138.
52. Ibid., p. 133.
53. Jowitt, *Revolutionary Breakthroughs,* pp. 132–37.
54. *Congresul al II-lea al PMR,* pp. 765–71, 834–42.
55. *Scinteia,* June 27, 1958; *Congresul al III-lea al Partidului Muncitoresc Romin* (Bucharest: Editura politica, 1960), p. 77. See also *Scinteia,* September 6, 1957.
56. At the third RWP congress in June 1960 membership was reported to be 834,600, and in April 1962 it was only "over 900,000"—a growth rate of less than 3,000 per month. Between December 1955 and June 1960 membership rose by nearly 240,000, or at the rate of nearly 4,500 per month.
57. *Scinteia,* May 17, 1962. Regarding one regional party organization's implementation of these directives, see *Dobrogea noua,* September 13, 1963.
58. The draft of the new statute was published in *Scinteia,* June 6, 1965. Other decisions regarding admission of members were discussed in ibid., June 8 and 9, 1965.
59. Ibid., August 13, 1969; *Statutul Partidului Comunist Roman* (Bucharest: Editura politica, 1974), pp. 22–28.
60. *Scinteia,* July 20, 1965, and April 24, 1976.
61. *World Marxist Review* 16, no. 5 (May 1973), pp. 128–29; *Scinteia,* March 24, 1978.
62. *Anuarul statistic al RSR, 1976,* p. 67.
63. *Scinteia,* March 20, 1970; April 25, 1972.
64. *Congresul al III-lea al PMR,* p. 77; *Scinteia,* May 17, 1962.
65. *Scinteia,* July 20, 1965; July 20 and 23, 1972.
66. Ibid., June 22, 1973; March 30 and 31, 1978.
67. Ibid., June 20, and July 4, 1973.
68. Elisabeta Ionita, "Cronologia miscarii organizate a femeilor din tara noastra," *Anale de istorie* 21, no. 4 (July–August 1975): 105–6.
69. *Congresul II-lea al PMR,* p. 340.
70. *Scinteia,* May 17, 1962.
71. Ibid., July 20, 1965.

72. According to the 1966 census, 87.7 percent of the population were ethnically Romanian; 8.5 percent Hungarian; 2.0 percent German; and 1.8 percent of other nationality. In 1975 the nationality composition of the party was 87.7 percent Romanian; 7.7 percent Hungarian; 1.9 percent German; and 2.7 percent other. *Scinteia,* April 24, 1976.

73. *Era socialista,* no. 6 (March), 1974, pp. 13–17.

74. *Anuarul statistic al RSR, 1975,* pp. 15–17.

75. *Scinteia,* April 17, 1965.

76. See "The New School Year in Party Education," *Lupta de clasa* 41, no. 9 (September 1961); *Scinteia,* August 26, 1958; Agerpres, May 23, 1960; *Dobrogea noua,* July 13, 1963.

77. *Scinteia,* March 20, 1970.

78. See, for example, the decision of the April 1974 CC plenum in *Scinteia,* April 3, 1974, and articles in *Munca de partid,* no. 1 (January) and no. 10 (May), 1974.

79. *Congresul al II-lea al PMR,* p. 132; *Scinteia,* March 30 and 31, 1978.

80. *Scinteia,* April 17, 1965; March 20, 1970.

4: The Character of the Party Elite

1. On this aspect of institutionalization as it relates to an elite, see Nelson W. Polsby, "The Institutionalization of the U.S. House of Representatives," *American Political Science Review* 62, no. 1 (March 1968): 144–68, and E. Spencer Wellhofer, "Dimensions of Party Development: A Study in Organizational Dynamics," *The Journal of Politics* 34, no. 1 (February 1972): 153–82.

2. This is evident in the CC resolutions on organizational matters that were issued during this time. See *Rezolutii si hotariri ale C.C. al P.M.R.* (Bucharest: Editura pentru literatura politica, 1952), vol. 1, pp. 11–27, 149–67, and vol. 2, pp. 36–55, 451–70.

3. For example, as was noted in the last chapter, in 1965 more than 76 percent of all party activists had been serving in party positions for more than five years; by 1970, 23 percent had served ten to fifteen years and 40 percent over fifteen years. *Scinteia,* April 17, 1965; March 20, 1970.

4. Article 14, *Statutul Partidului Comunist Roman* (Bucharest: Editura politica, 1974). Although these provisions were not formally adopted until the congress in November 1974, they were first presented at a CC plenum several months earlier. See *Scinteia,* July 30, 1974.

5. Radio Bucharest, November 26, 1974.

6. For some ideas on this event, see Robert R. King, "Ceausescu's Role at the 11th RCP Congress in Perspective," RAD Background Report/35, *Radio Free Europe Research,* February 28, 1975.

7. The exchange on this topic was included in the published account of the final day's proceedings. *Scinteia,* November 29, 1974.

8. Article 14, *Statutul P.C.R.*

9. *Scinteia,* November 28, 1974.

10. Ibid., November 29, 1974.

11. See Lester G. Seligman, "Political Parties and the Recruitment of Political Leadership," in Lewis J. Edinger, ed., *Political Leadership in Industrialized Societies* (New York: John Wiley and Sons, 1967), pp. 297–98.

12. Samuel P. Huntington, *Political Order in Changing Societies* (New Haven: Yale University Press, 1968), p. 22. For an excellent discussion of the problem of cohesion within the Romanian party, see Kenneth Jowitt, *Revolutionary Breakthroughs and National Development: The Case of Romania, 1944–1965* (Berkeley and Los Angeles: University of California Press, 1971), pp. 131–49.

13. *Scinteia,* July 19, 1967.

14. Ibid., December 7, 1961.

15. The Gheorghiu-Dej speech is in ibid.; the Ceausescu speech in ibid., December 13, 1961; and the Draghici speech in ibid., December 15, 1961.

16. See, for example, the resolution of the CC plenary session of June 10–11, 1948. *Rezolutii,* I, pp. 11–27.

17. Ibid., pp. 149–67.

18. Ibid., pp. 36–55, 451–70.

19. For analyses of the purge, see Jowitt, *Revolutionary Breakthroughs,* pp. 139–42; Ghita Ionescu, *Communism in Rumania, 1944–1962* (London: Oxford University Press, 1964), pp. 208–15; and Stephen Fischer-Galati, *The New Rumania* (Cambridge, Mass.: MIT Press, 1967), pp. 17–43.

20. For an analysis of the Ceausescu consolidation of power, see Mary Ellen Fischer, "Ceausescu and the Romanian Political Leadership: A Study in the Transfer and Consolidation of Power" (Ph.D. diss., Harvard University, 1974).

21. Wellhofer, "Dimensions of Party Development," pp. 170–71.

22. For biographical data on Ceausescu, see "The Rumanian Party Leadership," Rumanian Background Report 4, *Radio Free Europe Research,* March 30, 1973, pp. 22–28.

23. *Scinteia,* February 13, 1971.

24. Ibid., April 19, 1972.

25. Ibid., July 23, 1972.

26. Ibid., February 25, 1971.

27. Ibid., July 10, 1971.

28. For reports on similar phenomena, see Rein Taagepera and Robert Dale Chapman, "A Note on the Aging of the Politburo," *Soviet Studies* 29, no. 2 (April 1977): 296–305, analyzing the increasing age of the CPSU Politburo over time, and Thomas Arthur Baylis, *The Technical Intelligentsia and the East German Elite* (Berkeley, Los Angeles, and London: University of California Press, 1974), pp. 172–73, discussing the long period of party membership of a group of leading young technical specialists holding high-level positions in the regime.

29. Wellhofer, "Dimensions of Party Development," p. 172.

30. Ibid., pp. 172–77.

31. Anthony Downs, *Inside Bureaucracy* (Boston: Little, Brown & Co., 1967), pp. 96–101.

32. This point is made in T. H. Rigby, "The Soviet Leadership: Towards a Self-Stabilizing Oligarchy?" *Soviet Studies* 22, no. 2 (October 1970): 191.

5: Party and Society: Emerging Patterns of Authority

1. Alfred G. Meyer, "Authority in Communist Political Systems," in Lewis J. Edinger, ed., *Political Leadership in Industrialized Societies* (New York: John Wiley and Sons, 1967), pp. 84–107; Samuel P. Huntington, "Social and Institutional Dynamics of One-Party Systems," in Samuel P. Huntington and Clement H. Moore, eds., *Authoritarian Politics in Modern Society: The Dynamics of Established One-Party Systems* (New York and London: Basic Books, 1970), pp. 3–47; and Kenneth Jowitt, "Inclusion and Mobilization in European Leninist Regimes," *World Politics* 28, no. 1 (October 1975): 69–96.

2. Meyer, "Authority in Communist Political Systems," p. 107.

3. Ibid., p. 89.

4. Ibid., p. 91.

5. See Kenneth Jowitt, *Revolutionary Breakthroughs and National Development: The Case of Romania 1944–1965* (Berkeley and Los Angeles: University of California Press, 1971), pp. 114–30.

6. Jowitt, "Inclusion and Mobilization," p. 70.

7. Meyer, "Authority in Communist Political Systems," pp. 91–93.

8. Peter Christian Ludz, *The Changing Party Elite in East Germany* (Cambridge, Mass.: MIT Press, 1972), p. 32.

9. For an excellent discussion of the system-building phase and its impact on political culture with particular emphasis on Romania, see Kenneth Jowitt, "An Organizational Approach to the Study of Political Culture in Marxist-Leninist Systems," *American Political Science Review* 68, no. 3 (September 1974): esp. 1175–82. Other more descriptive works on this and the earlier transformation phases of RCP development are Ghita Ionescu, *Communism in Rumania, 1944–1962* (London: Oxford University Press, 1964); Alexandre Cretzianu, ed., *Captive Rumania* (New York: Praeger, 1956); and Stephen A. Fischer-Galati, *Romania* (New York: Praeger, 1957).

10. In fact, it is far from certain whether any of even the most developed of the East European states (East Germany, Czechoslovakia, or Poland) has fully entered this postmobilization phase. See Melvin Croan, "The Leading Role of the Party: Concepts and Contexts," in Andrew C. Janos, ed., *Authoritarian Politics in Communist Europe,* Institute of International Studies Research Series, no. 28 (Berkeley: University of California, 1976) p. 155.

11. Jowitt, "Inclusion and Mobilization," p. 79.

12. Gordon Skilling, "Interest Groups and Communist Politics," *World Politics* 18, no. 3 (April 1966), pp. 435–51. See also Huntington, "Social and Institutional Dynamics," pp. 34–36; Zygmunt Bauman, "The Party in the System-Management Phase: Change and Continuity," in Janos, ed., *Authoritarian Politics,* pp. 90–93; and Richard Lowenthal, "On 'Established' Communist Party Regimes," *Studies in Comparative Communism* 7, no. 4 (Winter 1974): 344–47.

13. See William F. Robinson, *The Pattern of Reform in Hungary* (New York: Praeger, 1973), pp. 233–73, and Skilling, "Interest Groups and Communist Politics."

14. From a speech at a conference of cadres in social sciences and political education, published in *Scinteia,* October 8, 1976.

15. This theme has been a frequent one in speeches of the Romanian party leader. In 1968 he called for reduction of top salaries and narrower differentials between categories of workers; this theme was reiterated in 1971. See *Scinteia,* June 20, 1968; July 13, 1971.

16. Radu Florian, *Procese definitorii ale dezvoltarii societatii socialiste* (Bucharest: Editura stiintifica si enciclopedica, 1975), p. 74. A review of the volume was published in the party's theoretical and sociopolitical review: Achim Mihu, "Contradictiile in Societatea Socialista," *Era socialista,* no. 17 (September), 1975, pp. 24–28.

17. *Programul Partidului Comunist Roman de faurire a societatii socialiste multilateral dezvoltate si inzintare a Romaniei spre comunism* (Bucharest: Editura politica, 1975), p. 107.

18. See Lowenthal, "On 'Established' Communist Party Regimes," pp. 339–43; and "Development vs. Utopia in Communist Policy," in Chalmers Johnson, ed., *Change in Communist Systems* (Stanford, California: Stanford University Press, 1970), pp. 33–116; and Huntington, "Social and Institutional Dynamics," pp. 33–34.

19. Jowitt, "Inclusion and Mobilization," pp. 77–78. Another defense of this view is to be found in George Fischer, *The Soviet System and Modern Society* (New York: Atherton, 1968).

20. Probably the most thorough examination of this topic is Jacob Bielasiak, "Political Change and Economic Development: A Study of Elite Composition in Eastern Europe," (Ph.D. diss., Cornell University, 1975). On Romania, see pp. 153–59, 241–51, 283–90.

21. *Lupta de Clasa,* no. 11, November 1969.

22. *Scinteia,* April 17, 1965.

23. Ibid., April 25, 1972.

24. *Congresul al III-lea al Partidului Muncitoresc Romin* (Bucharest: Editura politica, 1960) p. 76.

25. *Anuarul Statistic al R.P.R., 1961,* p. 108.

26. *Scinteia,* April 18, 1970.

27. *Lupta de Clasa,* no. 6, June 1967.

28. *Scinteia,* February 17, 1971.

29. Ibid., February 13, 1971.
30. Ibid., May 15, and October 8, 1976.
31. Ibid., October 2, 1976.
32. Ibid., July 20, 1972.
33. Ioan Bosuioc, "Organele cu dubla natura—de partid si de stat," *Viitorul social* 3, no. 3 (July–September 1974): 508–16.
34. For assessments of the "plurality of offices," primarily on the local level, see Ion Catrinescu in *Munca de Partid,* no. 16 (August 1973), pp. 12–16; Leonte Rautu, "Procesul de faurire a societatii socialiste multilateral dezvoltate in Romania," *Era socialista,* no. 22 (November), 1973, pp. 16–22; Ilie Radulescu, "Impletirea activitatii de partid si de stat," ibid., pp. 38–41; Petre Molcomete in *Scinteia,* December 19, 1973; and Petre Blajovici, "Impletirea activitatii de partid si de stat in procesul perfectionarii conducerii," *Era socialista,* no. 2 (January), 1974, pp. 12–15.
35. The most detailed discussion of such bodies is Ion Deleanu, "Organele de partid si de stat—expresie a cresterii rolului conducator al partidului si a dezvoltarii democratiei socialiste," *Revista romana de drept* 31, no. 6 (June 1975): 3–9. See also Mircea Anghene, "Rolulu si insemnatatea organelor cu dubla natura, de partid si de stat, in sistemul democratiei socialiste," ibid. 30, no. 4 (April 1974): 9–18; Radulescu, "Impletirea activitatii;" and Busuioc, "Organele cu dubla natura."
36. Decree 444/1972, published in *Buletinul oficial,* no. 130 (November 21, 1972).
37. See Robert R. King, "The Blending of Party and State in Romania," *East European Quarterly* 12, no. 4 (December 1978): 489–500.
38. Meyer, "Authority in Communist Systems," p. 101; see also Huntington, "Social and Institutional Dynamics," pp. 38–40.
39. Jowitt, "Inclusion and Mobilization," p. 79.
40. Thomas A. Baylis, "East Germany: In Quest of Legitimacy," *Problems of Communism,* no. 2 (March–April 1972), p. 53. See also Robert S. Sharlet, "Concept Formation in Political Science and Communist Studies: Conceptualizing Political Participation," in Frederic J. Fleron, Jr. ed., *Communist Studies and the Social Sciences* (Chicago: Rand McNally, 1969), pp. 144–253.
41. Baylis, "East Germany," p. 54.
42. The speech was published in *Scinteia,* July 20, 1972; the resolution appeared in the paper's July 23, 1972, issue.
43. *Programul partidului comunist Roman,* part 6.
44. *Scinteia,* February 9, 1971.
45. Ibid., September 10, 1972.
46. A very interesting account of the preparations for Ceausescu's visit to Turnu Severin in May 1972 is to be found in a dispatch by Jan Behre in *Hufvudstads Blade* (Helsinki), June 23, 1972.
47. An account of this part of Ceausescu's visit can be found in *Scinteia,* September 16, 1972.

48. His criticism is included in his speech as broadcast live by Radio Bucharest (October 2, 1972), but it was omitted from the published version in *Scinteia,* October 3, 1972.

49. *Scinteia,* July 16, 1976.

50. Ibid., April 14, 1976.

51. Decision 4012/1953 and Decree 534/1966, published in *Buletinul oficial,* June 24, 1966.

52. *Scinteia,* June 25, 1976.

53. Huntington considers electoral competition to be one of the key factors in the expansion of popular participation in one-party systems during the adaptation phase; "Social and Institutional Dynamics," pp. 38–40.

54. *Scinteia,* July 23, 1972, and *Programul partidului comunist Roman,* part 6.

55. The law of 1968, for example, provided for the nomination of "one or more candidates" for each constituency; see Article 40 of Law 28/1968, *Buletinul oficial,* November 22, 1968. The electoral law of 1952 also implied that more than one candidate could be nominated for a single post.

56. *Scinteia,* July 23, 1972; December 21, 1974.

57. Reports on this stage of the election process were published in *Romania libera* and *Scinteia tineretului,* February 17, 1975. Precise figures on the number of candidates were given by Ceausescu in a speech to a Central Committee plenum on March 17, and reported in *Scinteia* the following day. For an analysis of the election, see Robert R. King, "Ansaetze zu einer 'sozialistischen Demokratie' in Rumaenien: Mehrfachkandidaturen bei den Wahlen von 1975," *Osteuropa* 26, no. 5 (May 1976): 382–88.

58. Ion Ceterchi, "The State and the Public," in the symposium on "The Present-day Problems of Socialist Democracy and Its Perspectives," *World Marxist Review* 18, no. 2 (February 1975): 71–72.

59. One of these important indications, which will be discussed in the next chapter, is the role of the nation and the party's changed attitude toward the national heritage. This aspect has assumed such importance in the Romanian context and become such a hallmark of RCP policy that it deserves more detailed treatment.

60. Jeremy Azrael, "Varieties of Destalinization," in Johnson, ed., *Change in Communist Systems,* pp. 135–53.

61. Jowitt, "Inclusion and Mobilization," pp. 89–96.

62. See Charles Andras, "European Cooperation and Ideological Conflict," in Robert R. King and Robert W. Dean, eds., *East European Perspectives on European Security and Cooperation* (New York: Praeger Publishers, 1974), pp. 17–49.

63. See Robert R. King, "Ideological Mobilization in Romania," in Robert R. King and J. F. Brown, eds., *Eastern Europe's Uncertain Future* (New York: Praeger, 1977), pp. 266–82.

64. *Scinteia,* October 8, 1976.

65. Huntington, "Social and Institutional Dynamics," pp. 36–38.

66. *Scinteia,* June 3, 1976.

67. Ibid.

68. A study of Romanian agricultural workers who were aware of the role of non-material incentives in the economy indicated that they were far more concerned about the material incentives they received. The authors of the report blamed this upon the unsatisfactory level of the workers' socialist awareness. See *Revista economica,* no. 7, February 20, 1976.

6: Changing Attitudes toward the National Heritage and the Nation

1. Alfred G. Meyer, "Authority in Communist Political Systems," in Lewis J. Edinger, *Political Leadership in Industrialized Societies* (New York: John Wiley and Sons, 1967), p. 105. See also Richard Lowenthal, "On 'Established' Communist Party Regimes," *Studies in Comparative Communism* 7, no. 4 (Winter 1974): 349–51.

2. Kenneth Jowitt, "Inclusion and Mobilization in European Leninist Regimes,' *World Politics* 28, no. 1 (October 1975), pp. 81, 87–88.

3. Alexandru Szabo in *Tinarul leninist,* no. 7 (July 1957). Among the more descriptive analyses of nationalism in this period are those written for the instruction of youth. See, for example, in addition to the Szabo article, Joan Rebeden in *Viata studenteasca,* no. 12 (December 1957) and Al. Popescu in *Romania libera,* July 8, 1958.

4. One can get a good impression by comparing the titles of articles that appeared in this journal, *Analele Institutului de istorie a partidului de pe linga CC al P.M.R.,* during this period. The titles of the articles that appeared in 1958 and in 1968, dealing with the interwar period, reflect the change quite graphically. The articles on the interwar period published in 1958 issues were captioned as follows:

"Aspects of the Strike of Railway Workers in Iasi [1933]"

"The RCP—Leader of the Anti-war Movement in Romania. The Committee Against War (1932–1933)"

"The Struggle of the Workers of Timisoara in May–July 1924"

"The International Situation on the Eve of the Fifth Congress of the RCP [1931]"

"On Characteristic Problems and Revolutionary Prospects in Party Literature in Romania Before the Fifth Congress of the RCP"

"The Stockyard Demonstration in Bucharest Organized by the RCP on 7 November 1940"

"The Struggle of the Railway Workers of Cluj in 1933"

"From the History of the Statute of the RCP"

"Data on the Young Workers' Movement in Romania Between the Years 1917 and 1921"

"The First Issue of the Daily *Romania libera*"

The 1968 articles dealing with the interwar period bore the following titles:

"The Vienna *Diktat* [which assigned Northern Transylvania to Hungary in 1940]—A Brutal Infringement of Independence and Sovereignty"

"The Anschluss [of Austria to Germany] and its Political Consequences for the European Continent"

"New Data on the Moldavian Peasants' Struggle for Land in the Years 1918–1921"

"The Internal and International Significance of the Struggle of Romanian Workers in 1933"

"The Assistance Granted by Romania to Polish Refugees during the Second World War"

"The Economic Problems of Romania on the Eve of the Second World War"

"The Dynastic Crisis (1927–1930)"

"The Balkan Entente and its Efforts to Achieve Collective Security in Europe (1934–1936)"

"13 December 1918 [The anniversary of the unification of Transylvania with Romania]—A Heroic Page in the Struggle of the Workers in Our Country"

See "Bibliografia revistei Anale de istorie (1955–1969)," *Analele de istorie* 16, no. 1 (January–February 1970): 135–210.

5. *Programul Partidului Comunist Roman de faurire a societatii socialiste multilateral dezvoltate si inaintare Romaniei spre communism* (Bucharest: Editura politica, 1975), part 1.

6. See Ceausescu's speech on the occasion of the centennial celebration, *Scinteia,* May 10, 1977. On this interpretation of Romanian history, see "Programul Partidului Comunist Roman—sinteza profund stiintifica a drumului de lupta si creatie istorica a poporului nostru," *Anale de istorie* 20, no. 5 (September–October 1974); and Michael Cismarescu, "Das neue Programm der Rumaenischen Kommunistischen Partei: Historische Legitimitaet und nationaler Kommunismus," *Oesterreichische Osthefte* 18, no. 2 (May 1976).

7. See chapter 1.

8. On the treatment of these issues by Romanian historians in the period before 1960, see Robert R. King, *Minorities Under Communism: Nationalities as a Source of Tension Among Balkan Communist States* (Cambridge, Mass.: Harvard University Press, 1973), pp. 220–25; Michael J. Rura, *Reinterpretation of History as a Method of Furthering Communism in Rumania* (Washington, D.C.: Georgetown University Press, 1961), esp. pp. 50–56; Dionisie Ghermani, *Die kommunistische Umdeutung der Rumaenischen Geschichte unter besonderer Beruecksichtigung des Mittelalters,* Untersuchungen zur Gegenwartskunde Suedosteuropas, no. 6 (Munich: Oldenbourg, 1967); and Constantin Sporea, "Die sowjetische Umdeutung der rumaenischen Geschichte," *Saeculum* 11, no. 3 (1965): 220–46.

9. A. Otetea and S. Schwann, eds., *K. Marx—Insemnari despre Romani* (Bucharest: Editura Academici R.P.R., 1964).

10. *Scinteia,* May 8, 1966.

11. Ibid., June 3, 1976.

12. Among the most interesting articles in this regard are Gheorghe I. Ionita, "Activitatea teoretica desfasurata de PCR in perioada interbelica pentru apararea unitatii nationale, a independentei si suveranitatii tarii," *Anale de istorie* 21, no. 4 (July–August 1975): 53–73; M. C. Stanescu and N. Popescu, "Partidul Comunist Roman si congresele Internationalei a III-a," ibid. 21, no. 5 (September–October 1975): 48–68; Ion Ardeleanu and Mircea Musat, "1918—Socialistii romani in fruntea luptei maselor pentru incheierea procesului de formare a statului national unitar," ibid. 21, no. 6 (November–December 1975): 45–57. For an analysis of the historical arguments of the 1975–1976 debates, see Robert R. King, "Verschaerfter Disput um Bessarabien: Zur Auseinandersetzung zwischen rumaenischen und sowjetischen Historikern," *Osteuropa* 26, no. 12 (December 1976): 1079–87.

13. For examples of this see the following papers by George Cioranescu: "Michael the Brave—Evaluations and Revaluations of the Wallachian Prince," Background Report/191, *Radio Free Europe Research,* September 1, 1976; "The Political Significance of the Thracians," BR/218, *RFER,* October 22, 1976; and "Vlad the Impaler—Current Parallels with a Medieval Romanian Prince," BR/23, *RFER,* January 31, 1977.

14. *Scinteia,* July 20, 1965.

15. "Resolution of the RCP National Conference [July 1972] Concerning the Blossoming of the Socialist Nation and the National Problem in the Socialist Republic of Romania," *Scinteia,* July 23, 1972. This resolution and Ceausescu's speech to the conference (ibid., July 20, 1972) are two of the most detailed official RCP statements on the role of the nation.

16. Ibid., July 23, 1972.

17. For attempts to define and theoretically defend the concept of a "socialist nation" see the following: Ana Gavrila, "Natiunea socialista—etapa superioara in viata natiunilor, *Analele inst. istorice* 14, no. 5 (September–October 1968): 101–8; the symposium "Natiunea si natiunea in socialism," ibid., 13, no. 6 (November–December 1967): 40–79; Ion Ceterchi and Elena Florea, "Consideratii privind rolul natiunii socialist in dezvoltarea societatii romanesti contemporane," *Anale de istorie* 20, no. 3 (May–June 1974): 91–99; and Elena Florea, *Natiunea romana si socialismul* (Bucharest: Editura Academiei Republicii Socialiste Romania, 1974).

18. *Scinteia,* July 23, 1972.

19. Among the earliest and most authoritative assertions was "The Statement of the Stand of the Romanian Workers' Party Concerning the Problems of the International Communist and Working-Class Movement," *Scinteia,* April 23, 1964. The full text appears in English in William E. Griffith, *Sino-Soviet Relations, 1964–1965* (Cambridge, Mass.: MIT Press, 1967), pp. 269–96. For a recent reiteration of this principle, see the RCP response to the Soviet attack on Spanish communist leader Santiago Carrillo in *Scinteia,* July 5, 1977.

20. See note 8 above.

21. In *Revolutionary Breakthroughs and National Development: The Case of Romania, 1944–1965* (Berkeley and Los Angeles: University of California Press, 1971), pp. 276–77.

22. *Scinteia,* June 9, 1976.

23. Ibid., June 3, 1976.

24. *Frankfurter Rundschau,* July 27, 1976.

25. An indication of the strength of feeling on certain of these questions can be sensed from some of the scholarly polemics that have appeared in academic journals. While the Hungarian party has made some effort to confine the discussion to scholarly circles, the Romanian party has permitted it to appear in the mass media. See, for example, Constantin C. Giurescu in *Revista de istorie* 28, no. 6 (June 1975): 941–48, and ibid. 29, no. 8 (August 1976): 1231–35; Aureliu Goci in *Flacara,* March 27, 1976; Dumitru Berciu in *Era socialista,* no. 7 (April), 1976, pp. 41–44; Dan Berindei in ibid., no. 8 (April), 1976, p. 59; Dan Zamfirescu in *Contemporanul,* April 16, 1976; Manole Neagoe in *Saptamina,* April 23, 1976; and Dumitru Tudor in *Scinteia,* April 26, 1976.

26. On the treatment of the minorities, see King, *Minorities Under Communism,* pp. 35–44, 82–85, 146–69; Mary Ellen Fischer, "Nation and Nationality in Romania," a paper prepared for the annual meeting of the American Association for the Advancement of Slavic Studies, October 1975; Trond Gilberg, "Ethnic Minorities in Romania Under Socialism," *East European Quarterly* 7, no. 4 (January 1974): 435–57.

27. See also Georges Castellan, "The Germans of Rumania," *Journal of Contemporary History* 6, no. 1 (1971): 52–75; G. C. Paikert, *The Danube Swabians* (The Hague: Martinus Nijhoff, 1967); and Joseph B. Schechtman, *Postwar Population Transfers in Europe* (Philadelphia: University of Pennsylvania Press, 1962), pp. 50–98, 263–86.

28. See also Peter Meyer et al., *The Jews in the Soviet Satellites* (Syracuse, N.Y.: Syracuse University Press, 1953), pp. 493–556.

29. Resolution of the Central Committee plenum of June 10–11, 1948, in *Resolutii si hotariri ale Comitetul Central al PMR,* 2d ed. (Bucharest: Editura de stat pentru literatura politica, 1952).

30. King, *Minorities Under Communism,* pp. 82–85.

31. On these events see *Scinteia,* August 27 and 31, September 1 and 3, October 25, and November 16, 1968.

32. See *Nepszabadsag* (Budapest), June 25, 1971; *Scinteia,* July 9 and 12, 1971. On the policy toward the minorities during this period, see Robert R. King, "Rumanian Concern for the National Minorities," *Radio Free Europe Research,* Rumanian Background Report/19, July 23, 1971.

33. The full texts of the letters from Karoly Kiraly have been published in English translation by the Committee for Human Rights in Romania, January 30, 1978. The official response from the Romanian government was the appearance in early 1978 of *A Living Reality in Romania Today: Full Harmony and Equality Between the Romanian People the Coinhabiting Nationalities* (n.p., n.d.).

34. Marilyn McArthur, "The Saxon Germans: Political Fate of an Ethnic Identity," *Dialectical Anthropology* 1 (1976): 349–64. Examples of the campaigns to discourage German emigration are found in *Neuer Weg* (German-language newspaper published in Bucharest), February 16, 27, and 28, and March 2, 3, and 5, 1971; and *Scinteia,* March 29 and 30, and April 1, 2, 3, and 6, 1977; *Neuer Weg,* April 1 and 2, 1977; and *Contemporanul,* April 1, 1977.

35. *Scinteia,* June 3, 1976.

36. Ibid., June 3 and October 8, 1976.

37. Ibid., September 19, 1976.

38. The Hungarians are unlikely to be enthusiastic about or convinced by an effort to show that Transylvania Hungarians welcomed the independence of the Romanian principalities in 1877; see Janos Fazekas, "Positia fortelor progresiste Maghiare fata de razboiul de independenta al Romaniei din 1877–1878," *Era socialista,* no. 13 (July), 1977, pp. 40–44.

7: The International Policy of the Party

1. Fritz Ermarth, *Internationalism, Security, and Legitimacy: The Challenge to Soviet Interests in East Europe, 1964–1968,* Rand Memorandum 5909PR (Santa Monica: The RAND Corporation, 1971).

2. Ceausescu's criticism appeared in a speech published in *Scinteia,* February 5, 1976. (It is significant that this criticism was noted and cited in the Soviet party daily *Pravda,* February 8, 1976.) Excerpts of the Marchais speech appeared in *Scinteia,* February 8, 1976, and the text of his comments on the dictatorship of the proletariat finally appeared in *Lumea,* no. 7 (February 22, 1976).

3. *Scinteia,* July 5, 1977.

4. Robert R. King, "Verschaerfter Disput um Bessarabien: Zur Auseinandersetzung zwischen rumaenischen und sowjetischen Historikern," *Osteuropa* 26, no. 12 (December 1976): 1079–87.

5. Stephen Fischer-Galati, *The New Rumania: From People's Democracy to Socialist Republic* (Cambridge, Mass.: The MIT Press, 1967), p. vii, suggests the earliest date; R. V. Burks, "Rumania and a Theory of Progress," *Problems of Communism* 21, no. 3 (May–June 1972): 83–5, and Robert Farlow, "Romanian Foreign Policy: A Case of Partial Alignment," ibid. 20, no. 6 (November–December 1971): 54–63, suggest the late 1950s, and J. F. Brown, "Rumania Steps Out of Line," *Survey,* no. 49 (October 1963): 19–34, and Kenneth Jowitt, *Revolutionary Breakthroughs and National Development: The Case of Romania, 1944–1965* (Berkeley and Los Angeles: University of California Press, 1971), pp. 198–224, suggest the early 1960s as the critical date. Jowitt's analysis of the process by which the RCP initiated its autonomous foreign policy is excellent.

6. On the background of the economic issues, see John Michael Montias, *Economic Development in Communist Romania* (Cambridge, Mass.: The MIT Press, 1967), pp. 187–230.

7. A number of articles and books deal with these aspects of Romanian foreign

policy: R. L. Braham, "Rumania: Onto the Separate Path," *Problems of Communism* 13, no. 3 (May–June 1964): 14–24; J. F. Brown, "Rumania Steps out of Line"; R. V. Burks, "The Rumanian National Deviation: An Accounting," in Kurt London, ed., *Eastern Europe in Transition* (Baltimore: The Johns Hopkins Press, 1966); Fischer-Galati, *The New Rumania*; David Floyd, *Rumania: Russia's Dissident Ally* (New York: Praeger, 1965); Graeme J. Gill, "Rumania: Background to Autonomy," *Survey,* no. 87 (Summer 1975), pp. 94–113; George Gross, "Rumania: Fruits of Autonomy," *Problems of Communism* 15, no. 1 (January–February 1966): 16–28; Jowitt, *Revolutionary Breakthroughs,* pp. 198–272.

8. "Statement on the Stand of the Romanian Workers' Party Concerning the Problems of the International Communist and Working-Class Movement Adopted by the Enlarged Plenum of the CC of the RWP in April 1964." The statement was published in *Scinteia,* April 23, 1964.

9. See Robin A. Remington, *The Warsaw Pact: Case Studies in Communist Conflict Resolution* (Cambridge, Mass.: The MIT Press, 1971), pp. 80–88; and Ermarth, *Internationalism, Security and Legitimacy,* pp. 33–40.

10. *Scinteia,* May 7, 1966.

11. J. F. Brown, "Rumania Today: The Strategy of Defiance," *Problems of Communism* 18, no. 2 (March–April 1969): 32–38.

12. *Scinteia,* June 7, 10, and 17, 1969.

13. The text of the treaty was published in *Scinteia,* July 8, 1970.

14. Robert R. King, "Autonomy and Detente: The Problems of Rumanian Foreign Policy," *Survey,* no. 91–92 (Spring–Summer 1974), pp. 105–20.

15. Robert R. King, "Rumaenien und die europaeische Sicherheit," *Europa Archiv* 27, no. 22 (November 25, 1972): 775–84.

16. Stephen Fischer-Galati, "Rumania and the Sino-Soviet Split," in Kurt London, ed., *Eastern Europe in Transition* (Baltimore: The Johns Hopkins Press, 1966); and Robert R. King, "Rumania and the Sino-Soviet Conflict," *Studies in Comparative Communism* 5, no. 4 (Winter 1972): 373–93.

17. Robert R. King, "Romania and the Third World," *Orbis* 21, no. 4 (Winter 1978): 875–92.

18. Robert R. King, "Romania's Struggle for an Autonomous Foreign Policy," *The World Today* 35, no. 8 (July 1979): 340–48.

19. *Scinteia,* December 9, 1978.

Bibliographical Note

The sources used are fully documented in the notes, hence it seems unnecesary to include in addition a bibliography of sources cited. Since no party history has been published in Romanian or in any Western language, however, general comments on available materials relevant to the history of the Romanian Communist Party will be useful.

A number of volumes have appeared in English on Romania. One of the best is Henry L. Roberts, *Rumania: Political Problems of an Agrarian State* (New Haven, Conn.: Yale University Press, 1951). Though it is dated, it contains very useful information, particularly on Romania before 1945. Roberts's account of the background and rise to power of the RCP is brief and incomplete, but it supplies a useful starting point. A number of books on Romania since 1944 deal with certain aspects of the party's history and development, though most are concerned with the political, economic, social, cultural, and foreign policies that the regime has pursued. The studies of the early postwar period include Alexandre Cretzianu, ed., *Captive Rumania: A Decade of Soviet Rule* (New York: Frederick A. Praeger, 1956); Stephen Fischer-Galati, ed., *Romania* (New York: Frederick A. Praeger, 1957); and Ghita Ionescu, *Communism in Rumania: 1944–1962* (London: Oxford University Press, 1964). Works that deal with later developments, including Romania's innovative foreign policy after the early 1960s, are the following: John Michael Montias, *Economic Development in Communist Rumania* (Cambridge, Mass.: The MIT Press, 1967); Stephen Fischer-Galati, *The New Rumania: From People's Democracy to Socialist Republic* (Cambridge, Mass.: The MIT Press, 1967), *The Socialist Republic of Rumania* (Baltimore: The Johns Hopkins Press, 1969), and *Twentieth Century Rumania* (New York: Columbia University Press, 1970); David Floyd, *Rumania: Russia's Dissident Ally* (New York: Frederick A. Praeger, 1965); and Trond Gilberg, *Modernization in Romania Since World War II* (New York: Praeger Publishers, 1975). An excellent exposition of the party's role in the development of Romania, which deals in more theoretical terms with the party and its evolution between 1944 and 1965, is Kenneth Jowitt, *Revolutionary Breakthroughs and National Development: The Case of Romania, 1944–1965* (Berkeley and Los Angeles: University of California Press, 1971).

Although no comprehensive party history has been published, materials on various aspects of the party history are voluminous. The best and most complete bibliographic guide is the multivolume work published by the Romanian Academy, *Bibliografia istorica a Romaniei* (Bucharest: Editura Academiei Republicii Socialiste

Romania, 1970 and later years). The first volume includes materials published between 1944 and 1969, while subsequent volumes cover materials that have appeared at intervals since that time.

The Institute of Party History has sponsored the publication of extensive materials. A listing of its work from 1951 to 1971 is published in "Activitatea editoriala a Institutului de studii istorice si social-politice de pe linga C.C. al P.C.R. in cei douazeci de ani de existenta (Martie 1951–Martie 1971)," *Anale de istorie* 17, no. 2 (March–April 1971): 69–91. A useful listing of publications sponsored by the institute for the 50th anniversary of the founding of the RCP, which was celebrated in 1971, is found in "Lucrari editate in anul sarbatoririi semicentenarului Partidului Comunist Roman de catre Institutul de studii istorice si social-politice de pe linga C.C. al P.C.R.," *Anale de istorie* 17, no. 6 (November–December 1971): 197–99.

The journal published by the Institute of Party History is one of the most useful sources of data on the party's history in all periods. It has appeared under three separate titles since it first appeared in 1955: *Analele Institutului de istorie a partidului de pe linga C.C. al P.M.R.* (1955–1966); *Analele Institutului de studii istorice si social-politice de pe linga C.C. al P.C.R.* (1966-1968); and *Anale de istorie* (since 1969). A helpful bibliography of all articles published during the first fifteen years of the journal's existence is "Bibliografia revistei 'Anale de istorie' (1955–1969)," *Anale de istorie* 16, no. 1 (January–February 1970): 135–210.

Several series of documents dealing with the interwar period have been published, although there are still significant gaps. A one-volume selection appeared in 1951: *Documente din istoria Partidului Comunist din Romania* [1917–1944] (Bucharest: Editura Partidului Muncitoresc Roman, 1951). Another slightly expanded edition of this volume was published in 1953. Publication was begun on a more complete multivolume collection in 1953: *Documente din istoria Partidului Comunist din Romania* (Bucharest: Editura pentru literatura politica, 1953–1957), vol. 1 (1917–1922), vol. 2 (1923–1928), vol. 3 (1929–1933), and vol. 4 (1934–1937). This collection has not gone beyond 1937. A third series was started in the 1960s when the earlier collections were criticized as unrepresentative and incomplete. The principal reason for the new series, however, was the changed relationship with the Soviet Union that had emerged by the mid-1960s; the new documents were selected to reflect the altered situation. The first volume to appear dealt with events leading up to the creation of the RCP, *Documente din istoria miscarii muncitoresti din Romania, 1916–1921* (Bucharest: Editura politica, 1966). Between 1968 and 1975 another six volumes were published covering the periods from 1821 to 1915 and May 1921 to August 1924. This series was discussed in a review of the volume published in 1975, which covers the period 1900–1909. See "Mostenirea documentara—monument elocvent al vechimii si fortei miscarii muncitoresti si socialiste din Romania," *Anale de istorie* 21, no. 5 (September–October 1975): 101ff.

Party documents since the RCP's accession to power in August 1944 have not been collected and published, but party decisions and statements of any importance have appeared in the party daily, *Scinteia,* since it began regular publication in 1944. Other party periodicals are also useful sources. Among the most important are the theoretical journal *Lupta de clasa* (published until 1972); the social-political-theoretical semimonthly *Era socialista* (published since 1972); and the periodical for party work

Munca de partid (also published since 1972).

Another important source of materials is the speeches of the party leaders. The more important speeches and articles of Gheorghe Gheorghiu-Dej (party leader from 1944–1965) have been published in a number of Romanian editions and in various other languages, but they have not been systematically and completely collected and published. Among the more important of the Gheorghiu-Dej works are: *Articole si cuvintari* (Bucharest: Editura politica, 1951); *Articole si cuvintari* (Bucharest: Editura politica, 1961); *Articole si cuvintari* (Bucharest: Editura politica, 1962); *Articole si cuvintari* (Bucharest: Editura politica, 1963). (The volumes are not numbered and the date of publication is the only way to distinguish them.) The complete works of Nicolae Ceausescu since he became secretary general of the party in 1965 have been published systematically and they form an important record of party activity and programs under his leadership. The period July 1965 to March 1969 appears as Nicolae Ceausescu, *Romania pe drumul desavirsirii constructiei socialiste* (Bucharest: Editura politica, 1968–1969), vols. 1–3. Since April 1969 they have appeared as Nicolae Ceausescu, *Romania pe drumul construirii societatii socialiste multilateral dezvoltate* (Bucharest: Editura politica, 1970–1979), vols. 4–15.

Index